John Adams, Giles Duncombe, John Q. Adams

Trials per Pais

or, The law of England concerning juries by nisi prius, &c. - With a compleat treatise

of the law of evidence, collected from all the books of reports - Vol. 2

John Adams, Giles Duncombe, John Q. Adams

Trials per Pais

or, The law of England concerning juries by nisi prius, &c. - With a compleat treatise of the law of evidence, collected from all the books of reports - Vol. 2

ISBN/EAN: 9783337844509

Printed in Europe, USA, Canada, Australia, Japan

Cover: Foto ©Suzi / pixelio.de

More available books at **www.hansebooks.com**

OR, THE

LAW of *ENGLAND*

CONCERNING

Juries by *Nisi Prius*, &c.

With a Compleat TREATISE of

The Law of EVIDENCE,

Collected from all the Books of Reports; together with
Precedents, and Forms of Challenges, Demurrers upon
Evidence, Bills of Exception, Pleas *Puis le Darrein
Continuance*, &c.

The Eighth Edition, with large Additions.

CONTINUED

Down to this present Year; together with such subsequent Resolutions, as
have been given in the Courts of *Westminster-Hall*: The Whole
put into a Method most useful and easy to the Practiser.

With a full and copious Table to the whole.

*Very Useful and Necessary for all Lawyers, Attornies, and other
Practisers, especially at the* A S S I Z E S.

Originally compiled by GILES DUNCOMB, heretofore of the
Inner-Temple, Esq; and continued by a Careful Hand.

In T W O V O L U M E S.

· V O L. II.

L O N D O N:

Printed by H. WOODFALL and W. STRAHAN, Law Printers to the
King's most Excellent Majesty: for T. WALLER, opposite to *Fetter-
Lane, Fleet Street.* M.DCC.LXVI.

I Do allow the Printing and Publishing of this B O O K, Entituled, *Trials per Pais:* Or, *The Law of* England *concerning Juries by* Nisi prius.

Fr. Pemberton.

This Day is published, Price 3 s.

Printed for T. WALLER.

THE *Laws concerning Game :* Of Hunting, Hawking, Fishing and Fowling, *&c.* And of Forests, Chases, Parks, Warrens, Deer, Doves, Dove-cotes, Conies: And also of Setting-dogs, Grey-hounds, Lurchers, Nets, Tunnels, Low-bels, Guns, and all Manner of Engines and Instruments mentioned in the several Statutes to destroy the Game ; shewing who are qualified by Law to keep and use them, and the Punishments of those who keep them, not being qualified. Likewise the proper Seasons allowed by Act of Parliament for Hunting, Fishing and following. Together with the Forest Laws: Shewing the Method of Chusing, and Oaths of the respective Officers; and the Authority, Power and Duty of Chief Justice in *Eyre*, Clerks of the Peace, Constables, Foresters, Game-keepers, Justices of Peace, Keepers, Lords of Manors, Parkers, Rangers, Regarders, Sheriffs, Stewards of Forest Courts, Stewards of Leets, Verderors, Wardens and Woodwards. By WILLIAM NELSON of the *Middle Temple*, Esq; To which are now added, *English* Forms of Convictions, Declarations, Indictments, Justifications, Licences, Mittimus's, Pleas Warrants, *&c.* Digested under proper Titles, in an alphabetical Order. *The Sixth Edition*, with all the Acts of Parliament and Cases in Print, and also a large Collection of Manuscript Cases, down to the present Time.

Trials per Pais.

VOL. II.

CHAP. XV.

Of Evidence (a) in general.

EVIDENCE, *Evidentia :* This Word in legal Underſtanding (ſaith *Coke,* 1 *Inſt.* 283.) doth not only contain Matters of Record, as Letters Patent, Fines, Recoveries, Inrolments, and the like ; and Wri-

(a) As the Diſcovery of Truth is of the utmoſt Conſequence to the Good of Society, ſo it lays Men under the ſtrongeſt Obligations, when called upon to give their Evidence, to adhere inviolably to Truth ; and this is a Matter not only enjoined by the Precepts of Religion, but alſo by thoſe of Reaſon ; the Violation of Truth being a Sin againſt human Society, as it breaks in upon that Correſpondence that is neceſſary to ſociable Creatures, by deſtroying the End of Language, which is the common Tie and Band of Society ; and as raiſing a different Idea in the Mind of the Hearer from that which is formed in the Mind of the Speaker, deſtroys all Intercourſe between Mankind; ſo it prevents that Truſt from being repoſed in them which is ſo neceſſary to their own Preſervation, and the good of others. 2 *Bac. Abr.* 284.

tings under Seal, as Charters and Deeds; and other Writings without Seal, as Court-rolls, Accounts, and the like, which are called Evidences, *Inftrumenta* : But in a larger Senfe, it containeth alfo *Teftimonia*, the Teftimony of Witneffes, and other Proofs to be produced and given to a Jury for finding of any Iffue joined between the Parties : And it is called Evidence, becaufe thereby the Point in Iffue is to be made evident to the Jury : *Probationes debent effe evidentes (id eft) perfpicuæ & faciles intelligi.*

And this Evidence (with *Bracton*) we may term *probatio duplex, viz. viva,* as Witneffes *viva voce* ; and *Mortua,* as by Deeds, Writings and Inftruments ; and *Violenta præfumptio,* in many Cafes, is *plena probatio* ; and therefore if all the Witnefs to a Deed be dead, then the Deed fhall receive Credit *per collationem figillorum fcripturæ, &c.* but efpecially if there hath been a continual and quiet Poffeffion ; which is a violent Prefumption, 1 *Inft.* 6. for no Man can keep his Witneffes alive.

If a Thing be generally referred to Proof, this fhall be intended Proof by Jury ; but if other Manner of Proof be agreed upon, that fhall take away the Proof which the Law generally intends by Jury. *Hob.* 127. As if I promife to pay what Money you prove *B.* borrowed ; this may be proved in the fame Action brought upon the Promife. *Vide Roll.* Tit. *Trial,* 594, 595.

The Teftimony of Witneffes *vivâ voce* is more effectual to difcover the Truth than their Depofition in Paper, by confronting them one with another, and applying Queftions for which they cannot be prepared. *Vin. Evidence,* 52.

Evidence

Evidence, in legal Underſtanding, not only contains *Matter of Record,* as Letters Patent, Fines, Recoveries, Inrollments, *&c. Writings* under Seal, as Court Rolls, Accounts, *&c.* but in a *large Senſe* it contains alſo the *Teſtimony of Witneſſes,* and other Proofs to be produced and given to a Jury for the finding any Iſſue joined between the Parties ; and it is called *Evidence,* becauſe the Point in Iſſue is thereby to be made *evident* to a Jury: *Proofs* ought to be perſpicuous and eaſy to be underſtood. *Ibm.*

Evidence to a Jury is what may be given in Evidence, as by *Parol Ore tenus,* or by *Writing* ; but nothing can be *delivered* in Evidence to a Jury, but what is of *Record* or *under Seal,* without Conſent. *Ibm.*

It is only given for the Information of Conſcience, yet if no Evidence be given on either Side, the Jury may notwithſtanding find a Verdict either for Plaintiff or Defendant, and even though the Evidence be given *excluſive,* they may find againſt it, and hazard an Attaint if they pleaſe. *Ibm.*

Evidence *vivâ voce* is always beſt ; and tho' the Law requires the *beſt Proof* that can be had, yet, when that cannot be had, it is ſatisfied with that which can. Evidence which is *contrary* to the *Matter in Iſſue,* or which is not agreeable to it, is not good ; but where the Evidence proves the *Effect* of the Iſſue, it is good ; and it ſuffices to prove the *Subſtance* without any preciſe Regard to the Circumſtances. *Ibm.*

In Caſe, the Declaration was for delivering Goods not merchandizable, *knowing* them to be naught, this *Sciens* need not be proved in Evidence. *Viner, Trial,* 348.

B 2   There

There is a Difference between Pleas of *Performance* and Pleas in *Excuse*; in the *latter* the Party is bound to prove it as *pleaded*, but not in the *former*. *Ibm.* 349.

Always when a Man pleads the *General Issue*, if his *Evidence* stands with his Issue, and proves it, the Evidence is good; but otherwise, where the Evidence doth not prove it. *Ibm.* 352.

In a Writ of *Right*, if the Mise be joined upon the *meer Right*, a *collateral Warranty* cannot be given in Evidence, for he hath no Right to it, it therefore ought to have been pleaded. *Ibm.* 354.

In Trespass, the Defendant pleads that the *Place where*, *&c.* is his Freehold, and gives in Evidence a Fine with Proclamations; this is good Evidence, because it is a Title. *Ibm.*

So in false Imprisonment, if the Defendant justifies by Warrant made *after* the Arrest, the Plaintiff may reply *de injuriâ suâ propriâ, &c.* And give the Matter in Evidence. *Ibm.*

A Fact alledged to be done on a *particular Day*, when no Fact was done, if it fall out upon the Evidence, that the Fact was done before the Action brought, it is sufficient. *Ibm.*

If the Point in Issue be a *bare Agreement*, or simple Contract, without complex Matter, and the Evidence proves an Agreement *Special*, yet this is good: So of a Feoffment *absolute*, and the Proof is of a Feoffment *conditional*. *Ibm.*

A Deed of Feoffment *without* Livery may be given in Evidence as a *Release*. *Ibm.*

Where

Where a Demife is pleaded to Hufband and Wife, a *Fine fur Releafe* to them, is no Evidence to prove the fame ; but in an Action on the Cafe by the Hufband of an *Affumpfit* made *to him* ; if the Evidence be that the *Affumpfit* was made to the *Wife*, and that he did agree to it, this is good. *Ibm.* 357.

When an Information or Action is brought upon any *Statute*, if the Defendant be *difcharged* by any *Provifo therein*, he may give it in Evidence ; but if it be any *Foreign Matter*, even though it be a Licence purfuant to a *Provifo of the Statute*, he muft plead it ; *per Turner J.* though *Hale* faid, that a Licence purfuant to a Provifo was the fame as a Provifo, and might be given in Evidence. *Ibm.* 359. See *Roll. Trial*, 683. *pl.* 11. and 2 *Roll. Rep.* 92.

In Affize, if the Tenant pleads *Nul Tort nul Diffeifin*, he cannot give a Releafe *after* the Diffeifin in Evidence ; but he may give in Evidence a Releafe *before* the Diffeifin, for then upon the Matter there is no Diffeifin.

In Trefpafs by the Warden of the *Fleet*, and Not guilty pleaded, it is good Evidence to fay he was *not* Warden. *Ibm.*

In Cafe, founded upon an Injury done, every Thing that fhews that the Defendant did what he might *lawfully* do, may be given in Evidence upon a *Not guilty*, for that proves he had done no Injury.

So upon a *Non affumpfit*, *Non dimifit*, or *Non detinet*, being in Iffue, *every Thing* may be given in Evidence which *difaffirms* the Contract, for that goes to the Gift of the Action ; for fince there is no Contract to be performed at the Commencement of the Action, there could therefore be no Trefpafs for Non-performance

of

of· it ; a *Releafe* therefore goes to the *Gift* of the Action, for it fhews there was *no Contract* at the Time the Action was commenced.

For as in Trover the Plaintiff claims a Right to the Thing he declares on, therefore *every Thing* that fhews the Contract to be void, as Nonage, or more Money loft at Play than the Statute allows of, may be given in Evidence on the General Iffue ; for on a *void Contract* the Plaintiff hath no Right to any Remedy ; this therefore, and the like, goes to the *Gift* of the Action.

Nota ; That the *Gift* of the Action is the *Fraud* and *Delufion* that the Defendant hath offered the Plaintiff in not performing the Promife he had made, and on relying on which the Plaintiff is hurt ; and therefore what goes to fhew that there was *no Contract*, or that it was *performed* or *paid*, or *releafed*, or that there was *no Confideration*, or difcharged, goes to the *Gift* of the Action, becaufe there could be no *Fraud* or *Delufion* to the Plaintiff at the Time of the Action brought, nor could he rely on that which had *no Being* ; thefe Matters therefore need not be pleaded but may be given in Evidence on the General Iffue. *Vin. Trial*, 359.

When a Man can have Advantage of the *Special Matter* by Way of *Pleading*, he fhall likewife in the *Evidence* ; as for Inftance, the Rule of Law is, that a Man cannot juftify the Killing or Death of another, and therefore in that Cafe he fhall be received to give the Special Matter in Evidence, as that it was *fe Defendendo*, or *in Defence of his Houfe*, or in the

the Night againſt Thieves and Robbers. *Ibm.* 362.

If an Attachment and Condemnation be, *before* a Writ purchaſed, it may be given in Evidence upon the General Iſſue, becauſe it is an Alteration of the Property before Action brought. *Ibm.*

Per Cur. If an Executor ſuffer Judgment to go againſt him by *Default*, upon executing a Writ of Inquiry he is eſtopped, and ſhall not give *the Want* of *Aſſets* in Evidence, as if it had been in the Caſe of an Heir, for he ſhould have pleaded *plene Adminiſtravit*, or ſpecially what Aſſets he had, *et non ultra. Vin. Evid.* 61.

When once a Perſon hath entred upon Evidence by *Deed*, if he fail in his Evidence, he cannot afterwards go to *parol* Evidence of *that Fact. Ibm.*

When a *Releaſe* is pleaded it muſt be *produced* in Evidence, for the Court is to judge of its Force in Law; but where Charters are *loſt or burnt*, in ſuch Caſes of *Neceſſity* the Law allows a Proof then without producing them. *Ibm.*

A Leaſe made upon an Outlawry produced in Evidence to prove a Title, the *Outlawry itſelf* muſt alſo be produced, for that is the Ground of the Leaſe, and by Conſequence of the Title; but if the *Leaſe* be produced to prove *other Matter* he need not produce the *Outlawry*, but may have the *Leaſe* only read in Evidence, though in both Caſes the Leaſe muſt be proved. *Ibm.*

So it is of an *Extent*, the Plaintiff muſt ſhew on what the Extent is grounded : So in *Debt for Rent* upon a *Leaſe parol*, and *Nil debet* pleaded, the Plaintiff muſt ſhew his Title to

B 4   the

the Land; but *contra* upon a Leafe *under Seal,* for the Defendant is eftopped by his Acceptance and Sealing a Counterpart. *Ibm.*

So in Debt for Tithe by a *Parfon,* he muft prove his *Inftitution* and *Induction,* and Reading the 39 *Articles,* for this is his Title to the Tithe. *Ibm.*

The Sheriff, upon an Affignment of a Bail-Bond doth not *part with* the Bond, becaufe he is to be *indemnified* if the Plaintiff be nonfuit, but he muft produce it at the Trial. *Ibm.* 62.

Confequential Damages may be given in Evidence in an *Action on the Stat. againft fuing in the Admiralty,* though 'not mentioned in the Declaration; as, that he *loft the Profits* of his Voyage. *Ibm.* 76.

When you have a *good Matter* in Bar, and an Opportunity to plead it, you fhall not give it in Evidence. *Ibm.*

In all Cafes, where a Man *admits* the Action were *it not for fpecial Matter,* that Matter may be fpecially pleaded; though it may likewife be given in Evidence on the General Iffue. *Ibm.* 77.

It is *not* a Rule, that becaufe a Matter *may* be given in Evidence, that therefore it *muft not* be pleaded fpecially; for it very often happens to be in the Election of the Defendant either to plead it fpecially or not, as he fhall be advifed. *Ibm.*

Where the Matter of the Plea confeffes the *Caufe* of Action, but *avoids, &c.* the Defendant may there plead fpecially, though he might have given it in Evidence; but otherwife where the Matter of the Plea doth not *avoid,* but *deny. Ibm.*

Where

Where there is a special Matter to avoid the Plaintiff's Action, which the Defendant *cannot* give in Evidence upon the General Issue, he must then plead it specially: So, where there is a *meer Matter of Fact*, to avoid the Plaintiff's Action it may be given in Evidence on the General Issue; but if the Matter of Fact contains likewise *Matter of Law*, the Defendant may either plead specially or generally, and give the special Matter in Evidence. *Ibm.* 78.

It was originally but an Indulgence to give Accord with Satisfaction in Evidence upon *Non assumpsit* pleaded, but it hath crept in, and is now settled.

Debt for Rent upon Demise, *Nil debet* as to Part, and *Nil habuit in Tenementis* as to other Part, this is ill, for in Construction of Law, *Nil habuit, &c.* goes to the whole, and *Nil debet* makes the Plea double, and on *Nil debet, Nil habuit, &c.* might have been given in Evidence, but by pleading *Nil debet* the Demise is admitted; and then by adding *Nil habuit* it is repugnant. *Ibm.*

Coverture, Infancy, &c. may be given in Evidence upon the General Issue; but upon a Not guilty in Trespass *Quare clausum fregit*, a *Highway* cannot be given in Evidence. *Ibm.* 79, 80.

Where a *general Jurisdiction* is *given by Statute*, and a Proviso excepts particular Persons or Things, all those may be given in Evidence; for if the Party or Thing is not within the Act, the Person accused is Not guilty; but where the *Jurisdiction is limited*, and confined to particular Persons or Things, with a Proviso of Exception, this must be pleaded, and you

must

muſt ſhew how the Perſon or Thing is within the Act. *Ibm.*

Whatever is a *Diſcharge* of the Action may be given in Evidence, as a Releaſe, &c. and whatever Promiſe is made by Parol, may be diſcharged by Parol. *Ibm.* 80.

In a Declaration about a Seat in a Church, you need not alledge the Repairing of the Pew, but upon the Trial you muſt prove it. *Ibm.*

In Felonies, &c. heretofore the Perſons that gave Evidence for the Priſoner againſt the King were not ſworn ; but ſee *Siderfin* 211. and Stat. 7 *W.* 3. *c.* 3. and Stat. 1 *Ann. c.* 9. and the Law now is, that they ſhall be ſworn.

B. was indicted for ſtriking *F.* in *Weſtminſter-Hall*, and the Witneſſes that gave Evidence for *B.* were admitted to be ſworn.

And ſo the Defendant's Witneſſes in Appeal of Murder. And the Court would not allow Evidence upon Oath, given upon the Indictment, although the Witneſs was dead ; nor is Evidence upon the Indictment of Treſpaſs Evidence upon an Action of Treſpaſs.

Upon Indictments and Informations concerning Criminal Offences, as againſt a Juſtice for compounding of Recognizances, &c. upon Motion the Court will order the Proſecutor to give particular Inſtances, that the Defendant may know what to defend. *Keb.* 2 Part 220.

A Jew being a Witneſs, is ſworn on the *Old Teſtament*, and Perjury upon the Statute 5 *Eliz. cap.* 9. may be aſſigned upon this Oath ; ſo if it be taken on the Common-Prayer Book, that hath the Epiſtles and Goſpels. *Keb.* 2 Part 314. *Hill.* 19, 20 *Car.* 2. *B. R.*

Proofs

Proofs to determine Matter of Fact, and to be offered to a Judge and Jury, are of two Sorts.   First *Living*, as by Witnesses, and to a Jury one Witness is sufficient.   And *dead*, as Matters of Record, as Letters Patent, Fines, Recoveries, Inrollments, &c.   Writings sealed and delivered; and Feoffments, Leases, Releases, &c.   And without Seal, as Court-Rolls, Accounts, &c.   And if the Case be between the King and a Prisoner, he is first to say what he can for himself, and then all that can say any Thing against him are to be heard upon Oath, and then others may be heard for him : And according to this Evidence on both Sides, or without any Evidence at all, the Jury are to give their Verdict, according to their Knowledge and Oath.

The Jury are obliged to take Cognizance of what is sufficient Evidence, on Pain of an Attaint.

Payment Time out of Mind, is good Evidence of an Endowment.

Where the Evidence proves the Effect and Substance of the Issue, it is good.

In Challenge to the Array, because made at the Denomination of the Sheriff's Clerk, Evidence at his Bailiff's Denomination is good, because favourably made is the Substance.   38 *H.* 6. 9.

Upon the General Issue the Defendant may give any Thing in Evidence, which proves the Plaintiff hath no Cause of Action, or which doth entitle the Defendant to the Thing in Question.

But if he hath Cause of Justification or Excuse, it must be pleaded ; wherefore upon *Non*
detinet

detinet in *Detinue*, the Defendant may give in Evidence a Gift from the Plaintiff; for that proveth that he doth not detain the Plaintiff's Goods; but he cannot give in Evidence that the Goods were pawned to him for Money, and that it is not paid, but he muſt plead it. 1 *Inſt.* 283. For the Property is in the Pledger.

Waſte was aſſigned *in Boſcis in ſuccidendo & vendendo decem Quercus.* The Defendant in Fact had only lopped them; held he might plead *Nul Waſt fait,* and give this ſpecial Matter in Evidence. *Dyer* 92. *pl.* 16.

Waſte was aſſigned *in fodiendo foſſam in quodam Prato.* The Defendant pleaded *Nul Waſt fait,* and the Jury found the Defendant made the Trench to drain the Water, whereby the Ground was better'd, and not damag'd. *Obj.* That this ought to have been pleaded, but it was held, it might be given in Evidence, being no Waſte. *Dyer* 361. *b. pl.* 12.

Waſte.

Upon the Plea, *Nul Waſt fait,* in an Action of Waſte, he may give in Evidence any Thing that proved it no Waſte; as by Tempeſt, by Lightning, by Enemies, &c. But he cannot give in Evidence any juſtifiable Waſte, as to repair the Houſe, or the like; nor a Reparation of the Waſte before the Action brought. For the Rule is, That the Evidence muſt ſtand and agree with the Iſſue. 1 *Inſt.* 283. See *Gilb. L. of Evid.* 274. So the Defendant may give in Evidence, that the Houſe was burned by Accident, for this is no Waſte, becauſe it cannot be ſuppoſed within the Party's Power to prevent. *Gilb. L. of Evid.* 274.

If

If a Man bring an Action of Waste, upon the General Issue of *Nullum fecit Vastum*, the Defendant cannot give in Evidence that the Houses were repaired, and the Waste set right before the Action brought, for this confesses the Waste and avoids the Action, by shewing that it is not lawful for the Plaintiff to bring his Action where the Injury is already redressed, and on the General Issue, the Plaintiff denies any cause of Action. *Gilb. L. of Evid.* 273, 4.

So upon this Issue the Defendant cannot give in Evidence a Licence to cut down Trees; for this is to confess, and not to deny the doing of the Waste. *Gilb. L. of Evid.* 274.

If the Defendant cut Timber, and lay it out in Repairs, he cannot give that in Evidence on the General Issue, but he ought to plead it specially; for this Evidence confesses and avoids the Declaration, and it admits the Fact of the Declaration, but brings those Circumstances in, which shew the Fact may be lawfully done; and therefore the foregoing Reasons ought to be offered to the Court. *Gilb. L. of Evid.* 274. *Objection:* But it may be said that this Evidence falsifies the Declaration, inasmuch as it proves that the cutting of the Timber is not the Disinheritance of the Lessor, and so it may be given in Evidence on the General Issue. *Answer:* If you admit any Fact, you allow all the Consequences of that Fact; now when the Defendant's own Evidence do attest the cutting of the Trees, he must allow the Consequences of that Fact, when it is to the Lessor's Disinheritance; for on the Issue nothing but the Truth of the Fact in the Declaration can be called in Question; you cannot therefore on this Issue allow the Truth of the Fact, and yet
offer

offer it to the Jury, and deny all the Confequences of the Law attending upon the Fact, for that is improper to the Jury, who are not Judges of the Law, and therefore muft be offered to the Court who are, and confequently notwithftanding this Objection ought to be pleaded. *Gilb. L. of Evid.* 275.

Upon Not guilty, in an Action upon the Statute *de parco fracto*, That the Plaintiff hath no Park, is god Evidence. 19 *H.* 8. 9. *Roll. Trial*, 683. *pl.* 6.

If the Defendant pleads Payment to a Bond or Bill, and it appears the Debt is very old, and it hath not been demanded, nor any Ufe paid for many Years, a common Prefumption is good Evidence, that the Money is paid, and the Juries ufe to find for the Defendants in fuch Cafes.

Evidence fhall never be pleaded, but the Matter of Fact fhall be pleaded; and if it be denied, the Evidence fhall be given to the Jury, not to the Court. *Lib.* 9. 9.

Evidence, that the Wife of every Copyholder fhall have the Land *durante viduitate*, will not maintain the Iffue, that the Cuftom of a Manor is, That fhe fhall have the Land during her Life, after her Hufband's Death, becaufe, though *durante viduitate* imports an Eftate for Life, yet an Eftate *durante vita*, is more large and beneficial. *Lib.* 4. 30.

Eftate for Life.

What may be given in Evidence.

Things done *before* the Memory of Man in another County, or in another Kingdom, may be given in Evidence to a Jury, as Affets in another County, &c. *Moor* 47. See *Lib.* 4. 22. 9. 27, 28, & 34. *Lib.* 6. 46,. 47.

Copy

Copy of a Record may be read at a Trial for a malicious Profecution, though not ordered by the Court. 2 *Str.* 1122.

Upon Iffue, *Payment at the Day*; Payment Payment. before or after the Day is no Evidence, *Moor* 47. but upon *Nihil debet*, it is good Evidence, becaufe it proves the Iffue.

In Attaint, the Plaintiff fhall not give more Attaint. Evidence, nor examine more Witneffes, than was before; but the Defendant may. *Dyer* 212.

In Actions upon the Cafe, Trefpafs, Battery, or falfe Imprifonment, againft any Juftice of Peace, Mayor or Bailiff of City or Town Cor- porate, Headborough, Portreve, Conftable, Ti- Special Evi- thingman, Collector of Subfidy or Fifteen, in dence upon any of his Majefty's Courts at *Weftminfter*, or the General elfewhere, concerning any Thing done by any Iffue, by whom. of them, by Reafon of any of their Offices afore- faid, and all other in their Aid or Affiftance, or by their Commandment, *&c.* They may plead the General Iffue, and give the fpecial Matter of their Excufe or Juftification in Evi- dence. 7 *Jac. cap.* 5.

Prohibition for fuing for Tithes in *Bocking- Park* in *Effex*, and furmifed, that the Lands were Parcel of the Poffeffions of the Priory of *Chrift-Church* in *Canterbury*, and the faid Prior and his Predeceffors had held it difcharged of Tithes *tempore diffolutionis*, and pleaded the A *non deci-* Statute of 31 *H.* 8. The Defendant pleads that *mando.* the Prior and his Predeceffors did not hold them difcharged, and upon Iffue joined there- on, the Evidence was, That the Prior or his Predeceffors, Time out of Mind, *&c.* never paid Tithes; but no Caufe was fhewn, either by Unity of Poffeffion, real Compofition, or
other

In *Nil debet*, upon the Statute for Tithes, a Lay Perfon cannot give a *Non decimando* in Evidence; but fo may the King and any other fpiritual Perfons. *Lib.* 2. other Caufe, to fhew it difcharged: *Cook* faid it was no Evidence, for it is a Prefcription *in non decimando. Curia contra* ; for a fpiritual Man may prefcribe *in non decimando*, and by the Statute of of 31 *H.* 8. he fhall hold it difcharged as the Prior held it ; and if he held it difcharged, *non refert* by what Means ; for it fhall be intended by lawful Means, and the Jury afterwards found it for the Plaintiff. *Cro.* 3 Part 2, 6. *Keb.* 2 Part 45.

Bp. of *Winchefter's* Cafe.

Suit in the Spiritual Court for Tithes, Defendant pleads, That Plaintiff did not read the Articles ; and held that Defendant muft prove this, tho' a Negative: For, fays the Book, the Law prefumes that none would lofe his Benefice rather than read the Articles. 1 *Roll. Rep.* 83.

In Ejectment for a Rectory, the Leffor of the Plaintiff muft prove not only his Admiffion, Inftitution and Induction, but alfo his Reading the Articles, and fubfcribing them, and his declaring his full and free Affent to the Book of *Common Prayer*, within the Time limited by the Statute. 1 *Sid.* 220.

Affidavit of one convicted of Forgery, not to be read to fupport a Complaint. 2 *Stra.* 1148.

A Church-Book is no Evidence. *Brownlow's* 1 Part 107. *Poftea.* 26 *Aff. pl.* 4. If a Church-Book, or any Thing elfe be given in Evidence, which ought not to be allowed, the Court above cannot quafh the Verdict, except it be certified and returned with the *Poftea. Brownlow's* 1 Part 207. But the Court may order a new Trial, upon caufe fhewed, as for exceffive Damage, &c.

The

The Court will not permit the Jury to carry any Writings out with them, but what are proved, and under Seal.

The Certificate of the King under his Sign Manual, was allowed in *Chancery* for Proof without Exception. *Hob.* 213.

Upon a Traverse of a Lease Parol for Years, *viz. Absque hoc, quod A. dimisit, &c. Nihil habuit in tenementis* may be given in Evidence. *Dyer* 122.

Shewing a Grant to dig Turfs, is no Evidence against a Prescription for the same, but the Grant being the same with the Prescription, shall be taken as a Confirmation. *Crew* and *Vernon, Moor* 819. *Quære tamen, vide Moor* 830. Where a Court of *Piepowder* is claimed by Prescription and Grant, and good. 2 *Cro.* 313. *Acc.*

The Confession of a Party must be taken whole, and not by Parts; as if to prove a Debt, it be sworn that the Defendant confessed it, but withal he said at the same Time, that he paid it; his confession shall be valid as to the Payment, as well as that he owed it; *per Hale* Chief Justice. And so is common Practice.

The Jury are to decide the Fact, and Evidence is not given but to inform them in their Conscience of the Truth; for although no Evidence is given of either Side, yet they may give their Verdict of one Side or other. 14 *H.* 7. 29. And therefore, although two Witnesses are necessary, where the Trial is by Witnesses, as in the Civil Law; yet they are not of Necessity, where the Trial is by Jury. And where Witnesses are joined with the Jury, yet they may be rejected, if they will not agree

Office of the Jury.

with the Twelve, and the Twelve may give their Verdict. *Roll. Trial*, 675.

Ibid. 676. *pl.* 7.

The Jury, after they are departed from the Bar, may return and hear their Evidence of any Thing they doubt before the Verdict.

Done in tayle.

Sur Traverse de done in Tayle, the Witnesses prove, That another made the *Done;* this doth not Warrant the Issue *Ibid. pl.* 13.

Extortion *verſ. vic.* Fee.

In an Action against the Sheriff upon the Statute of Extortion, that he took it for Bar-fee of one who was acquit, is good Evidence.

Poſſeſſion.

Poſſeſſion is an Evidence of Right, and he that hath Poſſeſſion may diſtrain the Cattle of him that hath no Title, for the Taking is in reſpect of the Poſſeſſion more than of the Title. *Roll. Trial*, 679. *pl.* 19.

A Receipt of the laſt half Year's Rent is Evidence that all before was paid.

Parſon.

Parſon or not Parſon, in ſuch Iſſue you may give in Evidence a Reſignation, although it be in another County and Spiritual. *Roll. Trial*, 677. *pl.* 28.

Fait.

In *Riens paſſe per le fait,* not his Deed may be given in Evidence.

In Waſte, the plaintiff declared of a Leaſe by *J. S.* to the Defendant, whereby *J. S.* granted him the Reverſion, to which the Defendant attorned; and the Queſtion was whether if the Defendant pleaded *Ne granta pas,* or *Riens paſſa per le fait,* he could give in Evidence, that he never *attorned* to the Plaintiff? *Shelly* thought he could not, but that he ought to traverſe the Attornment; but *Knightly* and *Fitzherbert* thought he might in either Caſe. *Dyer* 31. *pl.* 215.

To

To lay a Cuſtom to a Houſe and Land, Cuſtom.
to prove it to Land only, not good. *Godbolt*
234.

'Tis good Evidence to convict one upon the
Statute *Eliz.* for not coming to Church, to Church.
prove that the Party was not at his Pariſh
Church ſuch a Sunday, and the Party may ſhew
that he was at Church elſewhere.

After Evidence given, and the Jury ready Former Trial,
to give their Verdict ; and then the Attorney
General will not proceed, but draws a Juror,
and brings another Information, none of the
former Jurors ſhall be admitted to give in E-
vidence, that the Jury were ready to give their
Verdict againſt the King in the firſt Information ; for this ought not to be diſcovered, for
ſo no Benefit would accrue to the King by
his Prerogative to draw a Juror. *Roll. Trial,*
679. *pl.* 10.

But this may be given in Evidence in What may be
ano her Action, where the King is not con- given in Evi-
cerned. dence upon a
  ſpecial Iſſue.

Upon an Iſſue of Common appendant, *&c.* Common.
common pur cauſe de vicinage cannot be given in
Evidence. *Roll. Trial,* 680. *pl.* 2.

If an Advowſon be pleaded to be granted *Grant per fait,*
per fait, and this Iſſue is taken by a Stranger where it is
to the *Fait,* if it be found granted *ſans fait,* prove the
or by another *Fait* it is good ; for the Deed Effect of the
is Surplus, and the Effect of the Iſſue is up- Iſſue.
on the Grant, not upon the *Fait.* *Ibid.* 651.
pl. 1.

If a Man plead Not guilty, he cannot give What Things
in Evidence a Matter juſtifiable, which ſhall may be given
be a Confeſſion of the Act, for this is con- in Evidence
trary to the Iſſue. As *Son aſſault demeſne* in upon the Ge-
Battery upon Not guilty : But upon Not guilty Treſpaſs.
  in Battery,

C 2

in Trefpafs for beating one's Servant, *per quod servitium amifit*, you may give in Evidence, that the Plaintiff did not lofe his Service by the Battery. *Roll. Trial*, 682. *pl.* 1, 2, 5.

Wafte.

Nor upon *Null waft fait* can he fay, *fufficientment repair devant le brief purchafe. Ibid. pl.* 3.

Libel.

In an Information for Writing, Printing, and Publifhing a Libel, That Copies were found in the Defendant's Chamber, is no Publication, without difcourfing it, or Delivery of it out. *Keb.* 2 Part 502.

What Evidence the Jury may have with them.

Exemplifications.

The Jury can have nothing but what is delivered to them in open Court, and given in Evidence by the Party in Court: If an Exemplification come out of *Chancery* of Witnefles examined there upon Oath, who are dead, the Jury fhall have this with them; but if the Exemplification comprehend fome Witnefles alive, and fome dead, they fhall not have it with them. Neither fhall they have any Pedigree drawn by a Herald at Arms, for it is no Evidence, only Information for Direction.

Pedigree.

Nor an Office before an Efcheator, unlefs exemplified, nor a Teftimonial, nor a Part of a Fine indented, unlefs exemplified, but they may find the fame fpecially.

An old Terrier or Survey of a Manor, whether Ecclefiaftical or Temporal, may be given in Evidence, for there can be no other way of afcertaining old Tenures or Boundaries. *Gilb. L. of Evid.* 78.

Terror.

Conventicle of thirty or forty, is Evidence of Terror, &c. *Keb.* 2 Part 558.

Matter in Law.

Matter in law is not to be given in Evidence, for the Jury are only to try Matters of Fact.

Fact. The adverse Party may demur to such Vaughan's
Evidence. *3 H. 6. 36.*   Rep. 143.

A Writing or Answer permitted to be read *Totum & pars.*
in Part, may be read *in toto*.

The Council of that Party which doth begin to maintain the Issue, whether of Plaintiff
or Defendant, ought to conclude.

The Jury may carry from the Bar an Exemplification under the Great Seal, of Depositions in *Chancery* ; but if they are not exemplified, the Jury can only look upon them
at Bar, but not have them with them out of
Court.

Exemplifications of Depositions in Equity
shall be delivered to the Jury, if the Party be
dead ; but if they comprehend the Testimony
of some that are living, they shall not be given
in Evidence. *Gilb. L. of Evid.* 21.

In Evidence, he which affirms the Matter
in Issue, ought first to make the Proof to the
Jury. *Litt. R. 36. Godb. 23. 3 Leon. 162.*
Where there are several Issues, if there be one
Affirmative in any of them from the *Plaintiff*,
he shall first go through his Evidence as to *all*
of them ; but where the Affirmative lies upon
the *Defendant*, he shall first go through his Evidence. *Vin. Evidence*, 60.

On a *special* Issue no Body can run into any
Point that is out of the Issue ; but on the General Issue, whatever tends to satisfy the *Plaintiff's* cause of Complaint may be given in Evidence. *Gilb. L. of Evid.* 233, 4.

The King's Message or Letter shall not be
allowed for Evidence between Party and Party ; otherwise where the Matter was secret,
and that the King only had personal Know-

C 3   ledge,

ledge, as in Sir *George Reynel*'s Cafe, *Co.* 9 *Rep.*

2. B. R. 66.
Smith *verſus* Rawlins.
2 Keb 126.
Impropria
tion. Vicar.

Upon Evidence at Bar it was agreed, That an old Impropriation ſhall be preſumed to be well and lawfully made. A Vicar might anciently have been endowed without a Deed ſealed, being only an Ordination of the Biſhop, and Allotment of Maintenance.

Hand.

The Chief Juſtice ſaid, If a Man be over-ſea or dead, the Party ſhall be admitted to prove his Hand by Witneſſes, or comparing with other of his Writings; to which the Court agreed.

Marriage.
Starch *v.* Ely.
24 Car. 2.
Rot. 494.

In an Action brought by a Woman for ſlandering of her, by which ſhe loſt her Marriage with *J. S.* the Marriage of *J. S.* is not traverſable, but ought to be proved in Evidence.

Foreign Attachment.

Cuſtom of foreign Attachment may be pleaded, or given in Evidence. 3 *Keb.* 221.

Evidence may be given to mitigate Damages, in all Cafes where Damages are to be recovered; as in Waſte, that the Premiſſes were ruinous at the Time, &c. or burnt by Enemies, &c. See *Olive* and *Gwin*'s Cafe, in *Siderfin* 2 Part 155. in the *Exchequer*, good Matter concerning Evidence, where it was adjudged, that a Record had in *Brecknock* in *Wales*, under the Seal of *Brecknock*, might be given in Evidence. See *Hardr. Rep.* 118.

Refuſing to
give Evidence
is a Contempt,
and fineable.

Lord *Preſton* was committed by the Court of Quarter-Seſſions, for refuſing to be ſworn to give Evidence to the Grand Jury, on an Indictment of High Treaſon. He was brought by *Habeas Corpus* in *B. R.* and *Holt*, C. J. ſaid, it was a great Contempt, and that had he been there, he would have fined him, and committed
ted

ted him till he had paid the Fine ; but being otherwife he was bailed. *Rex* verfus *Prefton, Salk.* 278.

You may take out Execution on a Judgment in Paper figned by the Mafter, but you cannot give a Copy of it in Evidence till it is brought in Parchment. *Gilb. L. of Evid.* 22.

Charnock was indicted, for that he the 10th of *February*, 9 *W.* 3. *& diverfis aliis diebus & vicibus tam antea quam poftea*, in the Parifh of St. *Clement Danes*, did traiteroufly confpire to kill the King. *Et per Holt*, C. J. Evidence may be given of a treafonable Confpiracy, *&c.* at any Time before or after the Time alledged in the Indictment :

1ft, Becaufe it is only a Circumftance, and of Form, fome Day muft be alledged, but it is not material.

2dly, The Indictment lays it to be at divers Days and Times, as well before as after, and thereby comprehends what was done laft Year, as well as this ; and as the Evidence may be of Matters before that Time, fo it may be of Matters alfo at any Time after the Time fpecified in the Indictment, provided it be not *after the Time the Indictment was found* ; neither is the Evidence tied up to the Place ; for it may be of any Place, provided it be not out of the County ; and fo it is of all criminal Cafes. *Salk.* 288.

Indictment, That the Defendant, with others, at the Parifh of *St. Giles in the Fields*, riotoufly affembled, *& quoddam cubiculum cujufdam S. S. in Domo Manfionali cujufdam David James fregit & intravit*, and thirty Yards of Stuff took and carried away. On Evidence it appeared to be the Manfion-houfe of *David*

C 4   *Jamfon,*

Jamſon, and not *James*; and held by *Parker*, C. J. at *Niſi prius*, that this did not maintain the Indictment. 1 *Salk.* 385. *Regina* verſus *Cronage*.

Dureſs cannot be given in Evidence, but muſt be pleaded. *Gilb. L. of Evid.* 165, 166.

Perſon preſumed to be living, 'till Proof to the contrary.

Generally Perſons are preſumed to be living, if the contrary be not proved. 2 *Roll. Rep.* 461. *Throgmorton* verſus *Walton*.

Unleſs abſent for ſeven Years.

But by 19 *Car.* 2. *cap.* 6. If Perſons for whoſe Lives Eſtates are granted, remain beyond Sea, or abſent themſelves in this Kingdom ſeven Years together, and no evident Proof be made of their Lives, in any Action commenced by the Leſſors or Reverſioners for Recovery of ſuch Tenements, they ſhall be accounted as dead.

Provided, That if after any Perſons ſhall be evicted by Virtue of this Act, the Perſons, upon whoſe Lives ſuch Eſtates depend, ſhall return from beyond Sea, or on Proof in any Action for the ſame, be made appear to be living, or having been living at the Time of the Eviction; the Tenant, who has ouſted, his Executors, &c. may enter, &c. And upon Action againſt them that received the Profits, recover for Damages the full Profits, with lawful Intereſt.

Where one in Poſſeſſion of an Eſtate ſhall be concealed from the Reverſioner, and not ſhewn to him once a Year, ſuch Perſon ſhall be taken for dead without other Evidence.

And by 6 *Annæ, cap.* 18. Every Perſon who hath any Claim to any Remainder, Reverſion, or Expectancy of any Eſtate whatſoever, after the Death of any other Perſon, upon *Affidavit* in *Chancery*, by the Perſons claiming Title thereto, that they have cauſe to believe that ſuch other Perſon is dead, and ſuch death con-

cealed

cealed by the Guardian, Truftee, or other Perfon, may once a Year, if the Perfon grieved
think fit, move the Lord Chancellor to order
fuch Guardian, or fuch Perfon fufpected to
conceal, to produce to fuch Perfon and Perfons, fufpected to be concealed; and if
fuch Guardian, &c. fhall refufe or neglect to
produce the Perfon on whofe Life fuch Eftate
depends; then the faid Court is to order fuch
Guardian, &c. to produce the Perfon conceal'd,
in *Chancery*, or before Commiffioners appointed
by the Court, (two of which Commiffioners
to be named by the Profecutor.)   And if fuch
Guardian neglect to produce fuch Perfon fo
concealed, and the Return be filed in the Petit Bag, the Perfon concealed fhall be taken to
be dead; and the Perfon claiming may enter on
fuch Eftate.

By 11 *W. & M. Seff*. 1. *cap*. 16. It was enact- No Evidence
ed, That after the Death of any Perfon fimo- of a fimonia-
niacally promoted to a Benefice, the Offence cal Promotion
or Contract of *Simony* fhall neither by Way of after the
Title in Pleading, or in Evidence to a Jury, Death of the
or otherwife be alledged or pleaded to the Pre- cerned.
judice of any Patron innocent of *Simony*, or of
his Clerk, upon Pretence of Lapfe, or otherwife, unlefs the Parfon fimoniacally promoted,
or his Patron were convicted of fuch Offence
at the Common Law, or in fome Ecclefiaftical
Court, in the Life of the Perfon fimoniack.

A Peer produced as a Witnefs ought to be Peer fworn
fworn.   3 *Keb.* 631. Earl of *Shaftfbury* verfus as a Witnefs.
P. Digby.

The Wife is not obliged to difcover the Wife.
Hufband's Treafon.

Wife

Wife de facto *only may bring Trespass for an Assault by Husband.* On Not guilty in Trespass for an Assault, the Defendant gave in Evidence his Marriage with the Plaintiff; to encounter which, she proved a former Marriage to one *Westbrook*, who was alive at the Time of her second Marriage. For the Defendant it was insisted, the Plaintiff ought not to give Felony in Evidence to support her Action; but this was over-ruled, and she obtained a Verdict, her Marriage with the Defendant being void *ab initio.* T. 4 G. 1. *Westbrook* v. *Stratville*, before *King*, C. J. in *Middlesex*, 1 *Stra.* 79.

In an Action for Wages earned by the Plaintiff's Wife of the Defendant's Intestate, the Ch. Justice would not allow the Wife's owning the Receipt of 20*l.* to be given in Evidence against the Husband. 2 *Stra.* 1094.

In Escape what Evidence.

No Retaking shall be given in Evidence in an Action of Escape, unless specially pleaded, and Oath be made by the Keeper of the Prison, that such Escape was without his Consent; but if such *Affidavit* prove false, such Keeper shall forfeit 500*l.* 8 & 9 *W.* 3. *cap.* 27.

Every Keeper's refusing after one Day's Notice, to shew the Prisoner in Execution to the Creditor or his Attorney, shall be adjudged an Escape. *Ibid.*

A Note from the Gaoler, Evidence of a Person's being a Prisoner.

Persons desiring to charge any Person with an Action or Execution, shall, at their Request, have a Note in Writing from the Keeper of the Prison, whether such Person be a Prisoner, or not, under Forfeiture of 50*l.* And such Note shall be sufficient Evidence. *Ibid.*

Where

Where a Woman conceals the Death of her Concealment
Baftard-Child, it fhall be look'd upon as mur- Evidence of
dered by her, unlefs fhe can prove by one Wit- Murder.
nefs at leaft, that it was Still-born.   21 *Jac.* 1.
cap. 27.

In an Ejectment brought by the Leffee of Baftardy ad-
Pride on a Trial at Bar in the *King's Bench*, be- mitted to be
fore *Holt* C. J. and *Eyre* J. The Plaintiff inti- prov'd after
tled himfelf to the Lands in Queftion, as Heir the Party's Death.
to *George*, late Duke of *Albemarle*, by being
Son to a Daughter of *Monk*, who was elder
Brother to the Duke. (Suppofing the Duke
died without Iffue.)   The Defendant claimed
under a Deed, and alfo under a Will of *Chrifto-*
pher, fon to Duke *George*.

To which the Plaintiff replied, he was not
Son to Duke *George*, but a Baftard, becaufe at
the Time Duke *George* married the Mother of
the faid *Chriftopher*, fhe had a Hufband then
living ; and fo the Marriage was void ; and
the Plaintiff produced feveral Witneffes who
endeavoured to prove this Fact.   To this the
Council for the Defendant objected, That
they ought not to be admitted to give Evidence to baftardize a Man that was dead, and
after the Death of his Father and Mother,
who were married in 1653, and cohabited
together as Man and Wife continually, to the
Time of their Death, which was ten Years
after ; and Duke *Chriftopher* was acknowledged
as fon and Heir to Duke *George*, unto the
Time of his Death, which was in 1668 ; and
was called fon and Heir in the Settlement and
Will of Duke *George*, and enjoyed the Eftate
accordingly ; and the Defendant under him,
by Settlement, for above twenty Years: And

Duke

Duke *Chriſtopher* alſo ſat in Parliament as Son and Heir to Duke *George*; and in a Patent made by King *Charles* the Second, was ſo ſtiled, and in an Act of Parliament that paſſed to enable him to diſpoſe of Lands that were ſettled on him as ſuch; and therefore they inſiſted that no Evidence ſhould be given to baſtardize him: But the Judges were of Opinion, that if the Facts were true, the Marriage was null and void, and the Jury might find the Facts; and this Evidence was admitted.   3 *Lev.* 340. The Rule that one ſhall not be baſtardized after his Death, holds only in the Caſe of *Baſtard eigne* and *Mulier puiſne.   Pride* verſus the Earls of *Bath* and *Montague, Hill.* 6 *W.* 3. *B. R.* 3 *Lev.* 340. *Salk.* 120.

Deceit of the Factor beyond Sea, Evidence to charge the Merchant in an Action of Deceit.

In an Action on the Caſe for a Deceit, the Plaintiff ſet forth, That he bought ſeveral Parcels of Silk for———Silk: On Trial, upon Not guilty, it appeared that there was no actual Deceit in the Defendant, who was the Merchant, but that it was in his Factor beyond Sea; and the Doubt was, If this Deceit could charge the Merchant?   And *Holt* C. J. was of Opinion, that the Merchant was anſwerable for the Deceit of his Factor, tho' not *criminaliter*, yet *civiliter*; for ſeeing ſome Body muſt be a Loſer by this Deceit, it is more reaſonable that he that employs and puts a Truſt and Confidence in the Deceiver, ſhould be a Loſer than a Stranger; and upon this Opinion the Plaintiff had a Verdict. *Hern* verſus *Nichols, Salk* 289.

In an Ejectment upon an Elegit, you muſt prove not only the Judgment, and by the Judgment-Roll, that the Elegit iſſued, and was returned, but you muſt prove the Writ of Elegit

by

by a true Copy thereof, and the Inquisition
thereon, because the Notice of the Judgment-
Roll is no more than that the Party did elect
such Execution to issue, and it is the Elegit
and Inquisition upon it, that carves out the
Term, and gives the Title of Entry, so that
the Judgment-Roll is no more than a Memo-
randum, that it was issued and returned, and
the Copy thereof is no Evidence, being but a
Copy of that, which is but a Copy or Memo-
randum of the Thing itself, *sed Quære*; because
Holt was then of a different Opinion, and was
for allowing the Entry of the Roll to be good
Evidence that the Elegit had issued; for a
Notice on the Roll of the Being and Return of
the Elegit, is as good Evidence, that such Elegit was, as a Copy thereof. *Gilb. L. of Evid.*
9, 10.

    On general Acts of Parliament the printed Statutes,
Statute Book is Evidence; not that the printed where Evi-
Statutes are the perfect and Authentick Copies dence.
of the Records themselves, for there is no ab-
solute Assurance of their Exactness, but every
Person is supposed to apprehend and know the
Law which he is bound to observe, and there-
fore the printed Statutes are allowed to be
Evidence, because they are the Hints to that
which are supposed to be lodged in every
Man's Mind already. *Ibid.* 10.

    A saving Proviso may be given in Evidence
on the General Issue, because, if the Party be
within the Proviso, he is not guilty on the
Body of the Act, on which the Action is
founded, and consequently, if the Defendant
shew he is within the Proviso, he is Not guilty
contra Formam Statuti. *Ibid.* 11.

In

In *private* Acts of Parliament the printed Statute Book is not Evidence, though reduced into the same Vol. with the general Statute, but the Party ought to have a Copy compared with the Parliament-Roll; *Quære*, for it seems the better Opinion, that the Copy of private Acts allowed to be Evidence, ought to be under the Great Seal. But Lord Chief Justice *Parker* allowed the printed Statute to be Evidence, in the Case of the College of Physicians and Doctor *West*, of the Truth of a private Act of Parliament, touching the Institutions of the College of Physicians, *London. Gilb. Law of Evid.* 12, 13.

On Not guilty pleaded, the Defendant cannot give Evidence the taking the goods as a Deodand. 1 *Str.* 61.

It was held, that no Release could make the Bankrupt a Witness to prove his own Act of Bankruptcy. *H.* 2 *Geo.* 2. *Field* versus *Curtis,* 2 *Str.* 829.

What a Man himself that is living has sworn at one Trial, can never be given in Evidence at another Trial to support him ; tho' what the Witness has said in Discourse may be given in Evidence to support him ; because the same Oath at another Trial is no Evidence of the Truth of any Man's swearing; for if a Man be of that ill Mind to swear falsly at one Trial, he may do the same on the other, on the same Inducements ; but what a Man says in Discourse, without Premeditation or Expectation of the Cause in Question, is good Evidence to support him. But if a Man hath sworn at one Trial different from what he hath at another, this is good Evidence as to his Discredit. *Gilb. Law of Evid.* 69, 70.

Comparison

Comparison of Hands is Evidence in *civil* but not in *criminal* Cases; for the Comparison of Hands is no more than a Presumption, founded on the Likeness, and the Presumption is in Favour of the Defendant, that he is Not guilty, so there is no more than one Presumption against another. *Gilb. Law of Evid.* 54, 55.

On Oath that a Witness is dead, or unable to travel, or detained by Means of the Prisoner, or cannot be found, his Examination before the Coroner is good Evidence; but the Coroner must swear the Examinations are the same which were taken before him on Oath. *Gilb. Law of Evid.* 140, 141.

If a Man was blind, and the Deed mis-read to him, he may plead *non est Factum,* and such Evidence will maintain the issue, for then 'tis indeed none of his Contract. *Gilb. L. of Evid.* 164.

On Question on a Trial, whether the Property of a Parcel of Wine, was in the Defendant, in order to ascertain whether Alien or British Custom was due for them, a Paper under his Hand, being an Affidavit he had been at the Custom-house, was given in Evidence, he swearing in it that the Wine was his. *E. 4 G. 1. B. R. Vin. Abr.* Tit. *Evid.* 83. *pl.* 4.

The Plaintiff or Defendant may make an Affidavit in their own Cause depending here, and it may be filed; but it may not be admitted in Evidence in the Trial of the Cause betwixt them. *Ibid pl.* 2.

A Man being about to convey Lands to a Purchaser, made Oath before a Master in Chancery, that there was no Incumbrance on the Estate; in an Ejectment brought, this Affidavit was produced in Court, but not suffered

2   10

to be read but as a Note or Letter, unlefs the Plaintiff would produce a Witnefs to fwear that he was prefent when the Oath was taken before the Mafter. *Ibid. pl.* 1. cites 3 *Mod.* 36. *M.* 35 *Car.* 2. *B. R. Smith* verfus *Goodier.*

Though an Affidavit cannot be read in Evidence, yet if the Party who made the Affidavit be fworn, and gives Evidence, his own Affidavit may be read againft him; and this is allowable, to fhew in what Manner he contradicts himfelf. *M.* 5 *W. & M.* in *B. R.* The *Queen* verfus *Rachel Taylor, Skin.* 403.

Affidavit by a Plaintiff in *Holland,* attefted by a Publick Notary, fhall be admitted a good Evidence to hold Defendant to fpecial Bail here. *Vin. Abr.* Tit. *Evid.* 87. *pl.* 8. cites 8 *Mod.* 322.

Of Evidence by Witneffes.

It is a good Challenge to the Witnefs to fay, that he *was one of the Accufers quod Nota. Vin. Abr.* Tit. *Evid.* 1.

Oftentimes a Man may be challenged to be of a Jury, that cannot be challenged to be a Witnefs; and therefore though the Witnefs be of *neareft Alliance, or Kindred, or of Council, or Tenant, or Servant,* to either Party, (or any other Exception, that maketh him not infamous) or to want *Underftanding,* or *Difcretion,* or *a Party in Intereft,* though it be proved true, fhall not exclude the Witnefs to be fworn, but he fhall be fworn, and his Credit upon the Exceptions taken againft him left to thofe of the Jury, who are Tryers of the Fact; infomuch as fome Books have faid, that tho' the Witnefs to the Deed be named a Diffeifor in the Writ,

Writ, yet he fhall, be fworn as Witnefs to the Deed. *Vin. Abr.* Tit. *Evid.* 1. cites *Co. Lit.* 6. *b.*

If a Perfon be infamous, he fhall not be fworn as a Witnefs. 1 *Inft.* 6. *b.*

Men that are fo branded with infamy, that they cannot be Jurors, (for which fee before *who may be Jurors*) cannot be Witneffes; yet *per Glyn* Chief Juftice, and *Nudigate* Juftice, *Mich.* 1657. B. R. Conviction of common Barretry hinders not from being a Witnefs; but *Maynard*, Serjeant, held ftrongly againft it. *V.* 2 *Salk.* 690.

At Lent Affizes, *Suffolk*, 1657. *St. John* Chief Juftice C. B. would not allow one who had been whipped for Petty Larceny to be a Witnefs; but *Earl* Serjeant faid, they ought to be *ftigmatici* that are difabled from being Witneffes: Yet *per Rolle* Chief Juftice, one burnt in the Hand for Felony may be a Witnefs; for he is in Capacity to purchafe Lands, and his Fault is purged by his Punifhment. *Style* 388.

A bare Conviction of Perjury will take away a Perfon's Evidence, becaufe it is an infamous Crime; but *contra*, where, tho' the Punifhment is the Pillory, the Crime is not infamous. 2 *Salk.* 514. See *Co. Lit.* 6. *b.*

A Pardon of Felony reftores a Party to his Credit, and he may be a Witnefs. (*a.*) *Goldb.* 288. 1 *Vent.* 349.

The

(*a*) Where the *Difability* is only the *Confequence* of the Judgment, the King may pardon it; but where the *Difability* is *part of the Judgment* itfelf, the King's Pardon will not take it away; therefore, if a Man be convicted of *Perjury* on the Statute, the King's Pardon will not re-

The general Rule is, that the Husband cannot be a Witness *for or against* the Wife, nor the Wife *for or against* the Husband, being adjudged that the Husband cannot be a Witness against the Wife, nor the Wife against the Husband, to prove the first Marriage, on an Indictment on the Statute 1 *Jac.* 1. *c.* 11. for a second Marriage; but the *second* Husband or Wife may be allowed to give Evidence, such second Marriage being void, therefore they were never Husband and Wife. 2 *Bac. Abr.* 286.

But some Exceptions have been allowed to this general Rule, especially in Cases of evident Necessity; and therefore it hath been adjudged, and is the constant Practice at this Day, that on an Indictment for a forcible Marriage, grounded on 3 *H.* 7. the Wife may be a Witness against the Husband; so where Husband or Wife have cause to demand Sureties of the Peace against each other. 2 *Bac. Abr.* 286.

Also in Lord *Audley*'s Case, who held his Wife's Hands and Legs while his Servant, by his Command, ravished her; the Wife was admitted an Evidence. *Hutt.* 116. 2 *Hawk. P. C.* 432. But in *Raym.* 1. this Case is denied to be Law; and in *Vent.* 244. it is doubted

---

store; for it is not a Consequence, but Part of the Judgment, *viz. Quod imposterum non fit receptus ut Testis*, cites *Co. Ent.* 368. But a Pardon by Act of Parliament will restore him in that Case; *per Holt* Ch. J. 2 *Salk.* 689. *pl.* 1. E. 7 *W.* 3. B. R. in Case of *King* and *Crosby, ibid.* says *Quod Nota. Quære* of a Perjury at Common Law, and if the Law be the same; for there the *Disability* is only a Consequence, and not Part of the Judgment; otherwise, if a Jury be convict on an Attaint, and cites *Raft.* 56. *a.*

of

of by my Lord Chief Juſtice *Hale*, becauſe here is a Wife *de jure*, and ſo not like the Caſe, where a Woman is admitted to prove a forcible Marriage.

Alſo in *Raym.* 1. it is ſaid, that a Huſband and Wife may be Witneſſes againſt one another in Treaſon ; but the contrary is adjudged in 1 *Brownl.* 47. and with this laſt Book, 2 *Hawk.* P. C. 432. ſeems to agree.

In a *qui tam* on the Statute of Uſury, the *Chief Juſtice* refuſed to let the Party to the Contract be a Witneſs to prove the Repayment of the Money, becauſe till that was proved, he was no Witneſs at all. *T.* 11 *G.* 1. *Shank qui tam* v. *Payne*, 1 *Str.* 633.

On Indictment againſt the Huſband for an Aſſault upon the Wife, the Chief Juſtice allowed her to be a good Witneſs for the King, and cited Lord *Audley's* Caſe, *State Trial*, Vol. I. *T.* 11 *G.* 1. The *King* verſus *Azire.* 1 *Str.* 633.

Two were indicted for an Aſſault, one ſubmitted, and was fined 1s. and paid it, the other pleaded Not guilty, and, upon the Trial, the Chief Juſtice allowed him to call the other Defendant, the Matter being now at an End as to him. *T.* 11 *G.* 1. The *King* v. *Fletcher*, *Str.* 633.

In an Indictment proſecuted by the Huſband, for ſeducing away his Wife, and keeping her ſome Time in Adultery. The Wife was admitted to be a Witneſs againſt the Defendant, *Coram Judice Windham*, Lent Aſſizes at *Aleſbury*, and the Defendant was found guilty. She may be a Witneſs to prove a Cheat upon her and her Huſband. *Sid.* 431.

And ſo it was reſolved in *John Brown's* Caſe, *Trin.* 25 *Car.* 2. *B. R.* on the Statute of 3 *H.* 7. *cap.* 2. *vid.* 1 *Cro.* 492.

The Wife of a Bankrupt cannot be examined by the Commiſſioners under the Statute of Bankrupts. 1 *Brownl.* 47.

There was a Libel in the Spiritual Court, *cauſa jaEtitationis maritagii,* pending which, the Witneſſes who were to prove the Marriage were indicted for a Conſpiracy to carry the Woman away by Force, and marry her; and ſhe was allowed a good Witneſs. 4 *Mod.* 8. *Rex* verſus *Fegas.*

The King cannot be a Witneſs by his Letters under his Signet Manual: One attainted of Piracy cannot be a Witneſs to prove another guilty. If he accuſed another before he was attainted, and afterwards confeſſes he wronged him, this Confeſſion ſhall be rejected, becauſe he is attainted. A Woman cannot be a Witneſs to prove a Man to be a Villein. *Co. Lit.* 6. 8.

Roll. Trial, 686. H.

Neither can the Party to the uſurious Contract be a Witneſs againſt the Uſurer, in an Information upon the Statute of Uſury. But Kinſmen never ſo near, Tenants, Servants, Maſters, Councillors, and Attornies, *&c.* may be Witneſſes. A Councillor may be a Witneſs to the Agreement, *&c.* but not to the Validity of an Aſſurance, nor to the Council he gave. *March Rep.* 43. If a Witneſs being ſerved with Proceſs, and having Money ſufficient to bear his Charges, (or leſs, if he accept it) do not appear to give his Teſtimony, he forfeits 10 *l.* to the Party damnified, and muſt recompence his Damages, 5 *Eliz.* 9. If a Witneſs commit wilful Perjury, he loſeth 20 *l.* ſhall be impriſoned

Roll, Trial, 685. pl. 2.

But an Attorney cannot be a Witneſs againſt his Client for Matters ſubſequent to his being employed.

foned fix Months, without Bail, ftand in the Pillory, and be difabled to be a Witnefs; fo fhall the Suborner who procures the Perjury. *5 Eliz. 9.*

In an Indictment for Ufury, the Cafe was, The Defendant lent the Profecutor 45 *l.* on a Pawn of Jewels, for a Year, at 9 *l.* Intereft; and afterwards the Profecutor gave the Defendant a Bond for the fame Money. *Holt,* C. J. admitted the Profecutor to be an Evidence, *de bene effe,* to prove the Contract; it being a Queftion whether the new Bond were void or not? *Fareft.* 118. *Rex* verfus *Sewell.*

A Party robbed is allowed a good Witnefs in his own Action againft the Hundred, for he is not bound, nay he is to be blamed, to tell any one what Charge he carries with him; and if he fhould not teftify, the Law would be often fruitlefs for Want of Evidence, or elfe more Robberies committed by the Party's difcovering his Money.

An *Approver,* or an *Accomplice,* may be a Witnefs till he is indicted. *Vin. Abr.* Tit. *Evid.* 1. *pl.* 7.

A. and *B.* jointly committed in Execution to the *Fleet,* at the Suit of the Crown; in an Action againft the Warden for fuffering *A.* to efcape, *B.* was held a good Witnefs to prove it. *Fitzgib.* 80.

4 & 5 *Ann.* 16. All Witneffes who ought to be allowed good Witneffes upon Trials at Law, fhall be deemed good Witneffes to prove any Nuncupative Will.

Cafe againft Defendant for refcuing a Perfon arrefted on mean Procefs, the Party refcued was allowed to be a Witnefs for the Defendant.

Per

Per Holt C. J. *fed hæfitanter,* and his Credit left to the Jury. 6 *Mod.* 211. 2 *Salk.* 690.

Defendant was convicted of Deer-Stealing on the Oath of the Informer, who by Stat. 13 *Car.* 2. is to have a Moiety of the Forfeiture, being 20 *l.* It was moved to quafh the Conviction, the Informer not being a good Witnefs. The Court gave no Opinion, but it feems he is no Witnefs.

In the Cafe of *Brereton* and *Tatam, Mich.* 1656. *B. R. Glyn* Chief Juftice cited the Lord *Chandos's* Cafe in this Court, where one *Gates* an Executor was produced to prove the Will, as a Witnefs, to which he (as Council) excepted, becaufe of his Executorfhip. It was anfwered, that he had fully adminiftred : He replied, that Affets might afterwards come to his Hand ; but the Court refolved, that it would not be prefumed to bar his Teftimony, which was allowed in the principal Cafe, being in Ejectment.

Affumpfit for the Profits of the Office of Chancellor to the Bifhop of *Landaff:* A former Bifhop had granted it to one Dr. *Loyd* and the Plaintiff, and the Survivor of them, and Dr. *Loyd* was dead ; the prefent Bifhop had granted it to the Defendant ; and the Queftion was, whether there was any Ufage to grant this Office to two ; and the Bifhop was produced to prove no fuch Ufage ; and held no Witnefs. 4 *Mod.* 16.

It is no good Exception to a Witnefs, that he hath Common *per* Caufe of *Vicinage* in the Lands in Queftion, becaufe it is but an Excufe of Trefpafs, and no Intereft. *Clapham's* Cafe, *Mich.* 1657. B. R.

The fame of Common of *Shack.*

A Feoffment

A Feoffment in Fee was made to the Use of *J. S.* and two Witnesses subscribed as to the Execution of it by Livery and Seisin; afterwards one of the Witnesses had an Estate at Will in Part of these Lands, and being produced to prove the Livery and Seisin, at a Trial at Bar, it was objected to him that now he was a Party interested in the Land; but held a good Witness. 1 *Bulstr.* 202.

If the Obligee devises the Debt to the Obligor, and his Executors deliver up the Bond in Satisfaction of the Legacy, which is cancelled, and after the Validity of the Will is questioned, *viz.* whether the Testator was *compos*, &c. the Obligor is a good Witness for the Will, because by the cancelling of the Bond his Debt was discharged. But *contra* in case of Mortgage, for though the Deed be cancelled, if it be no good Will, he must pay the Money. *Goodman* versus *Turbervil, Mich.* 1657, *B. R.*

If *A.* gives a Bond to *B.* conditioned to pay all the Money due from *C.* to *B.* *C.* is a good Witness to prove what is due. *Lutw.* 663.

An Action was brought by the Corporation of the Weavers of *Norwich,* for a Penalty against a Weaver for working at his Trade in Harvest-time, contrary to an Ordinance by them made. And *Atkins* Justice, allowed one of the Corporation to be a Witness, though one Moiety of the Penalty was due to the Corporation. *Lent Assize* 1657.

In a Trial at Bar, where an Estate for Life is limited to *J. S.* Remainder to the Poor of the Parish of *Greenwich* by Will; the Inhabitants of *Greenwich* were allowed to be Witnesses to prove the Will. *Townsend* and *Roan, Mich.* 1658, *B. R. Siderfin,* 2 Part 109.

D 4   A special

A fpecial Iffue was directed to try, whether any Cuftom in a Manor for Fines, to be paid by Tenants on the Death of a Lord, to the Heir during his Minority. The Steward was produced to prove fuch Cuftom; and it was objected, that he had a Fee on every Admiffion; but *non allocatur,* and he was fworn.   *3 Keble* 90.

An Action of Debt was brought, *Summer Affizes, Suff.* 1669. by the Town of *Ipfwich,* for 50 *l.* a Fine fet upon one chofen Common Council Man (called their prime Conftable) for refufing to renounce the Covenant, *&c.* And the Town-Clerk (though a Freeman) was allowed a Witnefs to prove Election, Refufal, *&c.* and the Fine fet, which is for Neceffity, for that none other are or ought to be prefent at thofe Acts. *Rainsford* Juftice.

Per Hale Chief Juftice, *Norfolk* Summer Affizes, 1668. A Freeman of *Lyn* is not an allowable Witnefs to prove the Cuftom of Foreign bought and foreign fold in that Town. *Harwich* verfus *Twels.*

All Perfons may be Witneffes who appear to have fufficient (*a*) Difcretion, and who from their (*b*) Principles, muft be prefumed to have a right

(*a*) An Infant of the Age of Nine Years has been allowed to give Evidence, *H. P. C.* 263. See 1 *Str.* 700.

(*b*) But an Infidel cannot be a Witnefs, *i. e.* fuch a one as neither believes the *Old* or *New Teftament* to be the Word of God, or one to which our Laws require the Oath fhould be adminiftred. 2 *Keb.* 314. 2 *Hawk. P. C.* 434. The Anfwer of an Infidel taken by Commiffion at *Calcutta,* in *Bengal,* in the *Eaft Indies,* after the Manner of that Part of the World, was allowed good Evidence by the late Lord Chancellor *Hardwicke,* after hearing the Arguments of Lord Chief Juftice *Lee,* Lord
Chief

a right Senfe of the Sanctity of an Oath, and of the Obligations it lays them under to depofe the whole Truth ; therefore Infants, Aliens, Villains, Bond-Men, &c. May be Witneffes. 2 *Bac. Abr.* 285. cites *Co. Lit.* 6.

Note; No Man can be a Witnefs for himfelf, but he is the beft Witnefs that can be againft himfelf. *Gilb. L. of Evid.* 122.

Informer no Witnefs, where intitled to Part of the Penalty. 1 *Str.* 316.

Vendor, a good Witnefs as to Title, where no Covenant for Warranty, &c. 1 *Str.* 445.

Wife (a) of *Prochein Amy* allowed to be a good Witnefs in an Action by the Infant. *H.* 8 *G.* 1. *Dennifon* verfus *Spurling.* In *Middlefex*, before *Pratt* Chief Juftice. 1 *Str.* 506. But Defendant's Guardian upon Record not. Same *T. Clutterbuck* and Lord *Huntingtower. Ibid.*

An Infant brought an Action of Affault, and declared by Guardian. And to prove that this Witnefs was the Promoter of the Caufe, and at the Expence of it, the Chief Juftice allowed the Defendant to give the Guardian's Declaration to that Purpofe in Evidence, he being a Perfon liable to Cofts. *Hil.* 9 *G.* 1. *James* verfus *Hatfield* at *Guildhall*, before *King* Chief Juftice, 1 *Str.* 548.

Chief Juftice *Willes*, and Lord Chief Baron *Parker* at Lincoln's Inn Hall, 23 Keb. 1744. *Hil. Term* 18 *G.* 2. but his Lordfhip declared, it was permitted to be read on Account of the efpecial Circumftances of that particular Cafe, and that he carried it no further. *Omichund* and *Barker*, 2 *Eq. Abr.* 397. *pl.* 15.

(a) But *Prochein Amy* no Witnefs, he being liable to Cofts. 2 *Str.* 1026.

A Corporator

A Corporator who has acted under the right claimed, may be a Witneſs to prove the Uſage. 2 *Str.* 1069.

The Wife of one Defendant cannot be a Witneſs for the other, on an Indictment againſt two, 2 *Str.* 1095.

As to the Witneſſes Privileges.

One was ſubpœn'd *ad teſtificandum*, and prayed a Privilege from being arreſted, which was granted; and *per Cur.* It will ſuperſede an Arreſt upon mean Proceſs, but not upon an Execution; yet the Sheriff in that Caſe may be committed for his Contempt. *Hen. Nevil's Caſe, Mich.* 15 *Car.* 2. *B. R.*

Detaining of Witneſſes :

Sir *Jo. Jackſon* was convict upon an Information for preventing of Evidence to be given on an Indictment of Perjury againſt *Fenwick* and *Holt,* who had been Witneſſes for Sir *J. J.* he arreſted ſome Witneſſes, and gave Money to others, and ſo they were acquitted : He was fined one thouſand Marks, one Month's Impriſonment, Behaviour for twelve Months. *Hill.* 1663. *B. R.*

Such Perſons as are infamous, as are Perſons attainted of Felony, or of a falſe Verdict, or of a Conſpiracy, or of Perjury, or of Forgery, upon the Statute of 15 *Eliz. cap.* 14. and not upon the Statute of 1 *H.* 5. 3. and ſuch as have had Judgment to loſe their Ears, or ſtand on the Pillory or Tumbrel, or have been ſtigmatized or branded, and Infidels, Men not of ſound Memory, or not of Diſcretion, or ſuch as are intereſted in the Cauſe, or have Benefit, are not competent Witneſſes. *Co.* 1

Inſt.

Inst. 6. but we see Jews are daily admitted Witnesses.

By Order of Court, the Depositions taken of a sick Witness may be taken in Evidence.

'Tis dangerous to permit Evidence to a Ju- Deed.
ry by Witnesses, that there was such a Deed,
which they have seen or read, or prove the *Keb.* 2 Part
Deed by a Copy, because the Deed may be 546. Instan-
upon Condition, Limitation, or Power of Re- ces of a Copy
vocation ; and if this should be permitted, the not examined,
whole Reason of the Common Law, in shew- allowed and
ing Deeds to the Court, would be subverted ; Evidence ;
for the Deed might be imperfect and void, but I think
which the Witnesses could not perceive ; yet unless the
in Cases of Extremity, as where the Deed was Witness swear
burned, or lost by some other notorious Acci- that he re-
dent, the Judges may at their Discretion allow Contents of
them to be proved by Witnesses. *Lib.* 10. 92. the Deed, and
and so of a Record. that they are
as the Copy
is, the Copy ought not to be allowed Evidence, unless examined.

If a Man makes a Feoffment, and afterwards Who may be
makes another, with Covenants that he was Witnesses.
seized, &c. and afterwards an Issue is taken interested ei-
upon the first Feoffment, the Feoffee shall not ther in Law
be a Witness. *Roll. Trial,* 685. *pl.* 1. or Equity, *in*
præsenti or
futuro.
In an Information for Usury, the Party shall Usury.
not be a Witness, because he would thereby Rolls, Trial,
avoid his own Bonds, &c. and be *testis in pro-* 685. *pl.* 2.
pria causa. 1 Inst. 6. b.

In Case of Forgery, Perjury and Usury, the Party grieved may have Advantage by the Verdict, and therefore shall not be received as a Witness ; but in Case of an Indictment for Battery, he that was beaten may be Witness, becaufe

caufe he can reap no Benefit by the Verdict in another Suit. *Hardres Rep.* 331.

Perjury.
3 Rolls 685.
***pl.* 3.**

Three Men fwear an Arbitrament in three feveral Actions againſt them, upon the Statute 5 *Eliz.* of Perjury, each of them may be a Witneſs for the other ; but in an Indictment of Perjury upon 5 *Eliz.* the Party grieved ſhall not be a Witneſs, for he is to have 20 *l.*

Common Experience tells us, upon an Indictment for Battery, *&c.* the Party grieved may be a Witneſs, becaufe 'tis only for the King. *Ibid. pl.* 5.

Hundred.
Roll. Trial,
685. *pl.* 6.

In an Action againſt the Hundred upon the Statute of *Winton*, *&c.* the Leſſor living out of the Hundred may be a Witneſs ; for 'tis not Reafon that he and his Leſſee being an Inhabitant ſhould be both charged : If the Servant be robbed of the Maſter's Money, the Maſter may be a Witneſs to prove the Delivery of the Money to the Servant before the Robbery. *Roll.* Tit. *Trial,* 686. *Style* 233.

Juror.

A Juror who is a Witneſs, muſt be alfo fworn in open Court to give Evidence, if he be called for a Witneſs ; for the Court and Council are to hear the Evidence as well as the Jury.

Bail.

If a Witneſs be Bail, upon Motion the Court will give Leave to alter the Bail. *Style* 385.

Wife.
Charges.

Debt on 5 *Eliz.* 9. Becaufe the Wife did not appear, whereas he *fubpœna'd* her, and tendred to her her Charges, and though not laid what Damages, yet being for the 10 *l.* upon the Statute, not for his Damages for her not appearing, and a Feme Covert being within the Statute, 'twas held good enough.   3 *Cro.* 130. *Leon.* 122.   *Note* ; She being the Perfon who

was

was to appear, the Charges are to be tendred
to her or her Huſband.

Debt for 10 *l.* againſt a Witneſs, upon the *Charges.*
Statute 5 *Eliz.* doth not lie, unleſs the Witneſs
hath his Charges, and he is not bound to come
without his Charges firſt paid: But if he accept of 12 *d.* and a Promiſe for the reſt at the
Trial, he is bound, and an Action lieth againſt
him, if he doth not come. *Cro.* 1 Part 522,
540. *Goodwin* againſt *Weſt.*

A Copy of his Retainer by a Nobleman, *Chaplain.*
entred in the Court of Faculties, denied to
be given in Evidence. *Littleton, Rep.* 1. But
one that had ſeen it under the Hand and
Seal of the Nobleman, was allowed a good *Quare Impe-*
Witneſs, becauſe the Plaintiff was a Stranger, *dit.*
&c.

A Councilor may be examined as a Witneſs *Councillor.*
againſt his Client, ſo far as it is of his own
Knowledge, not what his Client reveals to him,
but what he knows only by his Client's Information.

Mr. *Aylet* having been Council for the De- *Councillor.*
fendant, deſired to be excuſed to be ſworn on *Spark* againſt
the general Oath, as Witneſs for the Plaintiff, *Middleton,*
to give the whole Truth in Evidence, which Keb. 1 Part
the Court after ſome Diſpute granted, and that 505.
he ſhould only reveal ſuch Things as he either
knew before he was of Counſel, or that came
to his Knowledge ſince by other Perſons; and
the Particulars to which he was to be ſworn
were particularly propoſed, *viz.* What he knew
touching a Will in Queſtion, and the Court
only put the Queſtion, whether he knew of his
own Knowledge, &c.

Tenant

Tenant at Will.

Tenant at Will of Part of the Lands was admitted to prove Livery of Seiſin, and the Execution of a Feoffment under which he held. *Bulſt.* 1 Part 202.

Attainted of Felony.

If one be attainted of Felony and pardoned, he ſhall not afterwards be ſworn of a Jury, for *Pœna mori poteſt, culpa perennis erit* ; and therefore is not fit to ſerve on the Inqueſt, nor yet to be an indifferent Witneſs ; and two ſuch perſons proving a Suggeſtion were rejected, and the Prohibition diſallowed. *Brown* againſt *Craſham, Bulſtr.* 2 Part 154.

Treſpaſs againſt ſeveral ; after Iſſue joined on Motion, one of the Defendants Name was ſtruck out, that he might be a Witneſs for the Plaintiff. 2 *Siderf.* 441. and the like done as to a Perſon named in the *Simul cum.* 1 *Mod.* 11.

Simul cum.

In Treſpaſs with a *Simul cum*, if nothing be proved againſt them in the *Simul cum*, they may be examined as a Witneſs. *Style's Rep.* 401.

Poors con-cerns.

Neither he that pays or takes Collection, can be a Witneſs in ſuch Caſes.

Witneſſes.

Ceſtui que Truſt is not to be admitted a Witneſs where the Title of the Land comes in Queſtion.

Truſt.

One who would have any collateral Title to the Land, as if he hath a good Deed by the Anceſtor, which would charge the Lands in the Hands of the Heir, is not to be admitted an Evidence.

But one who has an equitable collateral Title upon the Land is admittable to be a Witneſs.

Indictment

Indictment of Perjury doth not difable a ⟨Pafc. 20 Car.⟩
Witnefs; otherwife of a Conviction, whether ⟨2. Colt verf.⟩
it be by Common Law or Statute. ⟨Colt. Perjury.⟩

A Truftee cannot be a Witnefs concerning ⟨Truftee.⟩
the Title of the fame Land, the Intereft in the
Law being lodg'd in him.

By *Twifden* and *Wyndham*, if an Action be ⟨Mic. 19 Car.⟩
brought againft two, and no Evidence is given ⟨2 B. R. 67.⟩
againft one, he may be a Witnefs himfelf in ⟨Witnefs.⟩
the Cafe.

In Debt againft the Heir upon an Obliga- ⟨Joint Obli-⟩
tion made by his Anceftor and *J. S.* jointly ⟨gation.⟩
and feverally, *J. S.* was fworn a Witnefs for
the Plaintiff.

In Trefpafs againft *A. fimul cum B. & C.* ⟨Hill. 1651.⟩
B. & C. are admittable to be Witneffes, if ⟨Coram Roll.⟩
the Plaintiff hath not arrefted them, or at ⟨Trefpafs.⟩
the leaft demanded Procefs of the Sheriff to ⟨Simul cum.⟩
do it.

A Clerk attending upon a Grand Jury fhall ⟨Trin. 1650.⟩
not be compelled to be a Witnefs to reveal that ⟨Grand Jury.⟩
which was given them in Evidence.

Plaintiff recovers againft the Defendant upon ⟨Perjury.⟩
the fole Evidence of *J. S.* and has Judgment,
and afterwards *J. S.* was convicted of Perjury
upon the fame Evidence; notwithftanding the
Court would not fet afide the Judgment. But
if it had been after Verdict that an Indictment
of Perjury was depending againft *J. S.* the Court
would have ftopped entring the Judgment 'till
the Perjury tried.

It was doubted by *Twifden*, that if one up- ⟨Mic. 22 Car.⟩
on Evidence forfwear himfelf, and afterward ⟨2. B. R. Roy⟩
the principal Action is annulled by Writ of Er- ⟨verf. Ser-⟩
ror, if afterwards he is indictable for this. ⟨jeant.⟩

By

Felony.

By *Rolle*, If one Convict of Felony be pardoned, or is burnt in the Hand, he may be a Witness again.

After Conviction and Clergy allowed, one is capable to be a Witness; *per Cur'*.

24 Car. 1.
Radford's
Case.

Radford brings an Action of Debt upon the Statute of 5 *Eliz. cap.* 9. for 10 *l.* against *J. S.* and declares that he was warned by *Subpœna* to appear such a Day at one of the Clock in the Afternoon to be a Witness, *&c.* And upon *Nil debet* pleaded, the *Subpœna* given in Evidence was generally to appear at this Day,

Subpœna.

and not at such an Hour; and although a *Subpœna* to appear at such a Day be of that Effect, that the Party ought to attend the whole Day, and so, as it was objected, includes that he ought to appear at this Hour; yet in Respect of the Variance it cannot be said to be the *Subpœna* on which the Plaintiff did declare, and therefore he was nonsuited; and in this Case no Regard was had to the Ticket left with the Defendant, which was according to the Declaration.

Guardian.

Guardian in Socage shall be admitted to be a Witness for the Infant, for he is accountable.

Trustee.

A Trustee may be a Witness *against* his Trust, by *Hale* Chief Justice; but *Twisden* doubted thereof.

A Trustee may be a Witness if he *Releases*, but *not* if he hath conveyed it over, not even for the King. *Vin. Evidence*, 6.

In a Trial at Bar to avoid a Patent, the *Deputy* of the Party that would avoid it was admitted a Witness, because the Suit was between the *King* and *Patentee   Ibm.*

An

An Heir apparent may be a Witnefs concerning the Title of Land ; but a Remainder Man cannot. *Per Treby*, Chief Juftice. 1 *Salk.* 283.

At a Trial at Bar concerning the Boundaries of Lands lying in two Parifhes, the Parfon of one of the Parifhes was refufed to be a Witnefs, becaufe he might enlarge his own Tithes. *Farefly* 63.

Cafe againft a Stake-holder of a Wager ; and held, that a Perfon who had laid a Wager that the Plaintiff did not win, and been paid it, was a good Witnefs to prove that the Plaintiff had not won. 3 *Lev.* 152.

Cafe in a feigned iffue out of the Chancery, to try the Forgery of a Will of Sir —— *Cuts*, whereby he gave to his Coufin *Dorothy*, now *Pickering*'s Wife, fuch Lands for 99 Years, wherein it was faid, *That if fhe fo long live* was rafed out, and fo made abfolute for fo many Years. And one Mr. *Baker* was called a Witnefs for the Plaintiff, who defired the Direction of the Court, whether he fhould be fworn, becaufe he was Solicitor in the Cafe for the Defendant. The Court faid ; That about Matters before he was imployed he is to be fworn ; but we will not examine him about any Privacies, in what he is employed fince that Time ; and Mr. Attorney General faid, he demurred in Chancery for the fame Caufe, and was over-ruled to be examined. And it was held, a Man cannot give in Evidence an Hearfay, (a) hough the Man be dead ; but a Man

[margin notes: Cuts verfus Pickering, B. R. Pafc. 24 Car. 2 1 Vent. 197. Solicitor. Hearfay.]

(a) Meer Hearfay is no direct Evidence, *Gilb. Law of Evid.* 152 But may corroborate the Teftimony of a Witnefs, 153.

may

may give in Evidence an Hearſay of an Act at the preſent Time, thereby to fortify and corrobora:e what the other ſays.

Pasc. 13 Car. 2. B. R.
Truel *verſ.* Caſtel.
Coparcener.

One Coparcener not to be Evidence for another in Ejectment, becauſe ſhe claims by the ſame Title, though not Party to the Suit. But the Daughter of her Siſter may be ſworn, for although ſhe ſhould be Heir, yet her Mother may give the Lands to whom ſhe will, being Fee-ſimple.

King.

Witneſſes muſt now be ſworn againſt the King in all Criminal Cauſes.

Will.

A Legatee or Deviſee of an Annuity may be an Evidence to prove the Will, if he hath received it, or releaſed it ; and this though after the Action commenced. *Siderf. Rep.* 315.

Equitable Intereſt.

An Intereſt in Equity diſables a Man to be a Witneſs. 2 *Keb.* 345.

It was held on Debate in Chancery, That a Legatee named in a Will, may be an Evidence againſt the Will; for he ſwears againſt his Intereſt. 2 *Salk.* 291.

A Legatee whoſe Legacy was paid, and who had given no Security to refund, in Caſe the Aſſets were deficient, admitted a Witneſs in a Suit againſt the Executor. 1 *Keb.* 651.

The Mother of the Leſſor of the Plaintiff, who had made a Bargain with the Leſſor of the Plaintiff, to have a Third of the Eſtate, was refuſed to be a Witneſs. 3 *Mod.* 84.

In a Trial at Bar on a *Scire facias* to repeal a Patent, a Witneſs was allowed to be ſworn, to whom the Perſon that would avoid the Patent, had promiſed to name him Deputy ; by three Judges *contra Twiſden.* 1 *Mod.* 211.

After ·

After four Months that a Dividend is made, a Creditor is a good Witness; for no other Dividend shall be intended. 3 *Keb.* 348. *Bents* and *Mico.*

If a Witness be convicted of Felony, and afterwards pardoned, whether he shall be thereby restored to be a good Witness? And *Scroggs* Chief Justice, and *Raymond* Justice, were of Opinion that he could nor, because the Pardon doth take away the Punishment due to the Offence, but cannot restore the Person to his Reputation, and of that Opinion was Justice *Nichols, Moor* 872. in *Cuddington* and *Wilkins*'s Case: But Justice *Jones* and Justice *Dolbin, cont.* And afterwards *Raymond* was of their Opinion: For in *Hobart*'s Reports of *Cuddington* and *Wilkins*'s Case, it is said, That the Pardon takes away not only *pœnam* but *reatum.* Another Query was, Whether a Man convicted and burnt in the Hand be stigmatized as to his Testimony? And *Jones* Justice held he is not, because the Burning in the Hand is no Part of his Judgment; and is by 4 *H.* 7. *cap.* 13. only to notify to the Judge, that he hath had his Clergy before. 5 *Co.* 50. *a. Biggins*'s Case. But having examined the Case, do find no Judgment given therein, but compounded, as it is reported both 3 *Cro.* 682. and by *Moor* 571. And *Cro.* says there were two Judges against two. And *Moor* says, it was agreed, the King could not pardon the Burning in the Hand in an Appeal; and in Truth, it seems to be Part of the Judgment, for the Entry is, *Ideo consideratum est quod le Offender cauterizetur in manu sua lœva. Rast. Entries* 1. *b.* 56. *a.* But upon the whole Matter it appears by *Heston*'s Case, cited in

Mrs. Celier's Case, Pasch. 32 Car. 2. B R. Raymond 369.

Felons. Pardons.

Hob. 81.

E 2 *Foxley's*

Foxley's Cafe, 5 *Co.* 110. That the Burning in the Hand is (by Virtue of 18 *Eliz. cap.* 6. which faith the Prifoner fhall be forthwith enlarged) in the Nature of a Pardon.

Trin. 32
Car. 2. B. R.
en Count de
Caftlemain's
Cafe for intending to
kill the King.
Raymond
379.
1 Vent. 349.

Dangerfield was produced as a Witnefs, who had been found guilty of feveral Indictments of Felony for which he had his Clergy, and was burnt in the Hand. And upon other Indictments he had been on the Pillory for Cheating, but had obtained his Pardon under the Great Seal for all his faid Offences. A Queftion did arife, whether he might be a Witnefs? and thereupon the Prifoner did defire to have Counfel affigned him; and it was granted. And *Darnel* one of his Counfel urged, That *Dangerfield* ought not to be a Witnefs, for he was blemifhed, and the Pardon had not reftored him, and cited 2 *Brownl.* 7. where it is faid, That if the King pardoned a Man attainted for giving a falfe Verdict, yet he fhall not be at another Time impanelled upon a Jury; for though the Punifhment were pardoned, yet the Guilt remains. 2 *Bulftr.* 154. *Brown* verfus *Crafhaw.* In a Prohibition, the Suggeftion was proved only by two Perfons attainted of Felony. And *Coke* Chief Juftice cited *Hill.* 11 *H.* 4. 41. *b. pl.* 7. That if a Man be attainted of Felony and pardoned, he fhall not after be fworn upon a Jury, becaufe he is not *probus & legalis homo.* But the Court willing to be throughly fatisfied, fent Juftice *Raymond* to the Court of Common Pleas, to know their Opinion in this Point; and the Judges there

Clergy.

refolved, That the Burning in the Hand was *quafi* a Statute-Pardon to Felony, and as to that he was a good Witnefs, and the King's

Pardon.

Pardon made him a good Witnefs as to the

other

other Offences; but they ſaid, had he not been burnt in the Hand, the Pardon would not have reſtored him to his Credit again, becauſe in his Teſtimony the People are concerned, and conſequently the Pardon will not deprive them of their Intereſt. And thereupon the Judges here allowed him to be a good Witneſs; and with the Opinion of the Judges of the Common Pleas, as to the Burning of the Hand, agree the Books of 5 *Co.* 110. *a. Heſton's* Caſe. *Hob.* 292. and *Hob.* in *Cuddington* verſus *Wilkins.* But *Moor* 872. ſays, Juſtice *Nichols* was of Opinion, that if the Plaintiff had been convicted, the Judgment would have been otherwiſe. But *Caſtlemain* was found Not guilty on the whole Matter.

In an Action againſt the Hundred on the Statute of *Hue and Cry*; it was held, That one that has Lands in the Hundred, but lets them out, and doth not inhabit, may be a Witneſs for the Hundred; but one that inhabits, tho' he pays no Taxes, is no Witneſs; for he is compellable to Watch and Ward. 2 *Siderf.* 2. *Oliver w̄ Wallington*

Upon the Statute of *Hue and Cry*, at a Trial Robbery. ſome Houſe-keepers appeared as Witneſſes, that lived within the Hundred, who being examined ſaid they were poor and paid no Taxes or Pariſh Duties. And the Query was, whether they were good Witneſſes? *Twiſden* went down from the Bench to the Judges of the Common Pleas for their Opinions, who ſaid, Judge *Wylde* was confident that they ought not to be ſworn, but Judge *Tyrrel* doubted; but after was of the ſame Opinion, becauſe when the Money is recovered againſt the Hundred to be levied, they might be worth ſomething. 1 *Mod.* 71. 2 *Keb.* 713.

E 3   It

Parishioner.

It was held in the Case of *Meredith* against the Hundred of *Watlington, Pasch.* 1657. That a Parishioner is not a competent Witness to prove the Bounds of a Parish where he is an Inhabitant, although he pay neither Scot nor Lot, but receives Alms of the Parish, because he is subject to the Watch and Ward, and so is concerned something, though not so much as others. *Sty. N. P. R.* 571, 572.

Pardon.
Felons.

Excommu-
nicate.

If one be attainted of Felony and pardoned, he cannot be either Juror or Witness. *Contra per Coke.* 2 *Bulst.* 154. *Brown* and *Crashaw.* Nor can a Recusant Convict be a Witness, for he is a Person Excommunicate.

Mich. 21
Car 2 B. R.
The King
against Paris.
2 Keb. 572.
Feme Covert.
1 Vent. 49.
1 Siderf. 431.

In an Information against *P.* That whereas he hath cheated one *Lee* in a Match, to the Intent that the Lands of this *Lee* should be charged before Marriage, he procured the Feme to acknowledge a Judgment to him, where in Truth no Debt was due by the Feme; in this Case the Feme was admitted a Witness for the King, though the Profit of the Husband was collaterally concerned; for by this Evidence if it be found against *P.* the Judgment shall be set aside.

Trustee.
2 Keb. 128.

A Trustee may be a Witness if he release his Trust; so if he be in Possession of the Lands in Question as Servant. *Siderfin* 315.

On a Trial at Bar it was held *per Hale,* That an Executor may be a Witness in a Cause concerning the Estate, if he hath not the Residue given him. 1 *Mod.* 107.

Trustee.
Legatee.

In an Information of Forgery for publishing a forged Deed, importing the Revocation of a Will, to the Prejudice of the Executors and Legatees; 'twas resolved by all the Barons of the Exchequer, upon Conference with the

Judges

Judges of the King's Bench; 1. That a Truftee who has conveyed over his Eftate in Truft, or has affented thereunto, cannot be a Witnefs for the King in this Cafe; nor can a Legatee, or any other Perfon that is a Lofer by the Deed, or may receive any Advantage by the Verdict's being found for the King. *Hardres Rep.* 331. *Watts*'s Cafe.

But in Deceit for forging a Will, a Legatee was allowed and fworn as a Witnefs in the Trial for Forgery; for this makes nothing to the Probate of the Will, or Recovery of the Legacy in the Spiritual Court, nor do they take Notice of it.

It was refolved in one *Long*'s Cafe, That upon an Information upon the Statute of Ufury, the Perfon who borrows the Money may be a Witnefs after he hath paid the Money, but not before. *Mich.* 22 *Car.* 2. *B. R. per Twifden* Juftice. *Ufury. Per* Twifden 22 Car. 2. B. R. Raymond 191.

If *A.* indict *B.* on the Statute 5 *Eliz. cap.* 9. of Perjury, as a Party grieved, the Profecutor cannot be a Witnefs againft *B. Roll.* 685. 2 Part. *Perjury. Profecutor.*

Judgment ftaid, becaufe the Verdict was had upon the Teftimony of one Witnefs, and he fince convict of Perjury in the fame Thing. *Paf.* 17 *Car.* 2. *B. R.* *Perjury.*

There ought to be two, where the Trial is by Witneffes. *Two Witneffes.*

In *Bennet*'s Cafe, *Style* 223. In a Trial at Bar, it was faid by the Court, That if either of the Parties to a Trial defire that a Juror may give Evidence of fome Things of his own Knowledge to the reft of the Jurors, that the Court will examine him openly in Court upon his Oath, and he ought not to be examined in *Juror.*

E 4   private

private by his Companions.   And it was alſo
said, That if a Robbery be done *in Crepuſculo,*
the Hundred ſhall not be charged; but if it
be done by clear Day-light, whether it be before Sun-riſe, or after Sun ſet, it is all one, and
the Hundred ſhall be charged.

Robbery.

By 1 *Annæ, cap.* 9. Witneſſes for Priſoners
upon Trials of Treaſon, or Felony, ſhall be
sworn as Witneſſes for the Crown are, and be
Subject to like Puniſhment for Perjury.

Witneſſes for
Priſoners to
be ſworn.

By 1 *Annæ, cap.* 18. It is enacted, That in
all Informations and Indictments in any Court
of Record at *Weſtminſter,* or at the Aſſizes or
Quarter-Seſſions, for not repairing their Highways or Bridges, the Evidence of the Inhabitants of the Town or County in which ſuch
decayed Bridges or Highways lie, ſhall be admitted.

Inhabitants
may be Wit-
neſſes con-
cerning
Highways
and Bridges.

By 7 & 8 *Wil.* 3. *cap.* 34. It was enacted,
That every Quaker who ſhall be required to
take an Oath on any lawful Occaſion, inſtead
of the uſual Form, ſhall be permitted to do it
in the Form preſcribed by this Act: And if he
ſhall be convicted of having done it falſly or cor-
ruptly, he ſhall incur the ſame Penalties, as other
Perſons convicted of wilful Perjury: But that no
Quaker, or reputed Quaker, ſhould be qualified
to give Evidence in any criminal Cauſe by Virtue of this Act.

Quaker falſi-
fying on his
Affirmation,
to be puniſh-
ed as for wil-
ful Perjury.

Quaker diſ-
abled to give
Evidence in
Criminal
Cauſes.

By 4 & 5 *Annæ, cap.* 16. It was enacted,
That ſuch Perſons as are deemed good Witneſſes
in Trials at Common Law, ſhould be deemed
good Witneſſes to prove a nuncupative Will, or
any Thing relating thereto.

Witneſſes to
prove a nun-
cupative Will.

Perſons in Commiſſion for the Trial of Priſoners for High Treaſon, were allowed to be
good Witneſſes, and they came off the Bench,
                                                   and

Commiſſioners
for Trial of
Priſoners,
Witneſſes.

i

and gave Evidence accordingly. *Kelynge* 12. Witneffes may be examined apart by the Direction of the Court. 2 *Inft.* 131. *Guiliems & Ux'* verfus *Hulie & Ux'*.

The fame Perfons who are Witneffes to the Indictment in Treafon, may be Witneffes at the Trial *Kelynge* 18. If a Confpirator be examined before a Privy Councillor, or a Juftice of Peace, and upon his Examination, without Torture, confefs the Treafon, and this be proved by two Witneffes at the Trial; in this Cafe there needs no other Evidence to prove him guilty of the Treafon. *Kelynge* 18. *Quære*, if not altered by 7 *W.* 3. *cap.* 3. By which Statute, unlefs the Party confefs the Fact in open Court, two Witneffes are required to convict him there. *(Witneffes to the Indictment, Witneffes at the Trial. Confeffion allowed Evidence. Confeffion to convict one of Treafon, muft be in open Court.)*

At the Seffions at the *Old Baily,* 7 *Dec.* 1664. Exception was taken to a Witnefs, becaufe he had been burnt in the Hand for Felony. But *Hyde* Chief Juftice, *Kelynge,* and *Wylde* Recorder, held that to be no Exception; and in Civil Caufes fuch Perfons are frequently admitted Witneffes: That it differs from cutting off Ears, ftanding in the Pillory, &c. becaufe thofe Punifhments make the Perfons infamous, but burning in the Hand does not fo, becaufe it comes in the Place of Purgation at the Common Law, which fuppofeth he might be not Guilty, notwithftanding the Verdict; and therefore at the Common Law, he that confeffeth a Felony, could never be admitted to his Purgation; for there could be no Prefumption of Not guilty againft his own Confeffion. *Kelynge* 37, 38. *(Perfon burnt in the Hand allowed a Witnefs.)*

Wicks

Person convict of Perjury.

Wicks verſus *Smallbrook, Mich.* 13 *Car.* 2. *B. R.* Exception was taken to a Witneſs, for that he was convict of Perjury, and they offered the Copy of a Verdict, (whereupon there had never been any Judgment) in the Time of *Oliver* the Protector; but the Court would not receive or allow of it, becauſe all is gone and diſcontinued by the Alteration of the Government. But they agreed, that Evidence to prove him perjured, might now be given *viva voce*; and thoſe of the other Side, to make his Teſtimony valid, produced a Pardon

Pardon cannot reſtore him to be a Witneſs.

of the Perjury. But *per Cur.* that will not avail, for it cannot reſtore him to his Credit. 1 *Sid.* 51, 52.

In *Crosby's* Caſe, *Aaron Smith*, who had ſtood in the Pillory for inſtructing *Stephen College*, and had the Advantage of a general Pardon afterwards, was allowed to be a Witneſs. 5 *Mod.* 15. *Rex* verſus *Crosby*.

Persons who have ſtood in the Pillory, whether they may be Witneſſes.

Qu. If Perſons convicted of framing a Libel, who have ſtood on the Pillory for it, may not be Witneſſes; for the Diſability ſeems to have reſpect to the Offence rather than the Puniſhment. *Rex* verſus *Davis & Coſter*, 5 *Mod.* 74.

Davis and *Carter* being convicted for forging a Bank-Bill, moved againſt the Sheriff of *London* for oppreſſing them in *Newgate*; but the Court refuſed to read their *Affidavits.* 5 *Mod.* 74.

Parties in the Crime may be Witneſſes.

Perſons guilty of the ſame Crimes (while they remain unconvicted) may be made Uſe of as Witneſſes againſt their Fellows. *Kelynge* 17.

One

One who was taken and married by Force *Wife married* was allowed to be a good Witneſs againſt the *forcibly, a* Offender, although ſhe was his Wife *de Facto.* *good Witneſs of it.* 1 *Vent.* 243.   *Brown's Caſe, 3 Keb.* 193.

Indictment againſt *Mary Grigs* for marrying a ſecond Huſband, the former being alive ; held that the firſt Huſband is not a Witneſs to prove the firſt Marriage.   *Raym.* 1.

In an Indictment againſt the Lord *Audley,* *Wife Witneſs* for aſſiſting another to commit a Rape on his *againſt her* Wife, ſhe was admitted a Witneſs againſt him. *Huſband in a* *Hut.* 115.   2 *Hawk, P. C.* 432. *(a).* *by his Aſſiſt-*

Men who claim under the ſame Title, ſhall *ance.* not be Witneſſes for one another. *Hob.* 91.

In Ejectment, Defendant challenged a Witneſs produced by Plaintiff to prove a Leaſe made by the Dean and ſix Reſidentiaries of *Hereford,* becauſe he was a Prebend at large ; and held he was no Witneſs, becauſe might aſſent. 2 *Keb.* 126.

In the Caſe of the City of *London* concern- *Members of* ing the Duty of Water-Bailage, the Freemen *Corporations* of *London* were not allowed as Witneſſes *ſometimes allowed as* 1 *Vent.* 351. But there is no general Rule, *Witneſſes for* where Members of Corporations ſhall be ad- *them, and* mitted or refuſed to give Evidence, in Actions *ſometimes* brought by or againſt the Corporation, but *not.* every Caſe ſtands on its own Circumſtances, *viz.* Whether their Intereſt is ſo great that it may be preſumed to make them partial or not. 2 *Lev.* 231.   *nd aſſo* 1 *Lev.* 236.

Debt by the Company of Sadlers againſt *Jones,* on he Statue 1 *Jac.* 1. *cap.* 22. *ſect.* 44. for making Saddles inſufficiently, *contra formam Stat.* and ſo became indebted to them

---

(a) But in *Raym.* 1. this Caſe is denied to be Law; and in *Vent.* 244. it is doubted of by Ld. Ch. J. *Hale.*

for

for the Forfeiture ; and three of the Company were disfranchifed in order to be Witneffes. 6 *Mod.* 165.

The like was done in the Cafe of the City of *London* againft the Hawkers. 3 *Keb.* 295. and in Cafe of Lord *Dorfet* verfus *Carter.* 3 *Keb.* 300.

Cafe for a falfe Return to a *Mandamus* to reftore the Plaintiff to be an Alderman of *Canterbury* ; the Defendant called feven Freemen of *Canterbury* to prove the Return true ; and to take off their Evidence a By-Law was read, by which the Charges of this Return were to be paid by the Corporation ; the Defendant then read a Releafe, whereby he releafed to the Corporation all Advantages, Contributions and Demands which he could have by that or any other Order ; and *Rainsford* and *Twifden* held the Freemen could not be Witneffes ; but *Jones* J. *contra :* But on a Bill of Exceptions the Court held the Freemen ought to have been fworn. 2 *Lev.* 236. *Jones T.* 116.

Cafe againft the Town of *Uxbridge* for taking Toll on Market-Day ; none of the Corporation can be a Witnefs for the Town. 3 *Keb.* 12.

If an Infant brings an Action by Guardian, he cannot be a Witnefs. *Gilb. Law of Evid.* 122, 123.

Parifhioners may be Witneffes of Money mifpent by Churchwardens, &c. In all Actions to be brought in the Courts at *Weftminfter*, or at the Affizes, for Monies mifpent by the Churchwardens or Overfeers, the Evidence of the Parifhioners (other than fuch as receive Alms) of the Parifh where the Defendants are Inhabitants, fhall be taken and admitted. 3 & 4 *W. & M. cap.* 11.

4

In

In an Information againſt the Defendant for a Cheat, upon Trial the Fact appeared to be, that he had a Promiſe of a Note for 5 *l.* from his Mother-in-law, and by ſome Slight got her Hand to a Note of 100 *l. Et per Holt,* C. J. The Mother cannot be a Witneſs, being concerned in the Conſequence of the Suit, which is a Means to diſcharge her of the 100 *l.* for though the Verdict upon this Information cannot be given in Evidence in an Action upon the Note for the 100 *l.* yet we are ſure to hear of it to influence the Jury ; and he ſaid he could not diſtinguiſh this from the Caſes of Perjury or Forgery, where the Party whoſe Intereſt is defeated or prejudiced by the Deed, *&c.* is no Evidence to prove the Perjury or Forgery. *Rex* verſus *Whiting, Salk.* 283. *Indictment for a Cheat in procuring a Note from H. H. was not allowed a Witneſs.*

A Goldſmith's Note is Evidence of his receiving Money. *Ibid.*

Indictment for a Cheat done to *J. S.* by impoſing upon him a Quantity of Beer mix'd with Vinegar, and Grounds of Coffee, for Port-Wine ; one of the Defendants pretending to be a Broker, and the other a *Portugueze* Merchant, for the better carrying on of the Cheat. *Et per Holt* Ch. J. *J. S.* was allowed to be a Witneſs to prove the Fact upon the Trial ; for in ſuch private Tranſactions, no body elſe can be a Witneſs of the Circumſtances of the Fact, but he that ſuffers. *Regina* verſus *Mackartney & al', Salk.* 286. *One who was cheated admitted to prove the Fact in the Indictment.*

Caſe by a Silk Dyer againſt his Servant for Money received to his Uſe ; and on Evidence it appeared that *A.* ſent Silk to be dyed by the Plaintiff, that the Plaintiff ſent it home by the Defendant, and *A.* was called to prove he paid Defendant

Defendant for it; but held by *Holt* C. J. that he was not a Witnefs. *Mich.* 8 *Ann.* at *Guild-Hall, Tybbald* verfus *Treggot.* Report of Cafes in Queen *Anne's* Time 261.

Evidence in an Action for running over the Plaintiff's Barge with a Ship.

In an Action on the Cafe for managing the Defendant's Ship fo negligently, that it ran over the Plaintiff's Barge, the Declaration fet forth, That he was poffeffed of the faid Barge, laden with divers Goods and Merchandizes. And 1. *Holt* Ch. J. would not fuffer the Pilot to be a Witnefs, becaufe he was anfwerable, if faulty in fteering, to the Mafter. 2. He would not fuffer any Damages to be recovered for the Goods, becaufe not fet forth particularly, faying, they ought to be fet forth fpecially; as where an Action is brought for burning his Houfe: So in Cafe for Words *per quod* fhe loft her Marriage with *J. S. & aliis perfonis,* he faid, he would not fuffer them to give in Evidence a Lofs of Marriage with any Body but *J. S. Martin* verfus *Hendrickfon, Salk.* 287.

Son took the Father's Money, and gave it to H. and the Son's Evidence admitted in Trover againft H.

In Trover for Money, the Cafe was upon Evidence, That the Plaintiff's Son had a general Authority from his Father to receive and pay out his Father's Money. The Son took a Bill for Money due to his Father, and received it without a particular Authority for that Purpofe; and this Receipt was with an Intent to imbezil and fpend it; but he gave a Receipt as for Money had to his Father's Ufe, and this Money was given to the Defendant. The Queftions were, 1. If the Son could be a Witnefs in this Cafe to prove the Delivery? And 2. Whether the Father could maintain an Action of Trover? *Holt* Ch. J. was of Opinion, That the Son might be admitted as a good Witnefs,

Witness, his Testimony being corroborated by other Circumstances. And that the Action was maintainable by the Father, for that the general Authority the Son had to take his Father's Money, made the Receipt of the Money to be to his Father's Use, and a good Discharge of the Debt, so as the Father could not avoid the Payment, and charge the Person that paid the Money with an Action : And then if the Payment was a good Discharge, it is Reason it should be his Money, and the Possession of the Son is the Possession of the Father, the Son being to this Purpose as his Father's Servant : And according to this Opinion the Plaintiff had a Verdict ; but he said he was willing to have a Case made of it ; but the Defendant acquiesced in his Opinion. *Anonymus, Salk.* 289.

The Plaintiff brought an Action upon a *Quantum meruit* against the Defendant, for that he, at his Request, had served him as a Commissioner in a certain Commission out of the Exchequer, directed to him and others for Examination of Witnesses : After Verdict on *Non Assumpsit, Tremaine* moved in Arrest of Judgment, That the Plaintiff acted by Command of the Court, and could not therefore take a Promise of Reward for the Service, no more than a Sheriff or Bailiff ; *sed non allocatur* ; for he is appointed at the Nomination of the Party, who ought to pay him if he employs him. *Stockbold* versus *Collington, Salk.* 330.

Quantum meruit lies for serving as a Commissioner on a Commission to examine Witnesses.

Of

404

Of Evidence relating to Executorſhip, Wills and Adminiſtrations. (a)

Roll. Trial, 678. pl. 1. *Plene adminiſtravit.* Pedigree.

An Account given to and allowed by the Ordinary, is not good Evidence ; nor a Pedigree by a Herald at Arms, to prove an Heir ; but it muſt be proved by Deeds, Records, or Witneſſes.

A Witneſs to a Deed, becoming Adminiſtrator, &c. his Hand may be proved. 1 *Str.* 34.

Devaſtavit.

In Debt againſt an Executor, ſuggeſting a *Devaſtavit*, any Evidence that proves Aſſets, is not ſufficient, but an actual *Devaſtavit* muſt be proved ; for now the Party is chargeable in his own Right. *Keb.* 2 Part 676.

Aſſets.

Upon *Plene adminiſtravit*, if it be proved that the Executor hath Goods of the Teſtator's in his Hands, he may give in Evidence, that he hath paid of his own Money for the Teſtator, to the Value of theſe Goods. *Co. Lit.* 283. *Dyer* 2.

The Plaintiff may ſay, he ſold the Land by the Appointment of he Teſtator. 3 *H.* 6. 3. *Roll. Executor*, 920. *pl.* 2.

Aſſets.

If the Iſſue be in a Suit againſt an Executor, Adminiſtrator, or Heir, Aſſets in *London*, to prove Aſſets in another Place, is ſufficient. *Lib.* 6. 47. *Dyer* 271.

On *Plene Adminiſtravit*, it was proved, that on the Day of ſuing out the Writ, a Sum of Money more than the Plaintiff's Debt was

(a) The Act or Order of Eccleſiaſtical Court for granting Letters of Adminiſtration proved by the Book, is Evidence. *Vin. Abr.* Tit. *Evid.* 81. *pl.* 1.

brought

brought into the Spiritual Court, and was delivered to the Executors as a Debt due to the Testator; but that he immediately, by the Order
of that Court, paid the same to another Creditor. Held that this Sum was Assets, tho'
the Plaintiff's Writ was only purchased the same
Day. *Dyer* 108.

Upon *Plene Administravit*, it was proved at
the Trial, that the Executor had discharged a
Debtor of the Intestate out of *Ludgate*, taking
a Bond from him for the Debt; and tho' it appeared that this Debtor was so extreme poor
that he was starving, yet the Debt was judged
Assets in the Executor's Hands. *Report in* Holt's
Time 297. *Cases W.* 3. 346.

Upon *Plene administravit*, the Executor cannot give a Judgment in Evidence, *Keilw.* 59.
nor Payment of Debts by Contract, in Debt
brought upon an Obligation. A cup pawned
and redeemed with the Executor's own Money,
is good Evidence; but a Recovery ought to be
pleaded. *Roll. Trial,* 684. *pl.* 7, 9.

*Plene Admini-
stravit.* But an
Outlawry of
the Testator
is Evidence
upon *Plene
administravit.*
Keb. 2 Part
745.

Case against Executors, and on *Plene Administravit* pleaded, it was proved, that *J. S.*
was bound to the Testator in 100*l.* for Performance of Covenants which were broken,
that the Executors had sued this Bond; and
then referred it to Arbitrators, who awarded
J. S. to pay 70*l.* and Releases to be given.
Held, that the Executors were in Law to be
taken to have Assets to the whole 100*l.* 3
Leon. 53.

In Case against an Executor; whereas the
Testator was indebted to the Plaintiff, the
Executor promised to pay the Debt, in Con-
sideration the Plaintiff would forbear to sue

Executor.

him; the Executor may give in Evidence upon *Non Aſſumpſit*, that there was no Debt, or that he had no Aſſets *tempore promiſſionis*, for then there would be no Conſideration. *Lib.* 9. 94. *William Bane*'s Caſe. Upon the Iſſue *Ne unques Executor*, to prove an Adminiſtration granted to him, is good Evidence. *Dyer* 305.

Held *per Holt*, C. J. That on *Ne unques Executor* you cannot give Letters of Adminiſtration in Evidence, but Letters *ad Colligendum* you may (*a*). *Comberb.* 221.

Ne unques Executor. Spiritual Courts.

In Trover brought by an Executor, the Defendant pleaded *Ne unques Executor*. The Defendant ſhall not give in Evidence that the Will was forged, becauſe the Will was under the Seal of the Ordinary, to whoſe Examination it belongs, as to Goods; but Forgery of the Probate, or a Revocation, may be given in Evidence, becauſe theſe Things are in Affirmance of the Spiritual Proceedings; ſo of an Adminiſtration, that there are *bona notabilia*, may be given in Evidence, but not *Non compos mentis*. *Sid.* 359. *Keb.* 2 Part 337.

On *Plene Adminiſtravit*, the Plaintiff replied Aſſets *die exhibitionis Billæ, ſcilicet* 23d of *October*; and in Evidence it appeared, that the Bill was not filed till 14 Days in Term. Held, what the Defendant had paid before the actual filing of the Bill was not Aſſets. 1 *Siderf.* 432.

That the Executor paid a Legacy, is Evidence that he had Aſſets.

(*a*) If there be Judgment againſt an Adminiſtrator by the Name of Executor, and he be ſued afterwards as Adminiſtrator for the ſame Cauſe, he may give the former Judgment in Evidence. *Comb.* 221.

Will,

Will, the Probate is good for the perfonal What fhall be Eftate, but not to prove a Will in Writing of given in Evidence, and Land, by the Statute.   2 *Roll.* 678. what is good Evidence.

Upon this Plea the Executor may give in *Plene admini-* Evidence a Retainer for a Debt due to him- *ftravit.* felf of as high a Nature; or Payment of Debts 1 *Cro.* 128. with his own Money, and that he kept Goods of the Teftator in lieu; for this alters the Property. *Roll. Trial*, 684. *pl.* 8.

On *Plene Adminiftravit*, the Defendant cannot prove, that he promifed to pay *J. S.* the Teftator's Debt; but otherwife if he had given a Bond for it.   *Clayton* 88.

The Original need not be fhewed in Evidence upon this Plea; nor upon the Iffue Affets at the Day, *&c.* becaufe the Day is agreed in pleading; yet fee *Syd.* 462. 2 Sid. 226. Rogers *verf.* Rogers.

Debt againft an Adminiftrator; he pleads, That the Inteftate was indebted to him by diverfe Bonds, [*reciting them*] to the Sum of 80 *l.* and that he had not Affets *ultra.* The Plaintiff demurred, becaufe it amounted to the General Iffue of *Plene adminiftravit*; but held the Plea was good, and that this was no Caufe of Demurrer.   *Hob.* 127.

Agreed by the whole Court, that if in Evidence the Executor give in Evidence the Probate under the Seal of the Ordinary, nothing can be given to the contrary that he is not Executor; for Caufes Teftamentary belong intirely and originally to the Ordinary; and if the Will be forged, the Suit ought to be in the Spiritual Court to repeal the Probate, according to 4 *H.* 7. 12. So of Letters of Adminiftration, it cannot be alledged that there was a Will; but if there be a Suit, it Pafch. 2 Car. 2. B. R. 68. Nowel *verfus* Wilfon.

Will.

muft

muſt be in the Spiritual Court to repeal it. Yet ſome Books ſeem to the contrary, as *Fitz. Eſtoppel*, 9. *Bro. Teſtm.* 4. 22 *H.* 6. 52. 21 *E.* 4. 50. *a. Com.* 282. 9 *Co.* 31. *a. Old Entries* 325. 1 *Brownl.* 79. Alſo upon Evidence it may be proved, that the Probate or Letters of Adminiſtration were forged.

Adminiſtration.

In Debt by an Adminiſtrator upon an Obligation, the Defendant pleads *Non eſt faſtum*; the Plaintiff in Evidence need not to ſhew the Letters of Adminiſtration, for this is admitted by the Defendant's Plea of *Non eſt Faſtum*.

If Letters of Adminiſtration be given in Evidence, you may ſhew they were revoked. *Gilb. L. of Evid.* 75.

Will.

A Will, under which a Title to Land is made to the Plaintiff, muſt be ſhewn itſelf to the Court, and the Probate itſelf is not ſufficient. 1 *Keb.* 117. The ſame Caſe cited 2 *Roll.* 678. between *Bret* and *Bret*, 10 *Car.* 1.

Paſch. 1651.
Will.

The Copy of a Will, according to the Book of the Regiſter in the Court Chriſtian, ſhall not be admitted to prove a Will of Lands, except the Poſſeſſion has gone a long Time accordingly.

Probate.

2 *Roll.* 678. adjudged, That Probate of a Will by Witneſſes for Lands, is not Evidence at Common Law, although the Probate was good as to the Perſonal Eſtate deviſed. Between *Bret* and *Bret*, *Hill.* 10 *Car.* 1.

Plene adminiſtravit.

Upon *Plene adminiſtravit* pleaded, the Account given to the Ordinary ſhall not be given in Evidence, nor any Reſpeſt ſhewn to it. 2 *Roll.* 678. *Turvie's* Caſe, *Paſch.* 7 *Jac.* per *Cur'.*

Debt

Debt againſt an Executor, upon *Plene admi-* *Plene admini-*
niſtravit, it appeared that the Executor med- *ſtravit.*
dled and adminiſtred, and then refuſed in Court, *Adminiſtravit*
and Adminiſtration was granted to another; a Retainer
and that ſeveral Sums were recovered againſt may be given
the Adminiſtrator; it was ſaid by *Periam* Ju- in Evidence.
ſtice, 1. That if an Adminiſtrator (who is a
Stranger) adminiſter, without the Commandment of the Executor, the Executor cannot
give ſuch Adminiſtration in Evidence to prove
this iſſue. 2. That in the principal Caſe, the
Executor having adminiſtred, he could not refuſe, and ſo the Adminiſtration is granted without Cauſe, and what he did was without Warrant, and no Adminiſtration. 1 *Leon.* 154. *Haw-*
kins and *Lawſe's* Caſe. At *Bury* Aſſizes, 1682.
before Judge *Wyndham,* The Executor gave the
Adminiſtration of the Adminiſtrator in Evidence, and allowed; but there what the Ad- *Plene admini-*
miniſtrator did, was by the Executor's Conſent. *ſtravit.*
In Mr. *Lun* and his Mother's Caſe.

An Executor *de ſon Tort* cannot give in 5 Co. 30.
Evidence his Retaining of Goods to pay him- 1 Cro. 630.
ſelf; for he cannot retain; but if he take out An Executor
Letters of Adminiſtration, although *pendente lite,* pleads *Plene*
he may retain for a Debt of as high a Nature, *adminiſtravit*
and plead this in Bar; for the Adminiſtra- *præter* a Judg-
tion purges his Wrong; and although he ſhall ment: Re-
not abate the Writ by taking out Letters of plication and
Adminiſtration, yet he may plead this in Bar. Iſſue, that the
Style's Reports 338. Judgment
was fraudu-
lent. The
Obligee who
had the Judgment was denied to give Evidence about his Debt, for be
ſweareth to have Aſſets for himſelf, and is intereſted in the Thing
Before Judge *Wyndham;* at *Bedford* Aſſizes, 1682.

In

Aſſets.

In Debt againſt Executors, and Aſſets *inter manus* in Iſſue, 'tis good Evidence that they ſold Land, by the Will of the Teſtator, &c. and that they had the Money paid ; that they recovered Damages in Treſpaſs for Goods taken in the Life of the Teſtator, &c. 3 H. 6. 3. *Roll. Executor,* 920. *pl.* 1, 2, 4.

Debt againſt two Executors ; and on *Plene adminiſtravit* an Inventory exhibited by one ſhall not charge the other. *Clayton* 106.

Trover by Adminiſtrator on the Inteſtate's Poſſeſſion, Defendant cannot give in Evidence a Will on the General Iſſue.

The Plaintiff brought Trover as Adminiſtrator, and declared upon the Poſſeſſion of the Inteſtate; and upon Not guilty pleaded, at the Trial the Council for the Defendant offered to give in Evidence, that the pretended Inteſtate made a Will and an Executor. But *Holt* Ch. J. over-ruled it, and took this Diverſity, That where an Adminiſtrator brings Trover upon his own Poſſeſſion, the Defendant may give in Evidence a Will, and an Executor upon Not guilty : Otherwiſe if it be on the Poſſeſſion of the Inteſtate, (as in the principal Caſe) for there the Defendant ought to plead it in Abatement ; and if he does not, he ſhall not give it in Evidence. *Blainfield* verſus *March, Salk.* 285. *Farreſt.* 181.

Otherwiſe, If on the Adminiſtrator's own Poſſeſſion.

Payment of Money due to the Wife as Executrix, is not Evidence to maintain Action for Money received to Huſband's Uſe.

In an Action on the Caſe for Money had and received to the Plaintiff's Uſe ; upon the Evidence it appear'd, that the Plaintiff's Wife was Executrix, and that the Money was paid to the Defendant as due to her ; and the Plaintiff was nonſuited, becauſe the Action ought to have been brought by Huſband, and Wife as Executrix ; for it being paid without any Authority from the Huſband, it remains as a

Debt

Debt due to the Executrix; and if the Husband dies, the Wife may bring an Action for it: But if the Money had been received by Authority from the Husband, then it had been as his Receipt, and as his Money, and the Action might well have been brought in his Name; and the Money would have been Assets in her Hands. *Anonymus, Salk.* 282.

In an Action upon the Case against an Executor, upon *Plene administravit* pleaded, three Points were declared *per Holt,* Ch. J. 1. That the Plaintiff must prove his Debt, otherwise he shall recover but a Penny Damages, though there be Assets; for the Plea only admits the Debt but not the Quantity. 2. That all sperate Debts mentioned in the Inventory, shall be counted Assets in the Executor's Hands; for that is as much as to say, they may be had for demanding, unless the Demand or Refusal be proved. 3. That in Strictness no Funeral Expences are allowable against a Creditor, except for the Coffin, ringing the Bell, Parson, Clerk and Bearers Fees, but not for a Pall or Ornaments. *Shelley*'s Case, *Salk.* 296. *[margin: Evidence upon Plene administravit.]*

In Debt, *Plene administravit* admits the Debt; and if to Debt on Bond on *Plene administravit* you offer to prove Payment of a Bond, you must prove that that Bond was sealed and delivered. 1 *Shower* 81.

A Note had been made by the Defendant to the Plaintiff's Testator above six Years before the Action brought for Payment of the Money; and upon *Non assumpsit infra sex Annos,* at the Trial before *Holt* Ch. Justice, the Plaintiff gave Evidence of a Promise made to himself after the Arrest, and before the Bill exhibited; and whether this Evidence maintained the Declaration was the Queſtion : and the Caſe of *Heylin* and *Haſtings* was remembered, wherein upon Conference with all the Judges of *England*, it was held, that a Promiſe after the ſix Years brings the Matter out of the Statute of Limitations ; that owning the Debt does not go ſo far, but is Evidence of a Promiſe.

Note ; Here the Declaration was of a Promiſe to the Teſtator, and the Promiſe in Evidence was to the Executor.

And the Court ſaid, here the Executor might declare of a Promiſe to himſelf : But *adjournatur.* And in *Hillary* Term, upon Conference with all the Judges it was held, the Evidence did not maintain the Declaration. *M.* 3 *Ann. Dean v. Crane* in *B R.* 6 *Mod* 309. 1 *Salk.* 28. S. C. See Ld. *Raym.* 389, 422, 741, 838, 1101. *Caſ. temp. W.* 3. 223, 234, 444. *Caſ. temp. Mac.* 314. 2 *Wms.* 373. 3 *Wms.* 84, 89, 143, 144. *Comyns* 54.

Ordinary cannot refuſe Probate to an Executor becauſe *Incapax.* A *Mandamus* iſſued to grant Probate of the Will ; the Ordinary returned, That the Executor was an abſconding Perſon, *Incapax, &c.* And this Return was held inſufficient ; for that there is a Will is admitted ; and ſince the Teſtator has thought the Executor a proper Perſon to be intruſted with his Affairs, the Ordinary cannot adjudge him otherwiſe upon a Diſability by the Canon Law, for that is not admitted here, but as far as it has been received from Time immemorial. *Per Holt* C. J. and a peremptory *Mandamus* was granted : Neither can the Ordinary inſiſt upon Security from the Executor ; for the Teſtator has thought him able and qualified, and he has a temporal Right, which he cannot ſue for before Probate ; And there have been no Precedents
or

or Practice of this Nature.   The King *versus* Raynes, *Salk.* 299.

If an Executor confesses or suffers Judgment by Default, he admits Assets in his Hands, and is estopped to say the contrary. *Salk.* 310. *6 Mod.* 308. says, if an Executor suffer Judgment to go against him by Default, upon Executing Writ of Inquiry, he shall not give Evidence the want of Assets, for he is estopped, as if it had been in case of an Heir ; for he should have pleaded *Plene administravit*, or specially what Assets he had. *Per Cur'*.

In Debt upon a Bond against an Administrator, he pleaded several Judgments, & *riens ultra* 5 *s.* which was found : The Plaintiff as to one Judgment replied, there was but so much due, which the Debtee was willing and ready to accept in full, and that the Defendant by Fraud deferred the Payment of that Money, and the Judgment was kept in Force to defraud the Creditors, and replied the same Matter as to another Judgment, and demurred as to the rest.   The Defendant rejoin'd that as to one Judgment, it was not kept on Foot by Fraud, &c. and as to the other, no Assets *ultra* so much, which was liable to the Judgment ; and so to the third ; and as to the rest joined in Demurrer.   *Et per Cur'* ; 1. The best Way for an Administrator to plead, is to plead truly and honestly ; and though there is a Judgment for a Penalty, he ought to plead the Judgment, and shew how much is due.   2. If he pleads several Judgments, and any one Judgment be ill pleaded, or found fraudulent, the Plaintiff shall have Judgment.   3. If an Administrator a Confession of Assets to satisfy them, and the *Riens ultra* a certain Sum is not material.

[margin note:] Executor pleading Judgments with Penalties should shew how much is really due.

[margin note:] Pleading of Judgments is

pleads

pleads twenty Judgments, 'tis a Confeffion of Affets to fatisfy the twenty Judgments, and the *Riens ultra* 5 s. is but Form, not material nor traverfable. 4. If a Judgment being pleaded, and *per fraudem* replied, iffue is taken thereupon, and by Evidence it appears the Debtee was willing to take lefs than is recovered, it is Evidence of Fraud: But if it be fhewed that the Adminiftrator had not Affets to pay that Sum, it is no Fraud. 5. If an Adminiftrator pleads two or more Judgments, and the Plaintiff confeffes the Plea to be true, and prays Judgments of Affets *in futuro*; if afterwards Affets came to his Hands, he may fatisfy the Judgments pleaded, for the Judgment of Affets *de futuro*, is only to be paid off after the other Judgments are fatisfied; and therefore there is no Inconvenience in making the Pleading of fraudulent Judgments a Confeffion of Affets. 6. The Conclufion of the Replication with *hoc paratus eft verificare*, to every Judgment, is well; but a general Conclufion to the whole had been better. *Vide* 2 *Saund.* 338. *Salk.* 211. *Parker* verfus *Atfield.*

Will made by a Wife in purfuance of a Power referved before Marriage, is not properly a Will, nor provable by the Ordinary. A Woman by Deed fettled her Eftate in Truft, referving a Power to herfelf to give by her laft Will and Teftament, as fhe fhould think fit, fo much of her Eftate in Legacies; and this was done before Marriage, with the Confent and Privity of the intended Hufband, who refufed nevertheleſs to be a Witnefs or Party to the Deed: The Marriage took Effect. The Wife made a Will and died, and the Executors proved the Will. *Et per Holt* Ch. J. This is not a Will, neither ought the Ordinary to prove it; if he does, a Prohibition lies.

Where

Where a Woman is Executrix and marries, there she may make a Will with Consent of her Husband, and cannot without. 1 *Jones* 157. So if a Woman having Debts due to her marries, she may make a Will *quoad* these, and the Ordinary may prove it. In other Cases she cannot, for it is only a Writing in Form of a Will: However, in the principal Case, it appearing that the Ordinary had only granted Administration *quoad* the Goods in this Will, 'twas allowed as reasonable. *Cro. Car.* 219. *Shardelow* versus *Naylor, Salkeld* 313.

Sir *Charles Hopson* made *Churchill* and *Goodwin* his Executors, Men of Good Credit: *Goodwin* being a Banker received all the Money; but *Churchill* joined with him in the Receipts, taking his Note to shew that he received not the Money. *Et per Harcourt* Lord Chancellor; If two Trustees join in a Receipt, and one receives the Money, he only that receives shall be liable; if there be two Executors, and they join in a Receipt, and one only receives the Money, as to Creditors, who are to have the utmost Benefit of Law, each is liable for the whole, though one Executor alone might give a Discharge, and the joining of the other was unnecessary; but as to Legatees, and those claiming Distribution, who have no Remedy but in Equity, the Receipt of one Executor shall not charge the other; for the joining in the Receipt is only Matter of Form, the substantial Part is the actual receiving; and this only is regarded in Conscience. *Churchill* versus *Hopson, in Canc. Salkeld* 318.

Two Executors join in an Acquittance, but one only receives the Money, both are chargeable for it to Creditors; but the actual Receiver only to Legatees.

Parol Evidence not admitted to contradict the Words of a Will. *M.* 20 G. 2. *Lowfield v. Stoneham, Exec. in B. R.* 2 *Str.* 1261.

Parol Evidence.

In

In proving a Will according to the Statute of Frauds and Perjuries, if *one* Witneſs prove that the other *two* were there preſent, this is a Proof ſufficient of ſuch Will, without having all the Witneſſes thereto to prove it; for then it is proved by a Witneſs that the Will was executed according to the Method required by the Statute, unleſs they ſhew ſuch Characters of Fraud as will make it neceſſary to produce the reſt. *Gilb. Law of Evid.* cites *T. Aſſ.* 1701. in *Kent.* 2 *Wms* 509, 510.

Indictment for forging a Will relating to perſonal Eſtate; and on the Trial a Forgery was proved, but the Defendant producing a Probate, that was held to be concluſive Evidence in ſupport of the Will. 1 *Str.* 481.

Evidence in particular, under the following Heads.

1. *Acts of Court.*

Two Commoners *on Behalf of themſelves and all the Commoners in H.* preferred a Bill in the Dutchy Court againſt the Owner of the Land in which they claimed Common, and upon Hearing the Common was decreed. The Court was put down; and the *now Defendant* having purchaſed Land in *H.* the *now Plaintiff*, who was a Commoner when the Decree was made, tho' *no Plaintiff* in that Cauſe, brought his Bill againſt the *now Defendant*, to have the Uſe of the *Depoſitions* taken in the former Cauſe, at a Trial to be had at the Aſſizes; and the Defendant demurred to the Bill, and the Demurrer was allowed, as neither the *now Plaintiff* or *Defendant* were Parties to that Suit, though the

the Suit was of general Concernment, and the Suit *there* the fame with the *prefent*, and that the Defendant *here* claimed under the Defendant *there*. *Vin. Evidence*, 81.

2. *Acts of Parliament, Proclamations, Rolls*, &c.

An Act printed by the *King's Printer* is always allowed good Evidence of the Act to a Jury, but was never yet allowed to be a *Record* without an Exemplification under the Great Seal, and it muft be pleaded as exemplified. *Ibm.*

A *private* Act printed among the *public* Acts hath been allowed in Evidence ; even a *private* Act in print, which concerns the *whole County*, as that of *Bedford Levels*, may be given in Evidence without comparing it with the Record. *Ibm.*

Antient Ufage for 3 or 400 Years is good Evidence of *a Law*, if an Act of Parliament be loft or imbezilled, the Law ftill remains. *Ibm.*

A printed Copy of a *private* Act or Ordinance obfolete, was difallowed by all the Court to be given in Evidence, unlefs it had been examined by the Original. *Ibm.*

... Acts of Parliament, and the Inrolment of ... are deftroyed by Fire, Rebellion; or I... Time, yet, if by any Circumftances an... they may be manifefted, they have t... of Acts ; as by antient Copies, Tranf... ks, Pleadings, and Memorials ; but th... muft not permit the fame to be put in... a Plea of *nul tiel Record*. No p... is Evidence on *nul tiel Record*, b... be exemplified under the Great Seal, I...

Upon

Upon View of the Parliament Roll of the Statute 2 *E.* 6. for Payment of *Tithes*, and comparing it with the Declarations in the Causes between *Bowes* and *Broadhead*, and *Burreston* and *Herbert*, it was found that the Statute was rightly recited, notwithstanding the *Journal Book* of Parliament was produced to the contrary, and thereupon Judgment was given in both Cases; for the Court is to be ruled by the Parliament Roll, and not by the Journal Book. And the same Day in a like Case between *Boyer* and *Tantulyar* for the like Reason, and the Court ordered the Parliament Roll to be brought into Court, to shew whether an Adjournment in Parliament was well recited, and would not credit the Journal Book, *Ibm.* 123.

In Case of a Wager about the Day on which the Peace was proclaimed, it was held by *Holt* Ch. J. that a *printed Proclamation* was good Evidence, though not examined by the Record, inrolled in Chancery, nor proved to have been under the Great Seal; but must be examined by the Original. *Vin. Evidence,* 129.

3. *Admiffion of the Party.*

A finding by special Verdict, or the Admission on former Pleadings, is good Evidence, unless the contrary appear. *Vin. Evidence,* 82.

In an Action for Work done, &c. the Plaintiff to charge the Defendant gave in Evidence *a Copy* of *a Bill delivered* to the Defendant, and copied by Order of the Defendant, and divers Exceptions were taken to the Bill, as to Quantities, Values, and private Marks; and it was ruled by *Holt,* Ch. J. that this *Copy*
of

of a Bill delivered was Evidence, as a Copy of a *Bill*, and not Copy of a Copy; and the Objection to Price and Quantity is not Part of a Confeſſion, or more than a Cavil. *Ibm.*

4. *Affidavit.*

A Man being about to convey to a Purchaſer, made *Oath* before a Maſter in Chancery, that there was no Incumbrance on the Eſtate; in an Ejectment brought, this *Affidavit* was produced in Court, but not ſuffered to be read more than as a Note or Letter, unleſs the Plaintiff would produce a Witneſs to ſwear he was preſent when the Oath was taken before the Maſter. *Ibm.*

The Plaintiff or Defendant may make Affidavit in their own Cauſe, and it may be filed, but is not to be admitted in Evidence in the Trial of a Cauſe between them. *Ibm.*

Though an Affidavit cannot be read in Evidence, yet if the Party who made it be ſworn, and gives Evidence, his *own Affidavit* may be read *againſt him*, and this is allowable, to ſhew in what he contradicts himſelf. *Ibm.* 83.

On a Queſtion on a Trial, whether the Property of Wine, *&c.* was in the Defendant, in order to aſcertain whether Alien or *Britiſh* Cuſtom was due for them, an *Affidavit* the Defendant had made at the Cuſtom-houſe was given in Evidence, in which the Defendant ſwore the Wine was his. *Ibm.* 83.

5. *Antient*

5. *Antient Deeds*, &c.

An old Deed is good Evidence without Proof or Seal; but whether the Indorfement on a Bond by the Obligee, after his Death, and after thirty-five Years entring into it, fhall be given in Evidence at Law, to take off an Objection to the Antiquity of it? fee 8 *Mod.* 278.

A Deed found in the Archives of the Chapter of *Hereford* was read, to prove an Endowment of a Vicaridge, the only *concurrent* Evidence, as it appeared not to have been ever fealed or delivered. *Vin. Evid.* 84.

An *original antient Leafe* could not be produced, but the Grandfon of the Leffor produced a *Counterpart*, found amongft his Grandfather's Evidence, and though it had no fubfcribing Witnefs to it, it was yet allowed for Evidence; and *Wyndham* J. faid he had feen many Deeds in Q *Eliz.* Time without any.

Where a Deed before Time or Memory is fupported by Ufage after, is *pleadable and good*; but the Books which fay that Deeds before Time of Memory fhall *not* be pleaded, are to be intended of Deeds of fuch Liberties and Franchifes as cannot be claimed or fupported by Ufage *in Pais*, as if one claim *bona felonum* by Deed before Memory, he cannot fhew his Deed, and fay *Virtute cujus*, &c. but muft fhew an antient confirmation, or Claim and Allowance *in Eyre*; therefore to fhew the Deed in the prefent Cafe, and a Ufage to fupport it, is fufficient, and the other Way of Pleading it with a *Virtute cujus* would have been naught.

As

As to the *Date* of a Deed 'tis pleadable, tho'
Time out of Memory, where it is a *private*
Deed; but Grants of Franchifes and Liberties
muſt be allowed *in Eyre*, and ſo is 1 *Roll.* 4.
649. *pl.* 8. to be underſtood. *Ibm.* 8 $\frac{4}{7}$.

In the Caſe of Water Bailage in *London*,
Evidence of conſtant Payment, and their *antient* Tables of Duties imported, was judged
ſufficient, though there can be no Preſcription
for it. *Ibm.* 85.

6. *Baron and Feme.* See *Marriage.*

7. *Belief. Hearſay.*

It is no Satisfaction for a Witneſs to ſay, that
he *thinks* or *perſuades* himſelf, *&c.* for, *per Coke*,
the Judge is to give abſolute Judgment, and
to have more Ground than *Thinking*; and
Judges, as Judges, are always to give Judgment
ſecundum allegata & probata, whatever private
Perſons may think. *Ibm.* 86.

The Saying of *old Men* may be given in Evidence, in caſe of a *Modus*, but not on an Iſſue,
parcel or not parcel; yet in a Queſtion in E-
jectment, whether a particular *parcel* belonged
to one, or to the other, the Deed and Declaration of the Perſon who held *under both*, was
allowed as Evidence by *Hardwick* Ch. J. at
Exeter, 1735. *Vin. Evidence* 118.

In caſe of a *Murder*, what the *deceaſed* declared after the Wound given, may be given in
Evidence. *Ibm.* But in *Trowter's* Caſe, *P.* 8
Geo. B. R. the Court would not admit the *Declaration* of the Deceaſed, which had been reduced into *Writing*, to be given in Evidence
without producing the Writing. *Ibm.* 119.

Though

Though *Hearsay* is not to be allowed as *direct* Evidence, yet it will serve to prove a Man was *constant* to himself, whereby his Testimony is corroborated.

In a Suit between *A.* and *B. A.* produced a Deed in a subsequent Suit between *C.* and *A.* it was *vivâ voce* proved that *A.* in a Cause between *A.* and *B.* produced such a Deed which proved so and so in particular. *Per Curiam :* This is good Evidence, for here *A.* if he pleases, may give that Deed in Evidence to controul the parol Testimony, and having the Deed in his Custody, which *C.* hath not, nor can produce. *Ibm.* 118.

To prove a *Discharge of Tithe,* by Unity of Possession, in the Hands of the Abbot, at the Time of the Dissolution, two Persons testified they had seen a Deed of *Appropriation* of the Parsonage to the Abbot, for which Reason they *verily thought* there was an Unity of Possession at the Time of the Dissolution; but this was ruled to be no Proof, for it may be intended not to continue, but they said that *Hearsay* shall be allowed for Proof. *Ibm.*

On a *Modus* alledged, it was agreed, that where the Statute appoints Proof of the *Surmise* to be by *two,* it is sufficient if *two affirm* that they have *known* it to be so, or that the *common Fame* is so. So on a *Modus* and Issue, the Witnesses said that for a long Time, as they *heard say,* the Occupiers of that Farm, *&c.* had used to pay annually to the Parson 3 s. for all Tithe ; and it was agreed that this *hearsay* Proof was sufficient to maintain the Surmise within the Statute 2 *E.* 6. *Ibm.*

2   Being

Being *told* by Perſons of good Credit, all along the Road, of the *Prorogation* of the Parliament, is good Evidence of *Notice* in an Action of falſe Impriſonment.   So if a Witheſs ſwear in a Cauſe, and dies, *the Court* held, that in another Trial, one who heard him, may, upon Oath, repeat his Teſtimony, and it ſhall be good Evidence, if the *Record* of that Trial be produced, but not otherwiſe. *Ibm.* & 136.

8. *Books, Papers,* &c.

In *Caſe* for taking the Profits of the Under Clerk of the Treaſury, a *Note* obtained by Lord *Finch*, formerly Maſter of the Office, of the Officers Subſcription, that they were but Servants, which will not bind others, was refuſed to be given in Evidence *by the Court*, eſpecially as Part had been cut off. *Vin. Evidence,* 136.

To prove taking the Oath, &c. in the Act of Uniformity, a Certificate was produced that had only a ſmall bit of Wax upon it; yet, *per Twiſden,* it may be read, and ſo we read *Recoveries* after the Seal broken off, and ſaid he had ſeen Adminiſtration given in Evidence after the Seal broken off; and ſo of Wills and Deeds. *Ibm.*

Transfer Books of a Company have been allowed; as Evidence. *Ibm.* eſpecially being the Books of a publick Company, and kept for publick Tranſactions, in which the Publick are concerned. *Ibm.* 89.

To prove the Cuſtom of a Manor relating to Copyholders *cutting down Wood*, the Bookcaſe of 14 *E.* 3. *Fitz. Bar,*   was given in, and allowed for good Evidence: So a Year

Book

Book is good Evidence to prove the *Courſe of the Court. Ibm.* 138.

At a Trial at Bar concerning the Title of Land, a Copy of an *Inſcription* upon a *Grave Stone* in *London* was admitted Evidence to prove a *Pedigree*: But a Charter of a *Pedigree* is no Evidence of itſelf, without ſhewing the *Books and Records*, from whence it is deduced to prove a *Deſcent*, though the Heralds ſwore the Pedigree was deduced from the Records and antient Books in the Office. Yet, *negatively*, a Book out of the Heralds Office was allowed to prove the Plaintiff was *not* deſcended from *W. Z.* of *P.* as alſo an *old Book*, in Lord *Oxford's* Library, mentioning the Pedigree of *W. Z.* of *P.* which was ſigned by himſelf. *Ibm.* 244. See 1 *Str.* 162.

Though *Heralds Books* are allowed to prove a Pedigree, the Reaſon is from *neceſſity*, becauſe they have not better Evidence ; and this is their proper Employ, and ſome credit is to be given to them, but they do not deſerve much. *Ibm.*

Heralds Books were admitted Evidence to Triers of a Challenge, to prove *Coſinage* in the *Sheriff. Ibm.* 119.

So an Inquiſition *poſt mortem* is Evidence, though not concluſive : So an *antient* Heralds Book to prove a Pedigree ; but an Extract is not. So an original *Viſitation Book* by the Heralds hath been allowed as Evidence ; but *an Entry* in their Office is not good Evidence to prove a Pedigree *for an Heir*, for they are not Matters of *Record*, only *circumſtantial* Evidence, and not the Entries of any public Office. *Ibm.*

In

In a Trial at Bar concerning the Right of Vifiting *Univerfity Coll. Oxon'*, one of the Iffues was, whether *King Alfred* was Founder? and feveral Hiftorians to that Point were offered in Evidence; but the *Chief Juftice* declared fuch Evidence is never admitted, unlefs in Proof of a Point concerning *the Government*; and it was waived. *Ibm.*

Old MSS. found amongft the Evidences of a Family, may be Evidence, becaufe *Originals*, but not a *Copy*, for that is liable to the Miftake of the Tranfcriber. *Ibm.* 101, 120, 244.

The Regifter Book of a Dean and Chapter are public Books, and Evidence: So a *Church Book* hath been admitted Evidence to prove Nonage; but the Entry of the Names and Titles of Perfons in a *Church Book*, either for Births or Marriages, are not pofitive Evidence, without fully proving the *Identity* of the Perfons, and alfo ftrengthened with *Circumftances*, as Cohabitation, or the Allowance of the Perfons themfelves. *Vin. Evidence,* 89, 235.

It is generally true, that where Books, as *Parifh Books, public Corporation Books* are *common Evidence* for *both* Parties, they are like *Court Rolls*, which belong as well to the *Tenants* as to the *Lord* of the *Manor*, and each Party hath a Right to the Ufe of them. *Ibm.* 89, 90.

Survey Books, though antient, unlefs *figned* by the *Tenants*, or appear to be made at a *Court of Survey*, are no other than private Memorials, and no Evidence; but old *Court Rolls* are Evidence: So of *Rentals*, or *Accounts* of Money *received* by the *Steward*; but Rentals, *without* Money received and paid upon them, are nothing, 'tis the *Payment* makes them of

Effect.

Effect. *Ibm.* See *p.* 131, 132. *Vin.* Title *Evidence.*

A *printed Book*, being an *Inventory* of the *State* of the late *South Sea Stock*, which was directed to be made by *Act of Parliament*, and to be left with one of the Barons of the Exchequer, and published by the Authority of the Speaker, was allowed as Evidence. *Ibm.* 91.

Where Books are lost in an *Earthquake*, so that the Plaintiff could not charge the Defendant otherwise than by his own Books, the *same Books* were admitted to be his Discharge. *Eq. Ca. Abr.* 10. cited as then lately adjudged in the Case of *Mellish* and *Turner. Ibm.*

9. *Certificate.*

In *Debt* against the Sheriff for the *Reward* given by the 6 & 7 *W. & M.* to those who should discover and convict Clippers and Coiners, the Plaintiff had a *Certificate* from *Holt* Ch. J. who tried the Malefactor, on his having been convicted on the Plaintiff's Evidence, which being produced, though under the Ch. Justice's Hand, was yet proved by my Lord's Clerk to the Jury. *Ibm.*

By Statute 6 *Geo. c.* 20. §. 7. The *Certificates of Clerks of Assize or Peace* are made *Evidence* of a Person's being convicted, and ordered for *Transportation*, so as to make him guilty of Felony without Benefit of Clergy *for returning.*

10. *Circumstances.*

De Morte Viri in Dower by the Wife, after the Husband had been absent seven Years beyond Sea, may be proved by *Circumstances*;
for

for in fuch Cafes *qui melius probat, melius habet.*
Ibm. 94.

A Man hath two Manors of *D.* and levies a Fine of the Manor of *D.* generaly ; *Circumftances* may be given in Evidence to prove what Manor he intended. *Ibm.* See *Vin. Trial,* 345. and the Books there cited.

Circumftantial Evidence ought never to be admitted where *better* may be had, *ex natura Rei,* for *Circumftances* are doubtful and fallible, and it is upon this Reafon the Copy of a Record is good, where the Record itfelf cannot be had. *Ibm.* See *p.* 99, 101.

11. *Confeffion.*

The *Confeffion* of the *Under-fheriff* of an Efcape, is Evidence againft the *High-fheriff,* for though the *Sheriff* be fuable, yet the *Under-fheriff* gives him a Bond of Indemnity, and the whole will fall upon him ; his *Confeffion* therefore is good Evidence, becaufe in Effect he charges himfelf. *Ibm.* 95.

Confeffion of Delivery of Goods, in the Court of Requefts, may be given in Evidence againft the Defendant at Law : So in an Information for publifhing a Libel, the Defendant's *own Confeffion* is Evidence againft him ; but then the *whole* muft be taken together, and not *fo much only* as ferves to convict him. *Ibm.*

It is the worft Sort of Evidence that is, where there is *no Proof* of a Dealing or Tranfaction, or a Probability of Dealing between Parties. *Ibm.* 96.

12. *Copies.*

12. *Copies.*

Wherever an Original is of a *public Nature*, and would be Evidence if produced, as a Bargain and Sale, Deed inrolled, Church Regiftr, *&c.* in fuch Cafe, a *fworn Copy* thereof will be good Evidence; but where the original is of a *private Nature*, a *Copy* is not Evidence, unlefs the Original be burnt or loft. *Ibm.* 101, 102.

By Statute 8 *Geo. c.* 25. §. 2. *Copies* of Recognizances, in Nature of a Statute Staple, *figned* by the Clerk or his Deputy, where the Original is loft, is good Evidence.

13. *Coverture.* See *Marriage.*

14. *Court Roll.*

As to the *Time* of a Surrender made, or Court held, the *Rolls* of the Manor are no conclufive Evidence, but fhall be tried by the County. *Ibm.* 105.

Proclamation, whereby the Lord claims *Forfeiture* of a Copyhold, ought to be proved *vivâ voce*, and not only the *Court Rolls*; fo held in Evidence to a Jury. *Ibm.*

To maintain *cuftomary Defcents*, Prefidents in the *Court Rolls*, to prove the Ufage, ought to be fhewn, for without *fuch Proof*, though it had been *deemed*, or *reported* to have been the Cuftom, yet the Court cannot folely give Credit to the Proof by Witneffes.

If Proof be made of a *particular Benefit* which the Lord of the Manor is to have, the Court Rolls is the beft Proof of it, for no Proof can be more directly or particular than the Entries in the Rolls in certain. *Ibm.*

14. -*Examination.*

15. *Examination.*

Witneſſes, as well in *criminal* as *civil* Cauſes, may be *examined* before a Judge, by Leave of the Court, where ſufficient Reaſon appears to the Court ; as going to Sea, &c. and in ſuch Caſes, the other Side may croſs examine. *Ibm.* 114.

In a Trial at Bar of an Iſſue out of Chancery, to try if a Leaſe was made in purſuance of a Power, which was, to make Leaſes for the beſt Rent that could be got, a Witneſs was examined in Chancery concerning the Value of the Land, having been Collector of the Rents, and at the Time of his Examination in Chancery, he referred to, and conſulted his Rental ; but now at this Trial he was become blind, and therefore his *Examinations* and *Depoſitions* in Chancery were admitted to be read ; for if he had been ſo ill as that he could not have come to the Trial, they had been good Evidence ; and now by the Act of God he is diſabled to conſult his Rental, the ſame Reaſon therefore holds ; he alſo gave Evidence of what he *remembered* beſides. *Ibm.*

16. *Exemplification.*

See the Statute 3 & 4 *E.* 6. *c.* 4.   13 *Eliz.* *c.* 6. touching the *Exemplification,* or *conſtat* of Inrollment of Letters Patent, and making them Evidence ; and alſo Statute 17 *Eliz. c.* 9. § 8. touching the *Exemplification* of Records of any Fine or Recovery inrolled, or any Part thereof, in the twelve Shires of *Wales,* or Counties Palatine, and making them Evidence.

Exemplification

Exemplification of *Depofitions* taken in Chan_cery, to prove one's being of Age when he le_vied a Fine, was allowed as Evidence, and the Jury regarded it more than the Fine's being re_verfed for Nonage. *Vin. Evidence,* 115.

In Evidence to an *Effex* Jury at Bar in Ejeët_ment, *Maynard* for the Defendant, offered an *Exemplification* under the Great Seal in 1588. of *Depofitions* in Chancery, whereby a Conveyance made in 1586. and loft, was proved; and the *Court agreed,* that being *fo old,* and the Re_cords of the Rolls *burnt fince,* it is good Evi_dence, and alfo in regard it was given in Evi_dence in a former Trial at Bar. *Ibm.* 116.

Copy of Depofitions generally are not to be *ex_emplified or allowed,* nor is the Exemplification of *a Will* under the Great Seal. *Ibm.*

Exemplification of *Letters Patent,* of a Grant of Fee-Farm Rents, was produced, but fo far only as concerned this Grant, and held good in *Carth.* 209. Yet in *Chancery Pre.* 59. the Exemplification of *part* of a Patent was not allowed to be read in Evidence (notwithftand_ing the Statute 3 & 4 *E.* 6. and 13 *Eliz.*) in a Cafe where the other Side have not Time to confult the Patent Roll, and fo may be furprifed by an imperfeët Exemplification. *Ibm.* 116.

To prove the Delivery of Goods to a Mafter of a Ship, an Exemplification of the *Entry* thereof was offered in Evidence, which Entry was made in the Cuftom-Houfe Books at *Rot_terdam,* attefted by a public Notary, and fealed with the public Seal there; but the Court would not permit the Exemplification to be given in Evidence. *Ibm.* 117.

16. *Hand-*

17. *Hand-writing.*

In Debt upon a single Bill, upon *non est Factum* pleaded, one subscribing Witness gave full Evidence of the Sealing and Delivery; the other Side produced a Witness of the same Name and Sirname with the other subscribing Witness, who acknowledged that the Hand was very like his, but that it was *not his Hand,* and that he *never knew either of the Parties,* nor the *other Witness,* neither could the other Witness say that *he was the Man,* and both their Reputations being proved *good, Holt* Ch. J. ordered both to write their Names, which they did, and left it to the Jury, who found for the Plaintiff. *Ibm.* 133.

In the Trial of the seven Bishops, *Powel* J. declared, in the proving of *Lord Chichester's* Hand, that in *civil Actions* a *slender Proof* was sufficient to make out a Man's Hand, as by *Letter,* or the like; but *in criminal Cases,* the Proof ought to be *positive and substantial,* not by Belief; but the Court was divided. *Ibm.* 222.

Where there are two Witnesses to a Deed, who are dead, if there be *full* Evidence to prove *one* of their Hands, and *any* Evidence that Endeavours have been used to find one to prove the other's Hand, this is sufficient, for perhaps the Witness was a Stranger. *Ibm.* 223.

To prove a Hand-writing by *similitude,* and by those who have known the Hand, though the Party was not seen to write it, *in Sidney's Case* was allowed sufficient Proof of a treasonable Writing; for it is as much Proof as the Thing is capable of; though *Sidney* said, it had been
declared,

declared in *Lady Carr's Cafe*, to be no lawful Evidence in *criminal Cafes*. *Ibm.*

In *Crosby's Cafe*, *Camparifon of Hands* was held not to be good Evidence in Treafon, unlefs the Papers are found in the Cuftody of the Perfon himfelf, and not of another; nor is it fufficient for the original Foundation of an Attainder, but if the Eaƈt be otherwife proved, it may be well ufed as *circumftantial* Evidence; but to *conviƈt* on *fimilitude* of Hands, is to run into the *Error of Sidney's Cafe*. *Ibm.*

In Debt upon Bond, and *non eft Faƈtum* pleaded, a Witnefs fwore his Hand was fubfcribed as a Witnefs, but did not fee the Obligation fealed and delivered, and that he never fet his Hand as a Witnefs but where he faw the Sealing and Delivery; upon this, one was fworn to prove the Hand-writing of the other Witnefs, who was dead, which was oppofed; but *Holt* Ch. Juftice faid, a Man fhall not lofe his Obligation becaufe they have tampered with his Witnefs, and he allowed the Plaintiff to prove his Obligation by *Comparifon* of the Hand of the other Witnefs. *Ibm.*

A Deed at *Warwick* Affizes 1699 was produced, to which there were two Witneffes, one of whom was blind; and by *Holt* Ch. J. the Deed was admitted to be proved by the other Witnefs, and read, or it might be proved without proving the Death of the *blind* Witnefs, or even having of him at the Trial, proving only his Hand; and fo it was done here. *Ibm.*

Debt on Bond by *G.* as *Executor* of *C.* againft *N.* which *C.* happened to be the only furfurviving fubfcribing Witnefs, whofe Subfcription was proved by *Parity of Hands*, and, by *Parker* Ch. J. *G.* being difabled by proving the
Will,

Will, is, as if there was *no Witnefs*, where *Parity of Hands* may be allowed : So in Cafe of Depofitions in *Chancery* taken *before* any *Intereſt* accrues to the fubſcribing Witnefs, *&c. after* he had made his Subſcription, this may be proved by *Parity of Hands. Ibm.*

Where a Witnefs would fwear to the Handwriting of another, he muſt be able to fay, he has *ſeen him write,* unlefs where there hath been any fixed Correfpondence by *Letters,* and that it can be made out that the Party writing fuch Letters, is the fame Perſon who atteſted the Deed, and then that will be fufficient. *Ibm.* 224.

Cafe on a Promiffory Note for 10 *l.* atteſted by two Witneffes, one of them faid his Name was *very like* his Hand, but he never faw the Note executed, for he remembered the Time when he was called in to witnefs fome Writings, there were only *two half Sheets ſtamped,* but no fuch Paper as the Note was atteſted by him ; the *other Witnefs* faid the fame ; upon which the Plaintiff produced the two half Sheets, and the Witneffes fwore to the Execution of them : Whereupon *Pratt* Ch. J. left it to the Jury, on the *Similitude* of Hands between the Deeds proved and the Note, and the Jury found for the Plaintiff. *Ibm.*

Two Witneffes to a Bond, *one* mad, and in *Bedlam,* and the *other* in *Africa ;* on an Order to prove an Exhibit *vivâ voce in Chancery,* a Witnefs proved this Faɛt, and their Hands to the Bond, *as if dead :* But if both Witneffes are *beyond Sea,* proving the Hand of the Party is *not fufficient ;* it is ufual only to prove the Hand of one of the Witneffes, and that *they are beyond Sea. Ibm.*

17. *Inqueſt*

18. *Inqueft of Office.*

An *Inqueft of Office* is no conclufive Evidence; nor is an Inquifition, where there is no *Commif-fion* to warrant it, unlefs in the Cafe of an old Inquifition *poft mortem*, which may be read as Evidence, without producing the Commiffion. *Vin. Evid.* 120, 121.

19. *Inrolment of Deeds.*

Inrolment of a Deed, which needs no In-rollment, is no Evidence: Where the *Eftate paffes* by *the Inrollment*, as by Bargain and Sale, there it is Evidence; but where it is only for *fafe Cuftody*, there it is *not*, otherwife than againft the Party who fealed it, and all claiming under him, and fo far it fhall. *Ibm.* 121.

See 10 *An. c.* 18. how to make the Inrol-ment Evidence.

20. *Infpeximus.*

It is faid an *Infpeximus* of a Deed inrolled in Chancery, is not to be fhewn in Evidence, unlefs it be a *Bargain and Sale* inrolled there; for if it be a Deed of Feoffment, the Deed it-felf muft be produced, for the *Infpeximus* is no Matter of Record: But, by *Rolle* Ch. J. though it be the *Infpeximus* of the Inrolment, and not of the *Deed itfelf*, yet if it be of an *antient Deed*, it may be given in Evidence. *Ibm.*

In Ejectment at the Bar, the Defendant gave in Evidence an *Infpeximus* of *a Leafe* made by the Abbot of *B.* which the Court difallowed, being *a private Deed*, and may be forged, and

an

an *Infpeximus* lies only of Matter of *Record*; whereupon they fhewed an *Allowance* of the fame Deed in the Court of Augmentations, which *per Curiam* is good *againft* the King. *Ibm.*

A *Conftat* or *Infpeximus* of Letters Patent, made fince 27 *H.* 8. may be *pleaded* by the King's Patentees, or any claiming under them, as well againft the King as any other. *Ibm.* 122.

21. *Journal.*

Journal of the Houfe of Commons is no Evidence, for they have no Power to give *an Oath*: But the *Journal of the Houfe of Lords* was proved, and admitted in the Bifhops Trial to prove the *King's Speech* 1662. and the *Opinion* of the Houfe of Lords about the King's Power in Ecclefiaftical Affairs. *Ibm.* 122.

22. *Libels.*

The finding two or three Copies of a *Libel* in a Perfon's Chamber, without difcourfing of it, or delivering of it out, is no Publication. *Per Cur'. Ibm.* 228.

Depofitions before a Juftice of Peace, the Deponent being dead, is Evidence only *in Felony*, but not in an Information for *a Libel* againft the Government. *Ibm.*

If *a Libel* be made in Writing, and afterwards burnt and one remembers the Contents, and dictates to another, who writes it, the *Writer* is Maker of *a Libel*: He who takes a Copy of *a Libel* in Writing, though he be not the Author, is guilty of making *a Libel*; *per Holt* Ch. J. *Ibm.* See 2 *Salk.* 417. good Matter on this Diftinction.

Printing

Printing a Libel is *a Publication*; and if a Man is not able to give an Account how he came by it, it makes him the Printer, and of Confequence the Publisher; so the Delivery by a Printer to *S.* is a Publication by the Printer, and the *Receiver* is *an Actor* in that Publication, if he doth not forthwith carry it to a Magistrate: If a *Libellous Paper* be found in a Man's Custody, as upon a Shelf in one's House or Shop (which was the prefent Cafe) it shall be thought he printed it, unless he can give a good Account how he came by it, to excufe himself; *per Parker* Ch. J. *Hill. Vac.* 3 *Geo.* at *Guildhall. Rex* and *Strahan*, who was a Bookfeller, and found Guilty. *Ibm.* 229.

23. *Marriage, and Marriage Agreement.*

Conftant Reputation shall be allowed Proof of *Marriage and Orders*; *per Holt* Ch. J. *Ibm.* 235.

What can be a greater Evidence in a Court of Law, to shew there was *no Marriage*, than a *Sentence in the Spiritual Court*, by a regular Suit, and pronounced in the Life-time of the Parties, that they were guilty of Fornication, and Proof of the commutation Money by the fuppofed Father. *Ibm.* 129, 235.

For the Proof of a Marriage, was given in Evidence *Cohabitation for twenty Years*; that they came to Town, and lodged in Town; that the Husband was a Papist, and they were married by a Papist, to wit, the *Portugal* Ambaffador's Chaplain, for which Reafon no other Perfon was prefent: That the Husband in his Life-time *acknowledged* her *his Wife*, and defired the Witneffes to ufe her *as fuch*; and that a little

before

before, and on the Day of his Death, *declared* in the Prefence of his Phyfician, and feveral other Witneffes, that he was *married* to her. *Ibm.* And it was fo found.

A. and '*M.* were married *at the Fleet by diffe- rent Names*, and an Entry made in the Regifter there, of the Marriage on 'fuch a Day, by *their different Names*; in the *Spiritual Court* this was fentenced *a good Marriage*, and that Sentence *affirmed* in the Delegates : Now on a Trial at Bar between a Daughter of that Marriage, and a Daughter of a former Marriage; *the Father being dead*, it was found a Marriage. *Ibm.*

A Marriage was not allowed on a Trial, it being *fignified* to the Court, that a *Sentence* in the Arches had been given, that there was no *Marriage*, and the Temporal Courts muft give Credit thereto, till it is reverfed, for it is a Matter of meer fpiritual Cognifance. *Ibm.* 236.

In Debt upon an Obligation, *Coke* Ch. J. faid, and that fo was the Opinion of the *Civi- lians*, that a *Difagreement* to a Marriage had *under Age* of Confent, ought *at Age* to be *pub- lifhed in Court*, otherwife the Iffue may be ba- ftardized ; for a Difagreement *in Writing* is not fufficient, nor a good Proof. *Ibm.*

In *Affumpfit* on a *Contract to marry*, any *lawful Impediment* may be given in Evidence ; as that the Parties were within the *Levitical De- grees*, &c. for this makes the Promife void ; but it is otherwife of a Præ-contract. If fuch a Promife be not *in Writing*, the Defendant may give in Evidence the Statute 29 *C.* 2. *c.* 3. and if *the Woman*'s Promife does not bind, the *Man*'s *Promife* is but *nudum pactum*, the Pro- mife therefore muft be mutual. *Ibm.* Yet,

If there be an *exprefs Promife* of the Marriage by the *Man*, and the *Woman* countenance it, and by her Actions behaves herfelf fo as if fhe agreed to the Marriage, though there be no *actual* Promife, yet this fhall be fufficient Evidence of a Promife on the *Woman's Side*. *Ibm.*

24. *Notary Public, Certificate.*

It was refolved that a *Copy* of an Agreement *regiftred* in *Holland*, and attefted by a *Public Notary* there, may be given in Evidence for the Defendant, as he proved that the Plaintiff took out another *Copy* of the fame Agreement, but would not now produce it; for it is plain he knew of the Agreement, and could not be furprifed. *Ibm.* 123.

And in the above Cafe the *Court held*, that a Plaintiff who was in *Holland* might make Affidavit *there*, and get it attefted by a *Public Notary*, and that it fhould be fufficient Evidence to hold the Defendant *here* to Special Bail. *Ibm.*

25. *Perjury.*

Exception was taken to a Witnefs, that he was *convict* of Perjury, and a *Copy* of a *Verdict in Oliver's Time*, on which there was *no Judgment*, was offered; but the Court would not admit the Evidence, becaufe, by the Alteration of Government, all was difcontinued; but it was agreed, that Evidence *vivâ voce* might be given to prove him perjured: The other Side, to eftablifh the Witnefs's Credit, produced *a Pardon* of the Perjury; but *per Cur.* this will not do, for it cannot reftore him to his Credit. *Ibm.* 244.

A falfe

A falſe Oath any Way conducive to the *Mat-ter in Iſſue*, or a guide to the Jury, though *only circumſtantial*, it is Perjury ; ſo if it tend to the *Diſcovery of Truth*, though but a *Circumſtance*, it is Perjury ; but to tell an *impertinent Tale*, nothing to the Purpoſe, is not ſo. *Ibm.* Yet if a Man ſpeak to the *Credit* of a Witneſs, *not* directly to the Iſſue ; if his Evidence be falſe it is Perjury.

As at a Trial the Queſtion was *upon Money lent*, and it being objected that it was *improbable*, that the Plaintiff who was a cautious Man ſhould lend ſuch a Sum *without a Note*, a Wit-neſs was produced to prove that he had lent a *greater Sum* to a Perſon *then in Court* without a Note, *which Perſon ſwore he did not* : And upon Motion to file an Information of Perjury againſt him for the Oath, the Court held it reaſonable. *Ibm.*

To convict a Man of Perjury a *probable* Evidence is not enough, the Evidence muſt be *ſtrong and clear*, and more *numerous* than the Evidence for the Defendant ; it is otherwiſe only Oath againſt Oath. *Ibm.*

A Perſon ſwore he ſaw and read ſuch a *Deed*, and it proved on the Trial to be only the *Coun-terpart* which he ſaw, this is no other than a Miſtake, but no Perjury. *Ibm.*

Perjury may be committed in *circumſtantial Matter*, but the Circumſtance muſt be *very material*, and of that weight, that without it, there is no Hope to find Credit with the Jury *Ibm.*

26. *Presumption.*

Presumptions are of three Sorts, *Violent, Probable* and *Light*; *Violent* is many Times *plena Probatio,* a full Proof, the *Probable* moveth little; and the *Light* not at all. *Ibm.* 124.

If a Deed of *Feoffment,* of forty Years standing, be given in Evidence, and *Possession* hath always gone along with it; *per Coke* Ch. J. *Livery* shall be intended, though it cannot be proved; but if the Jury find all the Matter *specially,* the Court cannot adjudge it a good Feoffment without *Livery*; and though a Jury may find a Thing upon *Presumption,* yet the Court ought to judge upon what appears upon Record. *Ibm.* 125.

In Things of *great Antiquity Omnia præsumuntur solenniter esse acta. Ibm.* 125. See 12 *Rep.* 3, 4.

After *long Possession,* as for twenty-five Years, *Livery and Seisin* shall be presumed, for it is as much favoured *in Law* as *in Equity. Ibm.* 126.

After a great length of Time, as forty Years Possession of a Copyhold, under a Will, a *Surrender* to the Use of a Will shall be *presumed* and supplied; for they are kept by the Lord and his Stewards, who are often changed, and generally negligent, and Surrenders may be lost without the Default or Negligence *of the Party. Ibm.*

Length of Time is only a *Presumption* of Payment, and there is a Difference between *Debts and Legacies,* as to their Antiquity. *Legacies* always appear upon the Face of the *Will,* and so an Executor knows what he hath to pay, without request; but for *Debts* and other dormant

mant Demands againſt which the Executor cannot provide without Notice, the Statute had,
Reaſon to limit the Time. *Ibm.*

Where *two Facts* are alledged againſt the
ſame Man, and it be queſtioned whether it be
the ſame Man, it is ſufficient that it be ſo *reported,* unleſs another of the *ſame Name* be
produced. *Ibm.*

27. *Priority of Birth.*

A Man had *eight Sons,* the *three laſt* were
all born at *a Birth*; and in Ejectment (the *five
eldeſt* being all dead without Iſſue) the Queſtion
was, which of the *three* was *eldeſt*? They were
baptized by the Names of *Stephanus, Fortunatus,*
and *Achicus.* Declarations of the *Father* were
proved, that *Achicus* was the *Youngeſt,* and that
he took the Names from *St. Paul* in his *Epiſtles*:
The *Son of Fortunatus* was Leſſor of the Plaintiff; *et è con.* it was proved from the Declarations of one *M. F.* who was *a Relation, and at
the Birth,* that upon the Birth of the *ſecond
Child,* ſhe took a String and tied it round the
Arm to know one from the other, *&c.* Objection was made, that the Declaration of *this
Woman* was *not Evidence,* in regard *it was ſince
the Death* of the *fifth Son,* when there was a
Diſcourſe about this Matter; but what this
Woman ſaid ſoon *after the Birth* was allowed
in Evidence, when there was no Proſpect of
a Controverſy. *Ibm.* 247. *Per Reynolds,* C. B.
at *Lent* Aſſizes Com. *Devon* 1731.

28. *Probate.*

28. *Probate.*

Will proved under the *Seal of the Bishop* is only an Estoppel : And the *Probate* of a Will, where it respects *Lands*, is no Evidence at Common Law ; nor is the *Examination* of Witnesses of the *Probate* to be made use of at Common Law. *Ibm.* 126.

At *Rygate, Surrey*, Summer Assizes, 10 *W.* 3. it was ruled by *Holt* Ch. J. upon the Evidence, that, because in the Spiritual Court after *Probate* of a Will, *six Months* are allowed to register it, and when it is registred, it is by the *Original*, but the Probate is *signed by the Register only*, upon the *Attestation and Examination* of the *Proctor*, a Will therefore proved in 1666, in the Archdeacon's Court of *London*, and the *Office* in the Fire of *London* was *burnt* soon after, and the *Probate* produced in Evidence to prove the Will with all these Circumstances ; it was denied by *Holt* Ch. J. to be good Evidence to prove the Will. *Ibm.* 127.

In the Case of *Lady Jones and Lord Say and Seal*, M. 2 G. 2. *Canc.* Though the Will was made in 1685. the Court would not allow the *Probate* to be read, it being only in Nature of a *Copy*, and unless the *Original be lost* cannot be read *as to Lands*. *Nota* ; The Will in a former Cause *was proved*, and an Order obtained for reading the Depositions *in that Cause*, but the *Will produced* not being marked by the Examiner as *an Exhibit*, Objection was therefore made to its being read, but the Will being set forth in *his Verbis* in the *Interrogatory*, and being *examined in Court* with it, the *Will* was ordered to be *read*, but it was agreed it could not be read out of the *Interrogatory*, because
that

that is no more than *a Copy*, and only Evidence when the Original *is loft*. And *King Chancellor* examined the Officer who produced the Will where he had it, though no Order was in the Caufe to examine *vivâ vocc*. *Ibm.* See *Ibm.* 259, 260.

29. *Record.*

When the Party makes a Title *by Record,* he muft fhew it under the Great Seal, unlefs it be in the fame Court, for a Man in Pleading cannot make to himfelf a Title in any Cafe *by Record,* without fo fhewing of it. *Ibm.* 130.

A Deed of Ufes was *loft,* and to fupply it, Evidence was given that it had been formerly produced in Evidence in the *Exchequer,* upon an Alienation there queftioned, and *the Record* thereof was fhewed; and this was allowed for Evidence. *Ibm.* 131.

No particular Crime fhall be proved againft a Witnefs, unlefs the *Record* of his Conviction be produced. *Ibm.*

30. *Reputation.* See *Marriage.*

The Judges fhall conftrue Words as they are intended and underftood in the *Places* where the *Land* demanded *lies. Ibm.* 132.

Ufage may expound antient Charters where the *Words* are *obfcure and obfolete,* and may bear feveral Senfes; but *contra* where the Charter is of modern date. The *Reputation* and Declaration of People may be given in Evidence to explain *old Words,* in a Conveyance; in the Defcription of an Eftate or Lands, no Witneffes fhall be afked how the Defendant ftands affected, where the King is Party; but if the

H 4 Defendant

Defendant gives Evidence of a *general Reputation*, it may be anfwered for the King by *particular Inftances. Ibm.* 132. *Vide Ibm.* 249.

31. *Rule of Court.*

It was ruled by *Treby* Ch. J. at *Guildhall*, P. 10 *W.* 3. That at a Trial at *Nifi Prius*, a Rule of Court, produced under the Hand of the *proper Officer*, is in itfelf an Original, and there is no need to prove it a true Copy. *Ibm.* 132.

32. *Seals.*

The Seal of *Brecknock* is Evidence; fo is that of *Chefter*. And the Courts at *Weftminfter* ought to take Notice of the Seal of the *Grand Seffions* in *Wales*, their Authority being by Act of Parliament, and the Profits of thofe Seals are appointed to be paid into the Court of Exchequer; and by *Moreton* Serjeant, he never knew the Seal of *any Court* denied in Evidence. *Ibm.*

33. *Sentence in the Exchequer.*

' Upon a *Seifure* of Goods, as Brandy, *&c.* if the *Property* be once *determined* in the Exchequer upon an Information, *&c.* and the Defendant *acquitted*, the Trial fhall not afterwards be drawn over again in *another Action*. So if Goods be *condemned*, the Party is bound by it, and fhall not have Liberty afterwards to conteft this in a *collateral Action. Ibm.* 133.

*Of Evidence by Records, (a) Books, Deeds,
and other Writings.*

If the Iſſue be a Recognizance or not, a Recogni-
Recognizance with a Defeazance is good Evi- zance.
dence. *Plo.* 14. So of an Agreement, a ſpe- Agreement.
cial Agreement will prove it. *Plo.* 8.

A Licence to alien Land, or a Pardon for Tenure *in*
Alienation of Land, was held by a common *Capite.*
Preſumption, to be a good Proof that the Land
was held *in Capite.*

Ancient Deeds may be given in Evidence, 1 Keb. 877.
although the Execution of them cannot be Ancient
proved. Deeds.

Where there are two Witneſſes to a Deed,
who are dead, if there be full Evidence to
prove one of their Hands, and that there have
been Endeavours to find out Proof of the
other's Hand, it is ſufficient. *Comberbatch*
248.

He that takes out a Copy of Part of a Re- Copy of a
cord, muſt at leaſt take out ſo much as con- Record.
cerns the Matter in Queſtion, or elſe the Court
will not permit it to be read.

(*a*) The bare producing the *Poſtea* is no Evidence of the
Verdict, without ſhewing a Copy of the final Judgment.
(*b*) Becauſe it may happen, that the Judgment was arreſted, or a new Trial granted. But it is good Evidence,
that a Trial was had between the ſame Parties, ſo as to
introduce an Account of what a Witneſs ſwore at that
Trial, who is ſince dead. *Per Pratt* Ch. J. 1 *Str.* 162.

(*b*) Not enough to give in Evidence a Copy of a Judgment, though it be indorſed to have been examined by the
Clerk of the Treaſury, becauſe it is not Part of the neceſſary Office of ſuch Clerk, for he is only intruſted to keep
the Records, for the Benefit of all Men's peruſal, and not
to make out Copies of them. *Gilb. Law of Evid.* 25.

To

Feoffment.

To prove a Feoffment, a Deed of Feoffment is fhewed, but no Livery is indorfed, if Pof-feffion has gone with the Deed, it is good Evidence. *Roll. Rep.* 1 Part 132.

Provifo.

Upon Not guilty to an Information upon a penal Law, a Provifo to excufe him may be given in Evidence. *Jones Rep.* 38.

Non deci-mando.

If a Man prefcribe in a *Non decimando* generally, he cannot give a Bull in Evidence. *Palmer's Rep.* 38.

Deed.

A Deed with the Seals torn off was admitted to declare Ufes. *Palmer's Rep.* 403, 405.

Upon Motion, a Rule was made by Confent, that a, Deed fhould be allowed in Evidence at the Affizes without proving of it. *Vin. Abr.* Tit. *Evid.* 52. *pl.* 5. cites 1 *Sid.* 269. *pl.* 23. *Trin.* 17 *Car.* 2. *Anon'.*

Records.

Records prove themfelves, and cannot be proved by Witneffes; but Copies of them muft, and are good Evidence ; and fo may any Thing done in the County-Court, Court-Baron, or Hundred-Court, &c. be proved by Witneffes.

A Copy of a Record being fworn to be a true one, fhall be admitted to be given in Evidence, and no Rafure or Interlineation fhall be intended. 10 *Coke* 92. *Layfield's* Cafe.

Where a Record is loft, a Copy of it may be read, without fwearing a true Copy, for the Record is in Cuftody of the Law, and not of the Party, and therefore if loft, there ought to be no Injury arifing to the Party's private Right, and confequently, if it be loft, the Copy muft be admitted without fwearing any Examination concerning it, fince there is nothing with which the Copy can be compared, and therefore

therefore it muft be prefumed true without Ex-amination. *Gilb. Law of Evid.* 22, 23.

A Copy of a Conviction upon an Indictment of Trefpafs, *&c.* fhall not be admitted Evidence fingly by itfelf in an Action of Trefpafs, *&c.* but with Evidence it fhall.

The Copy of the Decree of Tithes in *London* has been often given in Evidence, without prov-ing it a true Copy, becaufe the Original is loft. 1 *Vent.* 257. *Gilb. L. of Evid.* 23.

So a Recovery of Lands in antient Demefne was given in Evidence, where the Original was loft, and Poffeffion had gone a long Time according to the Recovery. 1 *Vent.* 257. *Gilb. L. of Evid.* 23.

A Fine, or Common Recovery, may be given Fine. in Evidence, though it be not under the Great Seal, or Seal of the Court, and without vouch-ing the Roll of the Recovery; and the Part indented is the ufual Evidence that there is fuch a Fine, though they which faw the Fine are alfo good Evidence. *Plow.* 410. *Style* 22.

The Chirograph of a Fine is Evidence to all Perfons of fuch a Fine, for the Chirographer is appointed to give out Copies between the Parties of thofe Agreements that are lodged of Record, and therefore his Copy muft be admit-ted as Evidence without further difpute. *Trin.* Affizes 1701. *Gilb. L. of Evid.* 24. But where the Fine with Proclamations is to be a Bar to a Stranger, there the Proclamations muft be ex-amined from the Roll, for the Chirographer is authorized by the Common Law to make out Copies to the Parties of the Fine itfelf; yet is not appointed by the Statute to copy the Pro-clamations, and therefore his indorfement upon
the

the Back of the Fine is not binding. *Gilb. L. of Evid.* 26.

When a Writ out of a Court of Record is only Inducement to an Action, the taking out the Writ may be proved without a Copy of it ; for it is not of Record 'till it be returned. And so I think it may, to prove the Point in Action, by Witnesses, or Notes of it in a Book of Entries, &c.

Bevis *against* **Holloway.**

Summer Assizes 1683, In Debt upon an Escape upon a Judgment, and *Ca. fa.* in the Court of the Dean and Chapter of *Peterborough*, being an inferior Court of Pleas, the Plaintiff was nonsuited, because he had not a Copy of the Plaint or Judgment, but only the short Notes of the Book of the Court. *Aliter* in Court-Baron, &c.

Case for rescuing a Distress, and declared, that he was seised in Fee, and demised the Premisses to *J. S.* for a Year, and so from Year to Year, as long as both Parties should please, rendering Rent ; and for Rent arrear he distrained, and the Defendant rescued ; and on Evidence it appeared, that the Demise was for a Year certain, and so from Year to Year, and that the Lessee should not go away without giving a Quarter's Warning ; and *per Holt*, C. J. held no Variance, for that the Quarter's Warning was only collateral. 6 *Mod.* 215.

Lease.

So if a Lease be pleaded, a Lease upon Condition is good Evidence, 1 *H.* 8. 20. because the *Genus* comprehends the *Species.* So of a Feoffment pleaded, a Feoffment upon Condition, or a Fine which is a Feoffment of Record, is good Evidence. 44 *E.* 3. 39. A special Agreement is Evidence of an Agreement. *Plow.* 8.

Pope

Pope bring's Replevin againſt *Skinner*, who avows as a Commoner, becauſe the Beaſts were Damage-feaſant in the Common. The Plaintiff pleads in Bar, that *W.* was ſeized in Fee of an Houſe and Land, *&c.* whereunto he had Common, *&c.* and demiſed the ſame to Plaintiff on 30th of *March* 11 *Jac.* to hold from *Lady-day* next before for one Year; the Avowant traverſed the Leaſe *Modo & forma*, and the Jury found that *W.* made the Leaſe to Plaintiff on 25th *March* for one Year from thence next enſuing; and held the Plaintiff ſhould recover; for though this be not the ſame Leaſe, yet the Subſtance of the Iſſue is, whether Plaintiff had ſuch a Leaſe as would intitle him to Common, and that he had, and the *Modo & forma* as to the reſt is not material. *Hob.* 72. *Pope* v. *Skinner*.

But if a Feoffment be pleaded in Fee, upon Feoffment. Iſſue *non feoffavit modo & forma*, a Feoffment upon Condition is no Evidence, becauſe it doth not anſwer the Iſſue; and whereſoever Evidence is contrary to the Iſſue, and doth not maintain it, the Evidence is not good. 11 *H.* 4. 3. *Feoffments* 41. A Grant in Reverſion is no Evidence, but a Leaſe and Releaſe is, 20 *H.* 7. 5. If the Indorſement be of a Livery by Attorney, the Letter of Attorney muſt be ſhewed.

To prove the Sealing and Delivery of a Deed, and not know the Party that did it, is not good Evidence; but if he knows the Party upon Sight of him, it is good enough. *Kilw.* 59.

A Shop-Book no Evidence after a Year. *Stat.* Shop-Books. 7 *Jac. cap.* 12.

The

The Plaintiff being a Brewer, brought an Action againft the Earl of *Torrington* for Beer fold and delivered; and the Evidence given to charge the Defendant was, that the ufual Way of the Plaintiff's dealing was, that the Draymen came every Night to the Clerk of the Brew-houfe, and gave him an Account of the Beer they had delivered out, which he fet down in a Book kept for that Purpofe, to which the Draymen fet their Hands, and that the Drayman was dead, but that this was his Hand fet to the Book; and this was held good Evidence of a Delivery; *otherwife of the Shop Book of itfelf fingly, without more. T.* 2 *Ann. Price* v. Earl of *Torrington,* before *Holt* C. J. at *Nifi prius* at *Guild-Hall, Salk.* 285. *Holt* 300. S. C.

Indebitatus Affumpfit on a Taylor's Bill; at the Trial before *Holt,* and by *Holt* Ch. J. a Shop-Book was allowed for Evidence, it being proved that the Servant that writ the Book was dead, and this was his Hand; and he accuftomed to make the Entries; and no Proof was required of the Delivery of the Goods; and the Chief Juftice faid, it was as good Evidence as the Proof of a Witnefs's Hand to an Obligation; he held, that though the Statute 7 *Jac.* 1. *c.* 12. fays, a Shop-Book fhall not be Evidence *after* the Year, yet that it is not of *itfelf* Evidence *within* the Year. *Salk.* 690. Ld. *Raym.* 732, 733. S. C. held accordingly.

Scrivener's Book to prove a Confideration paid (as a Tradefman's Book) is no Evidence for himfelf, but for any other it is: So a Tradefman's Book after his death. We have allowed a Burfer's Book of a College for Evidence. *Per Holt, E.* 6 *W.* 3 in *B. R. Smart* v. *Williams. Cumb.* 249. *E.* 6 *W. & M. B. R. Per Holt* Ch.

Ch. J. The Book of a Man that keeps regular Entries, might be Evidence for him. *M. 7 W. 3. B. R. Blackeler* v. *Crofts, Cumb.* 249,

Shop-Books have fometimes been allowed to be read as Evidence at the Hearing, and fometimes rejected. *Toth.* 91. *Cary's Rep.* 45.

Upon Iffue Affets or no Affets, or feized or **Covin.** not feized, if one give a Feoffment, &c. in Evidence, Covin may be given in Evidence by the other, but not if the Iffue be infeoffed or not infeoffed; for it is a Feoffment *tiel quel*, though made by Covin. *Lib.* 5. 60. *Hob.* 72.

A voluntary Conveyance is not fraudulent be- **Voluntary** caufe voluntary, but 'tis Evidence of Fraud againft **Conveyance.** an after Purchafer *bona fide*; the Statute avoids fuch Deeds as are not *bona fide* and on Confidera-tion, if made *ea intentione* to defraud Purchafers; therefore this Fraud muft be found by the Jury. *Keb.* 1 Part 486.

The Book of Domefday brought in Court, **Domefday-** is good Evidence to prove the Land to be An- **Book.** cient Demefne. *Hob.* 188.

Copies of the Court-Rolls are the only Evi- **Court-Rolls** dence for Copyholders, for (as *Littleton, Sect.* **for Copy-** 75. tells you) they are called Tenants by Copy **holders Reco-** of Court-Rolls, becaufe they have no other E- **veries are fome** vidence, concerning their Tenements, but only **the Manor** the Copies of Court-Rolls. But *Coke* explains **bears an In-** the Text, and fays, This is to be underftood **tail of a Co-** of Evidences of Alienation; for a Releafe of a **pyhold, but** Right by Deed, a Copyholder (that cometh in **to fhew that** by Way of Admittance) may have, and that **Remainders** is fufficient to extinguifh the Right of the **(after an E-** Copyholder, which he that maketh the Releafe **ftate Tail** had. **fpent) to be enjoyed, is a better.**

2 General

Statutes.

Pardons.

General Acts of Parliament may be given in Evidence, and need not be pleaded; and fo may general Pardons given by Parliament, if they be without Exceptions; but commonly Advantage of the Act is given by the Act itfelf to the Offender, without pleading it; as by the late (moft truly fo called) general Act of Indemnity, every Perfon thereby pardoned, may plead the General Iffue, and give the Act in Evidence, for his Difcharge: Which are *general*, and which *particular* Statutes, fee *Lib.* 4. 76.

A private Act may be given in Evidence exemplified under the Great Seal, or a Copy of the Record; but a printed Copy is no Evidence unlefs it be proved; it ought to be pleaded, but the Jury may find it. *Dyer* 239.

Cafe on a Wager concerning the Day of the Conclufion of the Peace; and to prove it to be on the 10th *September*, the printed Proclamation was produced; it was objected, that it ought to have been examined by the Record inrolled; but *Holt* C. J. held it good Evidence; and that fuch Things as thefe are of as publick a Nature, as publick Acts of Parliament: And that even a private Act of Parliament in Print that concerns a whole County, may be given in Evidence without comparing it with the Record. *Reports in* Holt's *Time* 296. *Cafes W.* 3. 215.

Infpection of a Deed inrolled may be given in Evidence; *Contr.* of a bare Deed not inrolled, or of a Deed that needs no Inrolment. *Pafch.* 1655. B. R. *Goodfon's* Cafe, *Style* 445.

An

An *Inspeximus* lieth only of Matter of Record, and not of a private Deed. *Keb.* 2 Part 294.

A Deed to lead the Uses of a Fine was inrolled on the Acknowledgment of but one of the Parties to it, and was allowed by *Glyn* Chief Justice in Evidence, as *Rolle* Chief Justice had done before him, tho' no binding Evidence. *Turbet* verf. *Maddison, Paf.* 1655. *B. R. Style* 462.

An Office found at a Death, *&c.* may be given in Evidence.

A Verdict against one, under whom either Plaintiff or Defendant claims, may be given in Evidence against the Party so claiming. *Contra* if neither claim under it. *Duke* and *Ventres, Mich.* 1656. *B. R.*

If a Man has Title to several Lands held by several Tenants, and recovers in Ejectment against one, that Recovery shall not be read in Evidence against the rest. 3 *Mod.* 141. *Loch* v. *Norborn.*

If an Action be brought on a Statute, which has several Provisoes in it, the Defendant may plead Not guilty, and aid himself by any of the Provisoes in Evidence ; but if the *Provisoes* be made to that Statute, in another Statute of which the Defendant may take Advantage, he ought to plead it, and not give it in Evidence. *Per Rolle* Chief Justice, *Mich.* 1650. *B. R. Jones* 320. *Accord.*

Arreft and Imprisonment to prove a Bankruptcy must be proved by Record. *Newby* verfus *Bathurft, Pafch.* 1659. *B. R.* In a Trial at Bar, what Evidence proves a Bankrupt. See *Keb.* 2 Part 487.

Bankrupt.

Records, as Patents, Statutes, Judgments may be given in Evidence. *Hob.* 227. *contr.* to *Dyer* 129.

To prove an Extent upon a Statute or Judgment, you must prove a Copy of the Statute and Judgment, as well as the Copy of the Writ and Extent.

When Records are pleaded, they must be *sub pede Sigilli*; *contr.* if given in Evidence. *Style* 22. *White's* Case.

A Copy of a Deed is good Evidence where the Defendant has the Deed, and will not produce it. *Per Vernon* Justice, *Clayton* 15.

So, that there was a Revocation is sufficient for the Heir, without shewing the Deed itself, which was taken away by the Defendant; so that the Witnesses to the Release proved the Lease without shewing, being taken away by the other Side.

A Deed of Feoffment without Livery may be given in Evidence as a Release. *Per Berkley*, 11 *Car. Clayton* 32.

If a Fine be given in Evidence, with five Years Non-claim, &c. the Fine must be shewed with the Proclamations under Seal, and the Chirograph will not serve.

A Deed cancelled by Practice or Fraud, was allowed to be read in Evidence in an Action under that Deed, the Practice being proved. *Hetley* 138.

Against a Purchaser *bona fide*, Recital in a Deed of Money paid is not sufficient, nor Acquittance for the Money, unless it be of ancient standing, and then it shall be presumed.

The

The Deed to lead the Ufes of a Fine *fur conceffit*, need not be proved *per Teftes*.

If a Deed of Feoffment be fhewn, but no Livery, Poffeffion going with the Deed, is Evidence to a Jury to find Livery. .

At *Guildhall*, *Trin.* 23 *Car.* 2. *Hale* Chief Juftice cited the Cafe of Sir *Paul Pindar*. A *Levari*, &c. was proved by a Recital of it in another Record, and *Hale* and *Mainard* demurred on the Evidence; and adjudged againft them for this Caufe, *viz.* That it was proved there was fuch a Record; that it was filed; that it was taken off the File. But (by him) generally without fuch Proof, the Evidence is not good, becaufe one Record may recite one that never was.

Recital of other Grants by Letters Patent in Letters Patent, is fome Evidence, but not fit to be allowed, without fhewing the former Letters Patents, or a Copy. But the Jury may find them. 2 *Rolle* 673. *pl.* 2. 2 *Lev.* 108. Recital in Letters Patent.

The Proof of this Surmife in any Court of Record, fhall not be given in Evidence in another Action upon the fame Cuftom, becaufe the Defendant in the Prohibition cannot crofs-examine. Surrender. Prohibition.

The Record of Conviction of Recufance being burnt, may be proved by the Roll of Eftreats of the Clerk of Affize, figned by the Judge and delivered into the Pipe, or by other Evidence, as a *Fieri facias*, &c. may be proved by other Evidence. Recufant. Hard. 323. Knight *ver.* Dowler.

If the Iffue be whether the King's Tenant by Letters Patent furrendered to the King or not, the accepting of new Letters Patent, which is a Surrender in Law, is good Evidence. Surrender.

If

Dures.

If an Imprifonment by *Dures* at *D.* be in Iffue, 'tis not material whether he was ever at *D.* or not, for the Effect of the Iffue is, if the Deed was made by *Dures.*

Feoffment.

So if a Feoffment pleaded by Deed, a Feoffment without Deed, or another Deed, is good, for the Effect of the Iffue is upon the Feoffment, not upon the *Fait.*

Non demifit modo & forma.
Dyer 116.
2 Rolls 682.
pl. 6.

If in pleading an Indenture of Demife you miftake the Recital, and the Iffue is *Non dimifit modo & forma,* the Miftake fhall not hurt, for the Effect of the Iffue is upon the Demife.

If the Date or Number of Years be miftaken, 'tis fatal.

Upon *Non habuit feu tenuit ad firmam contra formam Statuti,* The Parfon may fay he took the Farm for Maintenance of his Houfe, according to the Provifo in Debt upon the Statute of 21 *H.* 8.

But upon the Statute of 5 *E.* 6. for ingroffing, upon Not guilty 'tis faid, That the Defendant cannot give in Evidence a Licence according to the Provifo of the Statute ; *fed quære rationem.*

Seifin. Feoffment.

In a *Scire facias* againft Tertenants, and a Feoffment pleaded before the Judgment, *abfque hoc,* that he was feifed *tempore Judicii,* and Iffue upon the Seifin, that the Feoffment was fraudulent, to defraud the Judgment, may be given in Evidence ; but otherwife, if the Iffue had been upon the Feoffment.

Copy of Records.
Clayton 142.
Nelthorp *v.* Johnfon.

A Copy of Part of a Record cannot be given in Evidence, unlefs 'tis proved, that the Part fhewed in Evidence, is all concerning the Matter in Queftion.

A Tranfcript

A Tranfcript of a Record or Enrolment of Tranfcript.
a Deed may be given in Evidence, for they are Enrolment.
Things to be credited, being made by Officers
of Truft.

Where a Deed is inrolled (by the proper Officer) the Indorfement of that Enrolment is Evidence, without further Proof of the Deed.
Gilb. L. of Evid. 24.

If one produce a Leafe made upon an Out- Leafe upon
lawry, to prove a Title, he muft alfo produce an Outlawry.
the Outlawry itfelf; but if it be to prove
other Matter, he needs not fhew the Outlawry.
And fo it is of an Extent, without fhewing the
Statute or Judgment on which the Extent is
grounded.

By *Rolle*, an Office found after the Death Office.
of a Tenant *in Capite* of Lands in another
County, may be given in Evidence to try the
Title of thofe Lands, if there was a fpecial Livery granted unto the Heir.

The Copy of a private Act of Parliament Style 462.
may be given in Evidence ; and if upon a Col- Mich. 1650.
lateral Iffue it is to be proved, that fuch a one *Coram* Roll.
was Juftice of the Peace, or Baronet, &c. Com- Littleton *ver.*
mon Reputation is fufficient Proof, without Poins.
fhewing the Commiffion, or Letters Patent of Private Act.
the Creation. Juft. of Peace.

A Copy of a Record is not true, unlefs it Record.
be tranfcribed in the fame Language, and there- Lawrence
fore a Tranflation fhall not be given in Evi- *verfus* Key.
dence ; as where the Record is in *Latin*, and
the Copy in *Englifh*.

A Copy of Copyhold Lands may be given Copyhold.
in Evidence, whether the Rolls are loft, or not 1 Keb. 567.
loft. *Mic.* 15 *Car.* 2 *B. R. Snow* v. *Cutler.*

If

If Copyhold Rolls make mention of a Surrender to the Ufe of the Tenant's laft Will, and then admit *A.* as Devifee to the Will, this was ruled to be no Evidence of the Seifin, or Title of *A.* without the Will itfelf, becaufe the Land doth not pafs by the Surrender, without the Will itfelf, and therefore the Will muft be fhewn as the beft Evidence of *A.*'s Poffeffion and Title. *Gilb. L. of Evid.* cites *Jenkins* and *Baker, per Tracy,* 1705.

Copy of a Recovery.

A Copy of a Recovery, after long Debate, fuffered to be given in Evidence, the Recovery itfelf being burnt. And *Hale* faid, the

Exemplification.

Exemplification of a Record under the Mayor of *Briftol*'s Hand was allowed for Evidence. 1 *Modern Rep.* 117. *Green* and *Proud*'s Cafe. 3 *Keb.* 310. *Hard.* 179.

In an Ejectment for Lands in *Brecknockfhire* in *Wales,* the Defendant made Title by a Recovery of thofe Lands in a *Quod ei deforceat in Brecknock,* (which is their Writ of Right), and to make this out, produced an Exemplification of the Record under the Seal of the Grand Seffions in *Brecknockfhire.* To this Evidence the Plaintiff demurred, and on great Debates in *Scac.* it was held, that this Exemplification was good Evidence; and Judgment for Defendant. *Hardres* 118. 2 *Siderf.* 145.

An Exemplification of a Recovery under the Seal of the Mayor of *Briftol,* was held good Evidence. *Whitehead*'s Cafe, *tempore Wild,* C. B. *Hardres* 179. 1 *Mod.* 117.

At a Trial at Bar in Ejectment, the Defendant fetting up an Entail, the Plaintiff exhibited an Exemplification of a Recovery in the Marquifs of *Winchefter*'s Court in Ancient Demefne ;

mefne; and held Evidence. 1 *Mod.* 117. *Green* v. *Proude.*

An Office before an Efcheator fhall not be given in Evidence, unlefs it be exemplified under the Great Seal of *England.* *Bro. Gen.* *Iſſue* 75.

On an old Recovery the Court allowed it, though no Tenant to the *Præcipe* could be proved, but it fhould be intended. 2 *Cro.* 455. *Mod Rep.* 117.

When any Record is exemplified, the whole Record muft be exemplified, for the Conftruction muft be taken from the View of the whole Matter taken together. *Gilb. L. of Evid.* 17.

A private Act that concerned *Rocheſter* Acts of Par-Bridge, though printed by *Raſtal,* was not al-liament. lowed in Evidence, not being examined by the Record. Otherwife of general Statutes, there the printed Book is good Evidence. *Lambart's Perambulation, Co. Rep.* and *F. N. B.* are good Evidence. 3 *Keb.* 91.

A Man's Book of accounts is no Evidence Book. for the Owner of the Book, but for the ad- Crouch *and* verfe Party; for his Book cannot be of better Drury, Paſc. Credit than his Oath, which would not ferve B. R. in his own Cafe. 1 Keb. 27.

The Book of any Merchant is no good Proof; nor may be allowed touching any Debt due to him; but as to any Debt againft himfelf it may be good enough: And this was agreed *per Cur'. Vin. Abr.* 91. *pl.* 20, 22.

If an Action be brought by a Shop-keeper, for Money due on Sale of Goods, we never inforce him to produce his Books; but if very flender Evidence be with him, then, if he will not produce his Books, it brings a great

Slur upon his Caufe : *Per Cur'. M.* 3 *Ann. B. R.* in Cafe of *Ward* v. *Apprice,* 6 *Mod.* 264.

Copy.
Deed.

A Copy of a Deed is good Evidence, where the Defendant has the Deed, and will not prove it. *Per Vernon,* Juftice, *Clay. Rep.* 15. *Modern Rep.* 4. 266. 2 *Keb.* 483, 540. *Moor* 297.

It is dangerous to permit any one, who in Pleading ought to produce the Deed, on the General Iffue, to give Evidence that *there was fuch a Deed,* by thofe that have feen and read it, or to prove the fame by a Copy ; but in great Extremity, when it appears the Deeds are burnt by a Fire, *&c.* it may be done. 10 *Coke* (*Layfield*'s Cafe) 92.

The Plaintiff's Title in Ejectment was a Leafe for 2000 Years ; the Leafe was loft, but Witneffes fwore there was fuch a Leafe, and that it was taken out of the Plaintiff's Trunk by Defendant and burnt ; and held good Evidence. 2 *Keb.* 483.

The Defendant would have it prefumed, that this Leafe was revoked or furrendered, by fhewing that the Defendant's Mother, who was feifed in Fee, had made a Will and Settlements of the fame Lands. But *per Cur.* A Revocation or Surrender fhall not be intended without Proof. 2 *Keb.* 483.

In Ejectment, a Leafe being recited in a Releafe, was admitted to be proved by the Witnefs to the Releafe, the Leafe being imbezilled by the Leffor of the Plaintiff. 1 *Keb.* 12. *Negus* v. *Reynall.*

The Recital of a Leafe in a Deed of Releafe, is good Evidence againft the Releafor, and thofe that claim under him. 6 *Mod.* 44.

Copy

Copy of a Counterpart of a Leafe, the Copy.
Leafe being loft, given in Evidence, and al- Leafe.
lowed. *Mich.* 15 *Car.* 2 *Stroud* verfus Dr.
Holt, B. R.

The Counterpart of an ancient Deed which
is loft, is good Evidence with other Circumftances, but not of itfelf; but the Counterpart
of a Deed to lead the Ufes of a Fine, is good
Evidence of itfelf. 6 *Mod.* 225.

The Copy of a Deed burnt in a Fire, which
the Witnefs made to carry to Council, but never examined with the Original, allowed to be
read as Evidence. 2 *Keb.* 546. 1 *Mod.* 4.

An Exemplification under the Great Seal of
the Depofitions of Witneffes who are dead,
may be left to the Jury; but *contra*, where
fome of the Witneffes are ftill living. 2 *Rolls
Abr.* 687. *pl.* 3. & 4.

Several Depofitions under the Great Seal are
given in Evidence; the Jury may have them
all with them, though they were not all read in
Court. *Littleton's Rep.* 69.

Depofitions taken in the Dutchy and exemplified, were refufed to be read in Evidence,
becaufe the Defendant's Anfwer was not alfo
exemplified. *Clayton* 9.

Tnough the Seals be broken off a Deed, yet Deed.
the Deed may be given in Evidence. *Mod.* Seals.
Rep. 11.

Defendant claimed by Patent to *Vanlore* in Patents.
22 *Jac. tot, talia, tanta,* &c. as *Dyer*; the *Tot, talia,*
Duke of *Somerfet,* or Abbey of *D.* had them; *tanta,* &c.
and though by Way of pleading, a lawful Ufage
be fufficient, yet on Iffue thereon, or in any
Evidence, it muft appear that the Duke or the
Abbey had a Subftantive of *bona* & *catalla
Felonum*; by *Hale,* Ch. J. and the whole Court:

For

For moſt Grants of Abbey Lands as theſe are Relative, and no Subſtantive Grants appearing, the other Evidence was diſallowed, eſpecially for that the Duke of *Somerſet* was attainted, and ſo his Privileges thereby extinct, unleſs regranted.   3 *Keb.* 456, in *Sanford* and *Clerk*'s Caſe. *Moor* 297.

Deed.
Seals.

Deeds with Seals torn off admitted to declare the Uſe of a Recovery. *Palmer's Rep.* 403.

Fine.
Recovery.

The Chirograph of a Fine may be given in Evidence, but not given to the Jury; but a Recovery may be delivered in Evidence. 2 *Siderfin* 145, 146. *Plow. Com.* in *Scolaſtica*'s Caſe, 410.

Recovery in Value in Evidence may be given in Evidence. 2 *Sid.* 145.

Recital.

Recital of a Patent in another Patent is no Evidence of the recited Patent.   2 *Roll.* 678. *B. pl.* 2. *Hardres* 323.

Pedigree.

Upon Evidence to a Jury to prove *J. S.* to be Heir to *W. S.* the Court would not accept the Pedigree drawn by an Herald at Arms for Evidence, nor would ſuffer the Jury to have it with them, but 'tis only Information for Direction. *Paſch.* 8 *Jac. B. R.* Sir *Edward Plumpton* and *Robinſon,* 2 *Roll.* 687. *I. pl.* 1.

In Ejectment for Lands, the Earl of *Thanet,* to prove his Diſcent from *Robert Clifford* in *Edward* II.'s Time, produced a Pedigree drawn by the Heralds; and Sir *William Dugdale* and other Heralds ſwore it was drawn truly from their Books in their Office; but held not ſufficient, without producing the Books and Records from which it was extracted. *T. Jones* 224.

The

The Queſtion being, Whether the Leſſor of the Plaintiff was Heir at Law to him that laſt died ſ·iſed? To prove the Pedigree, Chief Juſtice *Pratt* admitted a Viſitation in 1623. made by the Heralds, entred in their Books, and kept in their Office, to be read in Evidence: He alſo admitted the minute Book of a former Viſitation, ſigned by the Heads of the ſeveral Families, which was found in the Library of my Lord *Oxford.* H. 5 G. 1. *Pitton* v. *Walter*, at *Surrey* Aſſizes, 1 *Str.* 162.

In a Trial at Bar concerning the Cuſtom of the Salt Pits at *Droitwich*, *Camden's Britannia* was offered as Evidence, but it was not allowed. *Skinner* 623. See *poſtea* 468.

A Verdict for a Leſſee is good Evidence Ejectment. for the Reverſioner in an Ejectment. *Hardres Rep.* 472.

Secus in Caſe of Depoſitions, for the Leſſee, for the Reverſioner, without being Party to the Suit, can have no Advantage. 472, 473, *Ibid.*

The Act of general Pardon cannot be gi- *Non debet.* ven in Evidence on *Non debet modo & forma*, General Pardons. but ought to be pleaded, for that it is not the General Iſſue within the Intent of the Act. *Hardres Rep.* 421.

If a Condition be to pay Money at a cer- Payment at tain Day and Place to avoid a Feoffment, Ac- the Day. ceptance before the Day, although he make an Acquittance, doth not maintain the Iſſue joined on Payment at the Day and Place. *Moor* 47.

A Recovery in the Court of Antient De- A Record loſt meſne, to cut of an Intail which had been proved by ſuffered a long Time ſince, and the Poſſeſſion Teſtimony. gone accordingly, was loſt; and the Court admitted other Proof of it to be ſufficient: And said, faid, if a Record be loft, it may be proved to a Jury by Teftimony. *Anonymous,* B. R. 1 *Vent.* 257.

Deed fhall not be allow-ed in Evidence until it be ftamped. By 5 & 6 *W. & M. cap* 21. No Deed fhall be given in Evidence in any Court either of Law or Equity, until it be ftamped as the Law requires.

Where Exa-minations be-fore the Co-roner fhall be read in Evi-dence, and where not. Refolved by the Judges, that in Cafe Wit-neffes, who were examined before the Coroner, are dead or unable to travel, and Oath made thereof, That fuch Examinations are the fame which he took upon Oath, wi hout any Addi-tion or Alteration; or that in Cafe Oath fhould be made, That a Witnefs who had been examined by the Coroner, was detained by the Procurement of the Prifoner, fuch Examination may be read; but agreed alfo, That if a Wit-nefs, who was examined by the Coroner, be abfent, and Oath made that they have ufed all their Endeavours to find him, and cannot find him, That is not fufficient to authorize the read-ing fuch Examination. *Kelynge* 55.

What Things are neceffary to be proved, to charge the Indorfor of a Bill of Ex-change in an Action by the Indorfee. An Action on the Cafe was brought on a Bill of Exchange againft the Indorfor, and it was ruled by *Holt* Ch. J. upon Evidence, That there is no need to prove the Drawer's Hand, becaufe, though it be a forged Bill, the Indorfor is bound to pay it. 2. The Plaintiff muft prove, That he demanded it of the Drawer, or him upon whom it was drawn, and that he refufed to pay it, or elfe that he fought him and could not find him; for other-wife he cannot refort to the Indorfor. 3. That this was done in convenient Time; for if they ftand and are refponfible a convenient Time after the Affignment, and no Demand made, the Indorfee fhall not charge the Indorfor. The Time

Time for foreign Bills is three Days, and no Allowance is to be made for Sundays and Holy-days. Serjeant *Wright* cited a Cafe of one *Tracy*, who ftood a Week after the Indorfe-ment, and the Indorfee loft this Money; which *Holt*, Ch. J. thought too ftrait, but fuch Mat-ters muft be left to the Jury. 4. 'Tis a Que-ftion, whether Notice muft be given or no; but 'tis fair to give Notice. 5. That the De-mand muft be proved fubfequent to the Indorfe-ment, for if it was precedent, he would only act as Servant to the Indorfor, and fo the De-mand was infufficient to charge the Indorfor. 6. If a Man indorfes his Name upon the Back of the Bill Blank, he puts it in the Power of the Indorfee, to make what Ufe of it he will, and he may ufe it as an Acquittance to dif-charge the Bill, or as an Affignment to charge the Indorfor. 7. In Cafes of Bills purchafed at a Difcount, this is the Difference; if it be a Bill payable to *A.* or Bearer, 'tis an abfolute Purchafe; but if to *A.* or Order, and it is in-dorfed blank, and filled up with an Affignment, the Indorfor muft warrant it as much as if there had been no Difcount. *Lambert* verfus *Park, Salk.* 128.

Holt Ch. J. held, That the Drawing of a Bill is an actual Promife. *Ibid.*

Indebitatus affumpfit for 5 *l.* received to the Plaintiff's Ufe, being Fees of the Office of Clerk of the Peace in *Oxfordfhire*; upon *Non affumpfit* it was infifted on, That the Plaintiff had forfeited his Office by not qualifying him-felf according to Law. And a Record of Sef-fions was allowed in Evidence to prove the Plaintiff had not taken the Oaths. It was there held by *Holt* Ch. J. That if a Judge admits that

Record of Seffions al-lowed in Evidence

that for Evidence which is not, the other Side cannot demur for that Cause, but muſt tender á Bill of Exceptions ; and he ſaid, he remembred a Cauſe where the Univerſity of *Oxford* intitled themſelves to a Preſentation by a Conviction of the Earl of *Shrewsbury* for Recuſancy ;

The Matter of a Record loſt may be proved.

and upon giving ſome Evidence that the Record was loſt, the Univerſity was permitted to prove the Effect of it by other Evidence. *Thurſton* verſus *Slatford, Salk.* 284.

Counterpart, where Evidence.

Per Holt Ch. J. In a Caſe in my Lord *Hale's* Time, between *Combe* and *Mayo,* a Counterpart of an ancient Deed was admitted as Evidence of the Deed, and the ſpecial Verdict was drawn up, as finding the Deed with a *Prout patet* by the Counterpart, which he ſaid was done to preſerve the Precedent : And now, by all the Court, the Counterpart of a Deed without other Circumſtances, is not ſufficient Evidence, unleſs in Caſe of a Fine, in which Caſe a Counterpart is good Evidence of itſelf. *Anonymus, Salk.* 287.

Bill of Exceptions muſt be tendred at the Trial.

A Corporation-Book was offered in Evidence at the Affizes, to prove a Member of the Corporation not in Poſſeſſion, and refuſed. No Bill of Exceptions was then tendred, nor were the Exceptions reduced to Writing, ſo the Trial proceeded, and a Verdict was given for the Plaintiff. Next Term the Court was moved for a Bill of Exceptions, and it was ſtirred and debated in Court. It was urged that the Law requires *quod proponat exceptionem ſuam,* and no Time is appointed for the reducing of it into Writing ; and the Party is not grieved till a Verdict be given againſt him ; and the ſame Memory that ſerves the Judges for a new Trial, will ſerve for a Bill of Exceptions. On the

other

other Side, it was faid, that this Practice would prove a great Difficulty to Judges, and Delay of Juftice; that the Precedents and Entries fuppofe the Exception to be written down upon its being difallowed, and the Statute ought to be conftrued fo as to prevent Inconvenience: Befides, the Words of the Act are in the Prefent Tenfe, and fo is the Writ formed on the Act. *Holt* Ch. J. If this Practice fhould prevail, the Judge would be in a ftrange Condition: He forgets the Exception, and refufes to fign the Bill, fo an Action muft be brought; you fhould have infifted on your Exception at the Trial; you wave it if you acquiefce, and fhall not refort back to your Exception after a Verdict againft you, when perhaps, if you had ftood upon your Exception, the Party had other Evidence, and need not have put the Caufe on this Point: The Statute indeed appoints no Time, but the Nature and Reafon of the Thing requires the Exception fhould be reduced to Writing when taken and difallowed, like a fpecial Verdict or Demurrer to Evidence; not that they need be drawn up in Form, but the Subftance muft be reduced to Writing while the Thing is tranfacting, becaufe it is to become a Record; fo the Motion was denied. *Wright* verfus *Sharp, Salk*. 288.

Upon a Trial at Bar in this Cafe, a Deed of Bargain and Sale acknowledged by the Bargainee and enrolled, by which a Term for Years was affigned, was given in Evidence without any Proof made of the Bargainor's Sealing and Delivery thereof. And after Debate it was allowed *per Holt* Ch. J. and *Eyre* Juftice, & *tot. Cur.* for the Acknowledgment of

Indenture of Bargain and Sale inrolled, may be given in Evidence without proving the Execution.

4

of the Party in a Court of Record, or before a Mafter extraordinary in the Country, (as this was) is good Evidence of its being fealed and delivered: And fuch an Acknowledgment eſtops a Man from pleading *Non eſt faƈtum.* Alſo Inrolments of Deeds on the Sta ute, are admitted every Day in Evidence without Witneſſes of the Sealing and Delivery; and it is the Acknowledgment which gives it Credit, and not its Operation or Contents. Alſo they held a fworn Copy of a Deed good Evidence. *Smartle* verſus *Williams, Salk.* 280.

Depoſitions before a Juſtice, Evidence only in Felony.

In an Information for a Libel againſt the Government, Not guilty being pleaded, upon Trial the Attorney General offered in Evidence Depoſitions taken before a Juſtice of Peace, relating to the Faƈt, the Deponent being ſince dead. *Et per Cur.* upon Advice with the Juſtices of the Common Pleas; in Cafes of Felony, ſuch Depoſitions before a Juſtice, if the Deponent die, may be uſed in Evidence, by the Statute 1 & 2 *Ph. & Mar. cap.* 13. But this cannot be extended farther than the particular Cafe of Felony, and therefore not to this Cafe. *Rex* verſus *Paine, Salk.* 281. 5 *Mod.* 161.

A Hiftory may be Evidence to prove a Matter relating to the Kingdom in general, but not a particular Right.

An Iffue was direƈted out of Chancery, wherein the Queſtion was, Whether by the Cuſtom of *Droitwich,* Salt-pits could be funk in any Part of the Town, or in a certain Place only? And upon a Trial at Bar, *Camden's Britannia* was offered in Evidence, but refuſed: For the Court held, *That a general Hiſtory might be given in Evidence to prove a Matter relating to the Kingdom in general,* becauſe the Nature of the Thing requires it, *but not to prove a particular Right or Cuſtom;* fo in the Cafe of *St. Katharine's*

Katharine's Hospital. *Hale* Ch. Juſtice allowed a Chronicle to be Evidence of a particular Point of Hiſtory in *Edward* the Third's Time: So *Speed's* Chron. was admitted in Evidence to ſhew the Death of Queen *Iſabel,* Dowager of *Ed.* 2. *Vin. Evidence* 119, 120. So a *Year-Book* may be Evidence to prove the Courſe of the Court; yet in this Caſe it was admitted, That Heralds Books are good Evidence as to Pedigrees, and Pariſh-Regiſters as to Births and Marriages, upon the Nature of the Thing; and it was ſaid, That in the Exchequer the Queſtion being, Whether the Abbey *De Senti-bus* was an inferior Abbey or not? *Dugdale's Monaſticon Anglicanum* was refuſed for Evidence, becauſe the original Records might be had in the Augmentation-Office. *Stainer* verſus *The Burgeſſes* of *Droitwich, Salk.* 281.

Heralds Books, Pariſh-Regiſters, &c. allowed to be Evidence.

An Almanack, in which the Father wrote the Nativity of his Son, was admitted and allowed to be ſtrong Evidence at a Trial at Bar, to prove the Nonage of the Son. *Raym.* 84.

The Almanack is ſufficient Evidence to prove a Day *Sunday,* or what Day is the Return Day. 1 *Sid.* 300. *Cro. Eliz.* 227. 1 *Leon.* 242. 6 *Mod.* 41. See Lord *Raym.* 4, 281, 870, 1544, 1556. *Raym.* 84. 11 *Mod.* 41. *Note*; The Almanack to go by, is that annexed to the Common Prayer Book. 6 *Mod.* 81.

In Ejeĉtment for the Barony of *Cockermouth,* and all the Manors, &c. of *Joſcelin* late Earl of *Northumberland,* of the Family of *Piercy*; Sir *William Dugdale's Baronage of* England was refuſed to be read to prove a Diſcent. *T. Jones* 164.

The Impropriator and the Parifhioners having a Difpute concerning the Right of an Houfe, brought Ejectment, and moved for Leave to infpect the Parifh Books, and take Copies of what concerned his Title; but the Court denied it. 5 *Mod.* 395.

In an Action concerning *India Stock*, the Court ordered the Transfer-Books of the Company to be produced at the Trial, and that the Parties might have Copies. *Farefl.* 129.

In *Quare Impedit*, the Defendant pleads, that he was retained a Chaplain to the Countefs of *Derby*, and had a Difpenfation to hold two Livings; the King replied, that *Banks* and *Travers* were retained Chaplains to her before; and the Incumbent traverfed the Retainer of *Travers*; and to prove it, a Copy of the Retainer of *Travers* entred in the Court of Faculties was produced; but held not Evidence. *Lit. Rep.* 1.

A Verdict on a voidable Trial read in Evidence. 1 *Str.* 308.

A Special Verdict between two Parties, not received in Evidence of a Pedigree. 2 *Str.* 1151.

Affidavit of a Dead Man read to prove his Marriage, that was taken before a Surrogate, no Caufe being in Court. 1 *Str.* 35.

The Day-Book from whence the Parifh Regifter is made up, not allowed in a Queftion of Legitimacy. 2 *Str.* 1073.

Of

Of Evidence in Courts of Equity, and the Ecclefiaſtical Courts.

Office Copies of Depoſitions are Evidence in Chancery, but not at Common Law, without Examination with the Roll ; for the Court of Chancery have, for Convenience, allowed thoſe Office Copies to be Evidence in their own Court, and have impowered their Officers to make out ſuch Copies as ſhould be Evidence ; but the particular Rules of their Court are not taken Notice of by the Courts of Common Law. *Gilb. Law of Evid.* 26.

Cannot read Depoſitions of a Witneſs examined fifty Years before, without ſome Account of his Death. 2 *Str.* 920. in the Exchequer.

Depoſitions in the Ecclefiaſtical Court cannot be given in Evidence, tho' the Parties be dead, *March* 120. A Defendant's Anſwer in an *Engliſh* Court is good Evidence againſt him, but not againſt others. *Godbolt* 326.

I cannot make uſe of Depoſitions in a Cauſe wherein I was not a Party, (*a*) for as they can-

Depoſitions.

(*a*) Depoſitions cannot be given in Evidence againſt any Perſon who was not Party to the Suit ; and the Reaſon is, becauſe he hath not Liberty to croſs examine the Witneſſes ; and it is againſt natural Juſtice that a Man ſhould be concluded in a Cauſe to which he never was Party. *Hardr.* 22, 472. *Bunb.* 50. *pl.* 84. 91. *pl* 148. 321. *pl.* 403. 9 *Mod.* 229. *Carth.* 181. *Vern.* 113. *Gilb. Evid.* 62. *Prec. in Chanc.* 212. But if a Witneſs is examined in Chancery, you may read, without an Order, any other Depoſitions of the ſame Perſon in the Spiritual Court, or elſewhere, in any other Cauſe, ſo as you make uſe of them only to confront the Evidence he then gives.

not be read againſt me, no more can they be read for me, becauſe I am not bound by them, nor in a Capacity of examining Witneſſes in it, or preferring Interrogatories. And it is not like the Caſe of an Ejectment brought by a Reverſioner, or Debt upon the Statute of *Ed.* 6. brought by a Proprietor of Tithes, after a Verdict a Law; for the Leſſee or the preſent Proprietor, the Reverſioner of the Lands or Tithes, ſhall have Advantage of the *Verdict,* and give it in Evidence; and the Reaſons are, becauſe they cannot be immediate Parties to the Action or Suit, for that muſt be proſecuted by the Leſſee or preſent Tenant, and they may give it in Evidence, as well as the Plaintiff himſelf; but it is otherwiſe in Caſe of *Depoſitions,* for there only Parties to the Suit can examine or interrogate; likewiſe the Reverſioner or Seignioreſs, (whoſe Tenants were only Parties in the former Suit) might themſelves have been Parties in a Suit in Equity. The Counteſs of *Pembroke's* Caſe, *Hardr. Rep.* 472.

The Depoſitions of a Witneſs taken before Anſwer, to preſerve his Teſtimony, who dieth after Anſwer, ſhall not be given in Evidence, although he continued ſo ſick, that he could not be examined after Anſwer. *Hardr. Rep.* 315.

Depoſitions in Chancery of Witneſſes that are dead may be read at the Aſſizes betwixt the ſame Parties, proving the Bill and Anſwer.

See *Keb.* 2 Part 31. An old Exemplification of a Decree in Chancery given in Evidence, although the Bill and Anſwer were not in it; for above forty Years ſince it was not uſual to inſert Bill and Anſwer.

The

The Anfwer of one Defendant is not Evidence againft another Defendant, unlefs he refer to it..

If Witneffes are examined *de bene effe*, before Anfwer upon a Contempt, fuch Depfitions cannot be made ufe of in any other Court, but in the Court only where they were taken ; the Reafon feems to be, becaufe there was no Iffue joined, fo as there could be a legal Examination, and they were only taken to be read in the Court in which they were taken, upon a Contempt to that particular Court *Hardr. Rep.* 332.

If a Witnefs be examined *de bene effe*, and before the coming in of the Anfwer, the Defendant not being in Contempt, the Witnefs dies, yet his Depofition fhall not be read, becaufe the oppofite Party had not the Power to crofs-examine him ; and the Rule of the Common Law is ftrict to this, that no Evidence fhall be admitted, but what is or might be under the Examination of both Parties. *Gilb. L. of Evid.* 65. *Hard.* 315. 2 *Jon.* 164. 1 *Wms.* 414, 415. 2 *Wms.* 563.

An Anfwer in *Chancery* is Evidence againft the Defendant (*a*) himfelf ; but the Bill mutt be proved. *Godb.* 326.

If

(*a*) If a Bill in Chancery be Evidence againft the Complainant, how much more is the Anfwer againft the Defendant, which carries ftill a higher Weight of Probability along with it, becaufe this is delivered in upon Oath, and therefore over and above the fingle Confeffion ; it has an Authority from the Sanction of an Oath. But when you read an Anfwer, the Confeffion muft be all taken together ; and you muft not take only what makes againft him, and leave out what makes for him ; for the Anfwer is read as the Senfe of the Party himfelf, and if it is to be

taken

If the Party make Oath that he cannot find his Witnefs, then he is as it were dead, and his Depofitions in an *Englifh* Court may be given in Evidence betwixt the fame Parties. *Godb* 327. Not only the Plaintiff but any Stranger may give the Defendant's Anfwer in Evidence againft the Defendant, but not againft others. *Sid.* 222. A Bill in Chancery given in Evidence againft the Plaintiff himfelf, where there are Proceedings upon it. *Keb.* 2 Part 499. See *p.* 478.

To prove a Jointure in Ejectment, Depofitions in Chancery were produced, but the Bill and Anfwer were taken off the File and loft ; but to fhew that a Bill was once filed, the Six Clerks Book was produced, and an Inrolment of the Decree which mentioned both Bill and Anfwer ; and held fufficient. 5 *Mod.* 210. *Haines*'s Cafe.

Depofitions.
Roll. Trial,
679. pl. 7.
8. 9.

Depofitions in the Court Chriftian, or in the Court of the Council of *York*, touching the Title of Land, of which they have not Conufance, or in another fuit againft him, who claimeth not under thofe Parties, or by the Commiffioners upon a Commiffion of Bankrupt, becaufe the Party could not crofs-examine, fhall not be allowed in Evidence. But fee *Keb.* 2 Part 348.

Depofitions in a Court not of Record, as the Spiritual Court, though it be in a Cafe in

taken in this Manner, you muft take it intire and unbroken. *Gilb. Law of Evid.* 51.

An Infant's Anfwer by his Guardian fhall never be admitted in Evidence againft him on a Trial at Law, for the Law has that Tendernefs for the Affairs of Infants, that it will not fuffer them to be prejudiced by the Guardian's Oath. *Ibid.* 51.

which

which they have Jurifdiction, fhall not be given in Evidence to a Jury.. *Littleton Rep.* 167.

In an Action on the Cafe againft a Parifh Clerk, Depofitions taken in the Ecclefiaftical Court were permitted to be read, the Witneffes being dead ; but it was refufed to let the Jury have them with them. *Clayt.* 62.

But a Sentence given in the Spiritual Court touching Tithes, may be given in Evidence in an Action at Common Law; for this is a Judicial Act. Sentence. 2 Roll 679. pl. 6.

A Thing which is concluded in the Ecclefiaftical Court concerning Lands, is not to be given in Evidence to Juries, for the Courts of Common Law are not to be guided by their Proceedings. *Mich.* 22 *Car. B. R. Style* 10. Proceedings in Ecclefiaftical Court.

Regularly the Depofitions in Chancery of a Witnefs fhall not be given in Evidence if he be alive, although he be beyond Sea, as in *Ireland, &c.* Otherwife if he be in *France,* or another Kingdom not fubject to the Dominion of our King. See *p.* 476. Depofitions.

Note, That the Depofitions taken before the Commiffioners of Bankrupts fhall not be ufed as Evidence at a Trial, although the Witneffes be dead. But Depofitions taken before the Coroner, with Proof that the Party that made them is dead, fhall be good Evidence, as it was ruled in the Cafe of the King and *Browning, Pafch.* 18 *Car.* 2. *B. R.* Mich. 16 Car. 2. B. R. Roll. Trial, 679. pl. 9. Depofitions. Bankrupt. Coroner.

A Decree produced in Paper, is not to be given in Evidence without Bill and Anfwer; *per Twifden.* Otherwife if not in Paper. 1 Keb. 21.

A Decree in Chancery may be given in Evidence, and fo may a Sentence in the Ecclefiaftical Courts, for their Judgments muft be of Decree.

·K 4   Authority

Authority in thofe Cafes, where the Law gives them a Jurifdiction, for it were very abfurd that the Law fhould give them a Jurifdiction, and yet not to fuffer what is done by Force of that Jurifdiction to be a full Proof, for that were to fuppofe they were incompetent Judges, where they had Jurifdiction. *Gilb. Law of Evid.* 68. 2 *Mod.* 231. 2 *Str.* 960, 961.

The Father wrote a Leetter fignifying his Affent to the Marriage of his Daughter with *J. S.* and that he would give her 1500 *l.* but fignified in another Letter that he would not ftand to thefe Propofals: He fome Time afterwards declared, That he would agree to what was propofed in his firft Letter. It was held, that this verbal Declaration had re-eftablifhed the Promife in the firft Letter, and that it was a fufficient Promife in Writing within the Meaning of the Statute of Frauds. *Bird* verfus *Blofs* in *Chanc.* 2 *Vent.* 361.

Where a verbal Declaration fhall re-eftablifh a Promife in Writing that had been revoked.

In Ejectment at a Trial, Depofitions taken in *Chancery de bene effe,* where the Witnefs died before anfwer put in, were held to be good Evidence; and upon this Evidence a Verdict *pro Quer'.* It was held alfo, That Depofitions after Anfwer between the fame Parties might be read in Evidence, though the Witnefs were not dead, if he could not be found upon Search. *Howard* verfus *Tremaine, Mich.* 4 *W. & M. B. R. Shower* 363. *Salk.* 278. *Holt Hæfitavit.* See *p.* 475.

Depofitions taken in Chanc. de bene effe, are Evidence at Law where the Witnefs dies before Anfwer.

Depofitions after Anfwer read in Evidence where the Witnefs cannot be found.

On a Trial at Bar in *C. B.* this Point arofe, *viz.* Depofitions had been taken in *Chancery,*

Depofitions in perpetuam rei memoriam are not to be read in Evidence while Party lives.

in

in perpetuam rei memoriam. And it happened afterwards that the Inheritance of the same Land defcended to the Perfon, who was fworn as a Witnefs, and he was now a Party to the Suit in Ejectment. And the Queftion was, Whether thefe Depofitions could be read in the Caufe? *Trevor* Ch. J. held, That they ought; for that he was difabled to give Evidence by the Act of God, fo that it was in Effect the fame Thing as if he were dead. *Tracy* and *Blencow contr.* Hereupon *Tracy* came into B. R. to afk the Opinion of the Court; and the Court agreed, they ought not to be read: For per *Holt* Ch. J. The only Intent of fuch Depofitions was to perpetuate Teftimony in Cafe the Witneffes died, and they cannot be read in any Cafe between other Parties till after the Death of the Witnefs, who is to appear and give his Evidence *viva voce*, fo long as he lives; much lefs can they be read in this Cafe, where the Witnefs himfelf is Party. To which *Trevor* Ch. J. agreed. *Tilley's* Cafe, *Salk.* 286.

On an Appeal from the Commiffioners of Excife to the Commiffioners of Appeals, the Depofitions of the Witneffes taken before the Commiffioners of Excife ought not to be read, but they ought to examine the Witneffes *de novo viva voce*. And *Holt* C. J. faid he thought that if the Witneffes were dead their Depofitions might be read.

Bill and Anfwer.

Bill in Chancery allowed in *Dom' Proc'* as Evidence to confront a Woman who pretended Marriage. *Vin. Abr.* Title *Evid.* 88.*pl* 3. ci.es *Parl. Coll. N.* 88.

The Infant's Guardian's Anfwer in Chancery of a Feoffee in Truft, was refufed by the Court to be given as Evidence; becaufe he was living, and not Party to the Suit, which was only between the Heir and *Ceftui que Truft. Vin. Abr.* Tit. *Evid.* 88. *pl.* 1.

An Anfwer in an *Englifh* Court is good Evidence to a Jury againft the Defendant himfelf, but not againft other Parties; yet it is not binding to the Jury. *Godb.* 326. *pl.* 418. *E.* 21 *Jac. B. R. Anon'.* Not good Evidence againft his Alienee. 1 *Salk.* 286. 1 *Mod.* 301. 6 *Mod.* 44. *Mich.* 2 *Ann. B. R.* in Cafe of *Ford* v. Lord *Grey.*

If the Plaintiff will read the Defendant's Anfwer in Chancery againft him in Evidence, the Defendant may likewife take Advantage thereof; for all is Evidence, or none. *Per Holt* Ch. J. *Hil.* 8 *W.* 3. *B. R. Lynch* v. *Clerk,* 3 *Salk.* 154.

An Anfwer in Chancery cannot be given in Evidence for the Party who made it, or againft a third Perfon not deriving any Title under him. *T.* 9 *Geo.* 1. *Hilliard* v. *Phaley & al'.* 8 *Mod.* 181. *Vin. Abr.* 88. *pl.* 6.

Allegations by a Complainant in a Bill in Chancery fhall by a Copy be made ufe of as Evidence againft the Complainant, in a Suit at Law, for it fhall be intended to be exhibited by his Confent and Privity. But *per*
4   *Bridgman*

Bridgman, there is a Difference where there is
a Proceeding upon ſuch Bill, and where not;
for in the firſt Caſe, it ſhall be admitted in
Evidence, but in the ſecond not. If Bill be
preferred *ſans Privity* of the *Plaintiff*, an Action
lies. *Vin. Abr.* Tit. *Evid.* 88. *pl.* 2. See *p.* 474.

Of Evidence in Account.

Account pleaded before two; Account before one is good Evidence, *Hob.* 55. becauſe
the Account is the Subſtance.

In Debt for Arrearages of an Account, upon
Nil debet modo & forma, no Account is good
Evidence. 20 *H.* 6. 26. *Roll. Trial,* 677. *pl.*
26.

Upon *Ne unques ſon Receiver, &c.* the Defendant cannot ſay that he paid the Money according to Directions, *&c. Dyer* 196.

Againſt *S.* as Receiver of two 30 *l.* and as
Bailiff for receiving his Rents for ſeveral Years,
not ſaying any certain Sum of Rents: *Per Earl*
Serjeant, The proper Way is to find *quod Com-
putet,* as to what is certain in the Declaration,
and ſo proved, as the Money was, but not to
the Rents; and ſo he ſaid was the Opinion of
Hale. But *per Moreton* Juſtice, the Verdict
ſhall be general, and it may be both Ways.
Saye's Caſe, *Norf. Lent Aſſizes* 1667.

Debt for 10 *l. pro eo quod cum* the Defendant had accounted with the Plaintiff for di-
verſe Sums as due, and was found in Arrear
8 *l.* and a *Mutuatus* for 2 *l.* and on the Trial
it was proved, That Defendant and Plaintiff's
Wife reckoned that Defendant had borrowed
at one Time 40 *s.* at another Time 40 *s.* and
at another Time 4 *l.* and that he promiſed to

pay

pay the 8 *l.* and held by *Holt* Ch. J. That
this is good Evidence of an Account. 1 *Show.*
215.

Upon *Ne unques son Receiver,* the Defendant cannot give in Evidence a Releafe from
the Plaintiff. 1 *Brownlow* 24. *Willowly* verfus *Small.*

Harrington brought Account againft *Deane*
for 200 *l.* received by the Hands of Sir *J. Rotherham;* the Defendant pleads that he was
never his Receiver, and the Jury found, that
Sir *John Rotherham* was indebted to the Plaintiff 200 *l.* that the Plaintiff willed *Deane* to require and receive the Money of Sir *John Rotherham;* that thereupon *Rotherham* prayed
Deane to borrow the Money of any body, and
pay it the Plaintiff: That he accordingly borrowed 200 *l.* for *Rotherham* of *J. S.* and received it ; and that *Rotherham* gave *J. S.* a Bond
for the Money. Held the Action well maintained. *Hob.* 36.

Of Evidence in Actions on the Cafe.

In an Action on the *Cafe* for 20 Guineas,
the *Value* need not be fet forth in the Declaration, but it may be given in Evidence to the
Jury ; but in *Debt* for them it is otherwife,
and the Value muft appear, but in *Cafe* the
Action is brought for Damages. *Vin. Value*
938.

*Quare defendens Crimen feloniæ ei impofuit,
&c.* The Plaintiff cannot give in Evidence
Words only, but Acts ; as arrefting, charging
or conventing him before a Juftice of Peace for
Felony. *Saunders* verfus *Edwards, Mich.* 14
Car. 2. *B. R.* 1 *Keb.* 389.

Cafe

Case for maliciously prosecuting an Indictment of Perjury; and it appeared the Defendant was a Justice of Peace, and procured some as Witnesses to appear against the Plaintiff, and his own Name was indorsed on the Indictment; held this was not sufficient to prove him a Prosecutor. And on the other Side it was proved, that the Indictment was drawn by Order of the Sessions; and Plaintiff nonsuited, with a Reprimand. 1 *Vent.* 47. 2 *Keb.* 572.

Case by Baron and Feme for maliciously prosecuting the Defendant for Felony in stealing Goods, of which she was acquitted. And *Holt* Ch. J. allowed the Oath, which the Prosecutor (now Defendant) had made at the Trial of the Indictment, of the Felony being committed, to be given in Evidence for the Defendant, to prove a Felony committed; else, he said, one that was robbed alone, if he prosecuted the Felon, and he was acquitted, would be liable to an Action, without a Possibility of making a Defence. 6 *Mod.* 216.

Case for a malicious Prosecution of Plaintiff for Barretry; and set forth, that he was *inde legitimo modo acquietatus,* and to prove it at the Trial produced a *Nolle prosequi* by the Attorney General; and held the Action would not lie, for the *Nolle prosequi* is only a Discharge of the Indictment, but no Acquittal of the Crime. 1 *Salk.* 21. 6 *Mod.* 261.

If any Action arises on Request, as in Trover or special Promise, the Statute of Limitation goes only to the Request. *Juy*'s Case, *Mich.* 1562. C. B. 1 *Cro.* 139.

Declaration for Words spoken in the Presence of *A. B.* and others; in Evidence it sufficeth, that they were spoken in the Presence of

others

others only. *Winckfield* and *Coot, Lent Assizes Norfolk,* 1662, *per Hale* Ch. Baron.

In *Indebitatus* for carrying of Herrings; the Evidence was, he was a Porter at *Yarmouth,* and when Herring-Ships came Home, he went (of his own Head) and carried up to the Defendant's House, with other Porters, so many Herrings; and good by *Twisden,* Judge of Assise, *Norf. Summer* 1662. *Jermin* versus *Lucas.*

Pew.
Keb. 2 Part 342.
1 Sid 88.
1 Lev. 71.
1 Keb. 345.

In an Action for hindring to sit in a Pew, claimed by Prescription, *repaired, &c.* ought to be given in Evidence; and one may prescribe to sit in the uppermost Seat in a Pew. *Buckston* and *Bateman, Mich.* 14 *Car.* 2. *B. R.*

Case by Sir *H. Snelgrave* and *A. B.* against *Brograve,* for disturbing them of a Seat in the Church; and declare, That they, and those whose Estate they have, from Time immemorial used to have a Seat in the Church; the Defendant traverses, that the Plaintiffs, and those whose Estate they had, *&c.* had the Seat *modo & formâ:* And on Evidence it appeared the Plaintiffs were Tenants in Common; and held this did not prove the Issue, for they cannot join in a joint Prescription. *Palmer* 161.

Where-ever a Person intitles himself to a Seat in a Church by Prescription, though he do not alledge that he used to repair it, yet he shall be obliged at the Trial to prove, that he, or those whose Estate he had, used to repair; or else he will fail in his Prescription. 1 *Siderf.* 203.

In Action for executing an illegal Warrant, *&c.* It is good Evidence to prove the Justice of Peace acted as such, without shewing his Commission; so on the Statute of *Hue* and *Cry.* *Constable's*

Conſtable's Caſe, *Norf. Lent Aſſizes, per Hale* Chief Baron.

Action for ſtopping up Lights, *&c.* One had a Piece of Ground, and builds an Houſe on Part and leaſes it, then he ſells the other Part of the Ground to one who builds on it, and ſtops up the Lights of the firſt Houſe, the Leſſee has a good Action. But if two own two Pieces of Ground, and one builds, the other may alſo build and ſtop up his Lights. *Palmer* verſus *Fleſher, Mich.* 15 *Car.* 2. *B. R.* 1 *Keb.* 553.

If a Maſter always gives his Servant Mo- Maſter. ney to buy his Markets with, it is good Evidence to diſcharge the Maſter in an Action brought againſt him for Goods taken up on Truſt by that Servant. *Per Glyn* Chief Juſtice, *Mich.* 1658. at *Guildhall,* Sir *Thomas Rouſe*'s Caſe.

The Maſter declared, That the Defendant Maſter. dug a Pit, and as he was driving his Horſe, he fell in the Pit, *&c.* To prove the Servant drove the Horſe doth not maintain the Declaration. *Style* 335.

A Watercourſe runs through my Grounds to the Grounds of *J. S.* where is a Pit that Time out of Mind uſed to be filled with that Water; I may ſtop the Water in my Ground, and uſe it as I will, ſo I do no turn the Courſe another Way; but when I have done with it, I muſt let it fall into its own Courſe. *Per St. John* Chief Juſtice *C. B. Suff. Summer Aſſizes* 1657. *Smart* and *Tyſtead.*

Action for Words, *You forſwore yourſelf in your Anſwer in Chancery.* Defendant juſtifies. Plaintiff replies *de injuria ſua propria abſque tali Cauſa. Per Hale, Summer Aſſizes, Suffolk,*

It is a good Replication, and a small Mistake in an Answer shall not convict of Perjury, for the Counsel may mistake, or his Clerk.

Action for not scouring a Ditch, by which the Water overflowed his Land, &c. and declare *quod quidam Rivus* ran there, &c. Upon Evidence it appeared only a Land Flood, and good by Name of *Rivus*, though it be dry great Part of the Year; and it.was held the best Pleading of the Course of this River to put a Place from whence it comes, and so to the Plaintiff's Land, without mentioning mean Places by which it passes, which may be many, and must be proved if laid. *Per Whitfield* 1641. *York, Clayton* 96.

Case for maliciously turning away Part of a Course of Water, that ran from a Fountain in *Clerkenwell* to the Plaintiff's House in *White Fryers*; and on Evidence it appears that the Ancestors of the Defendant had caused a Leaden Pipe to be laid to the main Pipe, through which the Water ran, and that Defendant had used the Water, by opening the Cock when he pleased; and held the Defendant liable, and Judgment for the Plaintiff. *Dyer* 320. *Bendlows* 215.

Soldiers lying in an Inn fourteen Days, are Guests within the Custom of *England. Harland's* Case, *per Whitfield* 1647.

The Plaintiff in an Action of the Case intitles himself, by Prescription, to a Foldcourse for Sheep upon all the Lands in such a Field on *Michaelmas-day*, and so to *Lady-day*, the Lands being unsown, and for that the Defendant put on Sheep, &c. before *Michaelmas-day* and after, and thereby fed the Grounds, &c.

&c. the Plaintiff could not take fo good Feed, *actio inde.*

1. The Owner may put on Sheep, and feed his own Grounds before *Michaelmas*, unlefs a Cuftom be to the contrary, which ought to be laid in the Declaration. *Contra* of a Stranger.

2. It appearing that Part of the Lands, *&c.* had been the Lands of the Plaintiff, who was Lord of the Manor, and prefcribed as fuch, and there being no Exception of thofe Lands in the Prefcription, the Plaintiff was nonfuit; for as to thofe Lands the Prefcription is gone by Unity of Poffeffion. *Per Hale* Chief Baron, *Norfolk, Summer Affizes,* 1661. *Branthwait* verfus *Hunt.*

In Action upon the Cafe for retaining of his Servant, *per quod fervitium amifit,* the Plaintiff ought to prove that the Defendant had Conufance, that he was his Servant.

Eod. Termin. Servant.

In Cafe againft a Sheriff upon an Efcape fuffered by a Bailiff, the Plaintiff ought to prove that fuch Procefs and Warrant iffued, that fuch a Debt was due to him, and that the Party arrefted was now become infolvent; or elfe he is not intitled to recover Damages to the Value of the Debt. *Clayton* 84.

Cafe for falfely and fraudulently felling an Horfe to the Plaintiff, as Defendant's own Horfe, *ubi revera* it was the Horfe of *J. S.* the Plaintiff was nonfuited, becaufe he could not prove that Defendant knew it was not his own Horfe. *Aleyn* 91.

In an Action on the Cafe, when the Requeft is laid at one Time in the Declaration, a Requeft at another Time may be given in Evidence. *Sid. Rep.* 268.

Requeft another Day.

In an Action on the Case for the Profits of Master of the King's Wardrobe, it was infifted for the Defendant, That the Plaintiff's Patent having recited a former Grant, he muft prove that Grant to have been furrendered: To which it was anfwered, That if they took Advantage of the Recital, they muft admit all that was recited, as well the Surrender as the Grant. And of that Opinion was the Court.

And it was faid, That in an Action of this Nature, it is not neceffary to fhew every particular Sum received by the Defendant; but it is a good Evidence for the Damage to fhew the Profit of the Office *Communibus annis.* Earl of *Montague* verfus Lord *Prefton,* 2 *Vent.* 170.

In an Action on the Cafe for Money had and received to the Plaintiff's Ufe, it appeared upon Evidence, That *Layfield* and the other Defendants were Bankers and Partners, and that the Plaintiff had given *Layfield* 20 s. for which he received a Ticket in the double Exchange-Lottery, and *Layfield* undertook to pay what Benefit fhould happen thereupon. That the Ticket came up a 40 *l.* Benefit, and for that Money the Action was brought. And it was objected for the Defendant, That the Action was brought againft *Layfield* and his Partners; and it did not appear that any had undertaken to be Truftees in the Lottery but *Layfield,* and therefore he only oughr to be charged, and not his Partners. To which *Holt* Ch. J. anfwered, That it appeared they were Partners in their Trade, and Goldfmiths, and the Adventures put their Money in upon the Credit of the feveral Goldfmiths that had undertaken to pay the Benefits; and it fhould be

presumed

presumed the Act of *Layfield* was the Act of the other, and should bind him, unless he could shew a Disclaimer and a Refusal to be concerned in it; and accordingly the Plaintiff had a Verdict for forty Pounds.———Versus *Layfield & al'*, Salkeld 291.

Case for a Deceit, for that the Plaintiff bought of Defendant several Parcels of Silk for—— Silk, whereas it was another Sort, and that the Defendant well knowing this sold it him for —————— Silk; and on Evidence it appeared, that there was no actual Deceit in the Defendant, who was a Merchant, but that the Deceit was in his Factor abroad; and held by *Holt* Ch. J. that the Merchant was answerable for this Deceit of his Factor *Civiliter*, tho' not *Criminaliter*; and that it was more reasonable, that the Defendant, who trusted the Deceiver, should be a Loser than a Stranger. 1 *Salk.* 289. *Hern* v. *Nichols.*

An Action on the Case upon the Custom of the Realm was brought against the Defendant, being Master of a Stage-Coach, and the Plaintiff set forth that he took Place in the Coach for such a Town, and that in the Journey the Defendant by this Negligence lost a Trunk of the Plaintiff's: Upon Not guilty pleaded, upon the Evidence it appeared, That this Trunk was delivered to the Person that drove the Coach, and he promised to take Care of it, and that the Trunk was lost out of the Coachman's Possession; and if the Master was chargeable with this Action, was the Question. *Holt*, Ch. J. was of Opinion, That this Action did not lie against the Master, and that a Stage-Coachman was not within the Custom as a Carrier is, unless such as take a

Master of a Stage-Coach not chargeable for goods lost by the Driver, unless the Master takes a Price for the Carriage of Goods.

L 2   distinct

diftinct Price for carrying Goods as well as Perfons, as Waggons with Coaches ; and tho' Money be given to the Driver, yet that is a Gratuity, and cannot bring the Mafter within the Cuftom: For the Mafter is not chargeable with the Acts of his Servant, but when he acts in Execution of the Authority given by his Mafter; and then the Act of the Servant is the Act of the Mafter ; and the Plaintiff was nonfuited. *Middleton* verfus *Fowler, Salkeld* 282.

Cafe againft an Innkeeper, for that Plaintiff brought Goods into Defendant's Inn, was lodged there, and robbed by the Default of Defendant and his Servants ; Defendant pleads that Plaintiff was not robbed by the Default of him or his Servants ; and in Evidence it appeared, that Plaintiff came to lodge with Defendant, that Defendant told him that his Inn was full, and that he could not lodge him ; that notwithftanding, the Plaintiff would ftay, and lodged with another Man, without the Confent of Defendant or his Servants ; held that Defendant was not liable. *Dyer* 158. *b.* 1 *Anderfon* 29. See *p.* 489.

Cafe againft a Carrier on the Cuftom of the Realm, for not delivering a Box with Goods and 100 *l.* in Money in it ; and on Evidence it appeared the Plaintiff delivered the Box to the Defendant's Porter, and told him, there was a Book and Tobacco in the Box, but faid nothing of the Money ; and held by *Rolle*, That the Carrier was anfwerable for the Money, though he was not informed of it ; but told the Jury, in Regard of the intended Cheat to the Carrier, they might confider him in Damages. *Aleyn* 93.

In

In an Action on the Custom for safe Carriage, Evidence of the Delivery and Charge to carry them safe, good, without saying whither, because it shall be intended to the Place where he usually came. *Gilb. L. of Evid.* 242.

In an Action for safe Carriage, if no Price be set, it shall be intended for the Common Price; but if a special Agreement be set out to carry for 4 s. a hundred, it must be proved that the common rate is to carry for 4 s. an hundred. *Ibid.*

In an Action on the Case brought against an Innkeeper for suffering the Goods of the Plaintiff his Guest to be taken out of his House, and upon Not guilty pleaded, the Defendant may give in Evidence that he told the Plaintiff that his House was full, and that he could not lodge him, and that notwithstanding the Plaintiff went in and lodged in his House; for this Evidence falsifies the Declaration, for it proves that there was no Injury done to the Plaintiff as Guest to the Defendant. *Gilb. Law of Evid.* 259. See *p.* 488.

In Action against Acceptor of a Bill need not prove the Hand of the Drawer. *Str.* 648.

In Action against Indorsor must prove Demand on Drawer. *Str.* 649.

Of Evidence in Assumpsit.

In an *Assumpsit in Deed*, the very Contract must be set forth in the Declaration; but in *Assumpsit in Law*, if the Plaintiff shews Part of the Goods delivered, or Part of the Money lent, it is good. *Gilb. Law of Evid.* 193, 172.

In

Aſſumpſit.

In an *Aſſumpſit in Law*, actual Payment, or any other Matter that excuſes Payment, may be given in Evidence on *Non aſſumpſit* ; but in an *Aſſumpſit in Deed* it muſt be pleaded. *Gilb. L. of Evid.* 204, 205.

Upon an *Aſſumpſit* to the Huſband, an *Aſſumpſit* to the Wife and his Agreement is good Evidence. 27 *H.* 8. 29. Upon *Non Aſſumpſit* to a ſpecial Promiſe, Payment is no Evidence ; by three Judges.

Indebitatus Aſſumpſit.

Upon *Non Aſſumpſit* in a general *Indebitatus Aſſumpſit*, the Defendant may give in Evidence Payment at any Time before the Action brought; but upon a ſpecial Promiſe to pay Money, &c. it is otherwiſe ; *Cauſa patet* ; for in the firſt Caſe, if there be no Debt, the Law will infer no Promiſe. 1 *Mod.* 210.

In *Indebitatus,* Covenant to pay is no Evidence. 2 *Cro.* 505. Nor Money due for Rent by Specialty, or on Record. *Hob.* 284. *Hutt.* 35.

Indebitat. for Money lent, Money received to Plaintiff's Uſe, & *inſimul computaſſet.* Plaintiff gives in Evidence only a Letter, whereby the Defendant promiſed ſhortly to pay him 30 *l.* he owed him. Held *per Holt* Ch. J. that this would not do, for it might be due on Bond or otherwiſe ; it is true, a Note to pay a Sum of Money on Demand, is *prima facie* Evidence of Money lent, unleſs the contrary appear; but it is not ſo here, and the Plaintiff was nonſuit. *Comberb.* 349.

But an Account ſtated for Rent and other Things is good Evidence.

Baron and Feme.

Indebitatus Aſſumpſit againſt Baron for Neceſſaries for his Wife, they muſt be according to his Eſtate, as well as Degree. *Siderfin* 128.

If

If fhe doth not cohabit with him, the Action doth not lie. If the Goods bought by the Wife or Servant come to the Ufe of the Hufband, although this be no binding Evidence, yet this prefumptive Evidence fhall charge him.

He may forbid one or two, *&c.* to let her have Goods, but a general forbidding alfo is void. *Keb.* 2 Part 554.

If Hufband and Wife cohabit, and the Wife deals feparately, her Contracts fhall bind the Hufband ; for Cohabitation is fufficient Evidence of Notice. 1 *Salk.* 113. 6 *Mod.* 162.

Per Hale Ch. J. *deins* Age may be given in Infancy. Evidence on *Non Affumpfit,* in an *Indebitatus* 2 Lev. 144. *Affumpfit. Keb. Rep.* 2 Part 851. *Painter* and *Bowman*'s Cafe.

Infancy cannot be given in Evidence, but muft be pleaded. *Gilb. L. of Evid.* 165. *Qu.* For the contrary is in Ufe, and it goes to the Gift of the Action. See *p.* 498.

A Feme Covert may plead *Non Affumpfit,* and give Coverture in Evidence ; becaufe Coverture makes it no Promife. 6 *Mod.* 230. *Gilb. L. of Evid.* 165.

Indebitatus will not lie for Money won 1 Keb. 216. at Dice. *Wiche*'s Cafe, *Hill.* 14, 15 *Car.* 2. *B. R.*

An *Affumpfit* to pay 50 *l.* in Confideration Plaintiff would permit the Defendant to enjoy Lands from 10 *Aug.* till 1 *May* following, will lie on an exprefs Promife, but not on the Promife in Law. 3 *Lev.* 150. *Johnfon* verfus *May.*

If a Promife be made to pay at a Day certain, and the Day is paft, the Plaintiff may declare to pay on Requeft : So if he declare on

Payment at a Day certain, and give in Evidence a Promiſe on Requeſt, *i. e.* when it is created on Account which gives the Duty, for there the Time is *ex abundanti*; but where the Action is founded on the Contract, otherwiſe; for there the Evidence muſt purſue the Contract. *Hill.* 1650. *B. R. Child*'s Caſe.

Aſſumpſit, in Conſideration Plaintiff would deliver to *J. S.* 10 Quarters of Malt, to pay him on Requeſt, if *J. S.* did not; and avers that he delivered the Malt to *J. S.* who had not paid, that he requeſted Defendant to pay, and that he had not paid; on *Non Aſſumpſit*, held by *Twiſden* and *Windham*, that Plaintiff need not prove a Requeſt; for it was traverſable, and by not being traverſed was admitted. 1 *Lev.* 166.

Promiſe to reſtore a Horſe hired for a Journey, if the Horſe dies in the Journey without the Rider's Default, his Promiſe binds not. *Liſle*'s Caſe, cited in *Matraver*'s Caſe, *Trin.* 1651. *B. R.*

One brings an *Aſſumpſit* for 20 *l.* and gives in Evidence a Promiſe, if two would ſurrender, to pay them 20 *l.* a-piece, good. *Mich.* 1655. *B. R. Thomas* and *Gery*, *Style* 461.

Indebit. for 50 *l.* brought by *Edgar* againſt *Chetham* Clerk. The Evidence was *T.* was indebted to *Edgar* in 50 *l. Chetham* deſires *Edgar* to let him take the 50 *l.* of *T.* and he would give *Edgar* a Bill of Exchange to receive ſo much at *London:* Accordingly *T.* promiſes to pay *Chetham* the Money, which Promiſe he accepted, and gave a Bill of Exchange to *Edgar*; after *T.* became inſolvent; then *Chetham* prohibits the Payment of his Bill, whereupon this Action is brought. *Per Wadh.*

Wyndham Juſtice, *Aſſize Norf. Summer*, 1663. the Action lies ; for *Chetham* having accepted the Promiſe of *T*. and given a Bill, *&c.* is now become a Debtor to *Edgar*, until his Bill be paid, though he never receives the Money of *Thompſon*. This Caſe, though for another Point, is in 1 *Keb.* 592.

In *Indebit.* it is good Evidence againſt the Father, that Phyſick was delivered to his Daughter at his Requeſt. *Stonehouſe* verſus *Bodvil*, *Hill.* 14 *Car.* 2. *B. R.* 1 *Keb.* 439.

One promiſes a Bailiff, that if he would let one arreſted be in his Houſe that Night, he would deliver him in the Morning ; it's a good Promiſe, and the Bailiff or the Plaintiff may bring the Action. *Benſon* verſ. *French*, *Paſch.* 15 *Car.* 2. *B. R.* 1 *Keb.* 483. 1 *Siderf.* 132. 1 *Lev.* 98.

Indebitat. The Caſe was, the Plaintiff ſold ſixty Comb of Rye to the Defendant at fourteen Shillings *per* Comb, to be delivered before *Michaelmas* ; the Plaintiff delivered fifty Comb before the Time, and brought this Action for the Money for it, and good, though it was agreed the Money to be paid on the Delivery of the laſt Rye. *Per Hale* Chief Baron.

1. Though the Agreement is intire, yet the ſeveral Deliveries make ſeveral Contracts.

2. Though the Payment was to be on the laſt Delivery, yet a Time being ſet for Delivery, it's intended to be paid when the Delivery ſhould have been.

3. The Time being paſt, it's now a Duty, and ſo *Indebitatus* lies.

4. The Defendant hath his Remedy for delivering the Reſidue. *Barker* verſus *Sutton*, *Lent Aſſize Norf.* 1662.

The

An Account. The Court would not admit Evidence of an Account current to maintain *Indebitatus*, becauſe it would involve the Court in a tedious Examination ; but if the Account had been ſtated, then *Indebit.* upon the Account is uſual. *Keb.* 2 Part 781.   1 *Mod.* 268.

Indebitatus Aſſumpſit pro opere, or *pro diverſis mercimoniis*, or *pro ſervitio*, or *labore*, is good, and the Particulars may be given in Evidence : Otherwiſe of an *Indebitatus* generally, or *pro multis beneficiis*, &c. *Keb.* 3 Part 781. *Keb.* 2 Part 552.

Indebitatus lies for a Portion after the Jointure ſettled ; ſo for a thouſand Pounds on Promiſe for ſo much for every Horſhoe-Nail ; but the Jury may mitigate Damages. *Ibid.*

A Promiſe to marry *B.* within three Months, within a Fortnight after they meet, and the Party promiſes again to marry her within three Weeks, this laſt Promiſe is no Diſcharge of the former, being all within the Time of three Months ; but had the laſt Promiſe been to marry her within ſome other Time after the three Months, it had diſcharged the former. *Hite* verſus *Chaplin, Paſch.* 1658. *B. R.*

In an *Aſſumpſit*, the Plaintiff cannot give in Evidence a Specialty to prove his Cauſe of Action. *Moor* 240. *Cro Jac.* 505.

Aſſumpſit on a Contract to pay Money on the Marriage of his Daughter, the Defendant gave in Evidence a Diſcharge of the Contract. *Hale* held the Defendant ought to have pleaded it, and that it only went in Mitigation of Damages.   2 *Lev.* 81.

If a Man be ſaid to aſſume the 4th of *May*, and he be then proved to be dead, and the Party be proved to aſſume another Day, it

3   ſufficeth.

ſufficeth. But if a Man bring *Treſpaſs* againſt another, and lay it to be done the fourth of May, and the Party is proved to be Dead, this diſcharges the Action; for a perſonal Action, that complains of a Wrong done, dies with the Perſon. *Gilb. L. of Evid.* 241, 2.

Caſe by a Man, and declares, That in Conſideration he would marry the Defendant, ſhe would marry him; held a good Conſideration; and that on *Non Aſſumpſit* ſhe might give in Evidence any lawful Impediment; as Conſanguinity within the Levitical Degrees, but not a Præcontract. 5 *Mod.* 411.

If a Citizen of *London* promiſes his Daughter's Huſband to give him a Child's Portion, by the Cuſtom of *London* that is certain enough. 2 *Roll. Rep.* 104.

Indebitatus by one, Defendant gives Evidence that another was Partner with the Plaintiff at the Delivery of the Wares; Plaintiff nonſuit. *Franklin* verſus *Walker, Norf. Lent Aſſize* 1667. *Per Morton contr.* in *Treſpaſs*, for there Jointenancy muſt be pleaded.

In *Aſſumpſit* in Fact, and *Non Aſſumpſit* pleaded, a Releaſe cannot be given in Evidence, unleſs only to mitigate Damages; but it may upon an *Aſſumpſit* in Law, to maintain *Non Aſſumpſit. Siderf.* 236.

Indebitatus for 9 *l.* Defendant pleaded *Non Aſſumpſit infra ſex annos*, Iſſue *inde*, the Plaintiff proved a Debt of 9 *l.* due ten Years before, and an Acknowledgment of the Debt within ſix Years, and an Offer to pay 5 *l.* for the whole.

Per Hale: The Plaintiff nonſuit; for the Acknowledgment of the Debt is no more than is done by the Plea, but there muſt be a new

Promiſe

Promife of the Debt within fix Years, to
make the Action hold, and here the Promife
or Offer to pay 5 *l.* gives no Action for the
9 *l. Bafs* verfus *Smith, Suffolk, Summer Affize,*
1668.

Non Affumpfit. In a fpecial Promife to pay 20 *l.* if the Plaintiff would pay 10 *l.* &c. Upon an Averment
that he paid the 10 *l.* upon *Non Affumpf:*, the
Defendant fhall not give in Evidence that the
Plaintiff did not pay the 10 *l.* neither is the
Plaintiff bound to prove it, for the Iffue is
upon the *Affumpfit*, and not upon the Payment of the 10 *l.* which might have been traverfed.   And although it was faid, That in all
Actions there is a General Iffue to be taken,
which fhall put all the Declaration in Iffue,
and that muft in this be *Non Affumpfit*, or
nothing ; yet by the Advice of all the Juftices
of *Serjeants Inn* in *Fleetftreet*, it was ruled as
abovefaid. *Mich.* 16 *Car. B. R.* between *Hol-*
2 Roll. 681. *dich* and *Brodrig.*   I have been the more par-
pl. 6.   ticular in this, becaufe I have known Plaintiffs
nonfuited in fuch Cafes at the Affize for want
of proving the Averment: Although I muft
confefs I never agreed with the Judge herein
that did it.   For it is a Miftake to fay, the
Plaintiff muft in all Cafes prove his whole Declaration ; if he proves the Matter in Iffue,
he ought not to be nonfuited. *Roll.* Tit. *Trial,*
681.

Delivery of the Goods is Evidence of the
Sale in the *Quantum Meruit*, becaufe they fhall
be fuppofed to be delivered on the Bargain,
and with Expectation of the Price of them.
Gilb. L. of Evid. 187.

Indebitat

Indebita!' Affumpfit for 750 *l.* laid out ; on
Non Affumpfit it appeared, that Defendant and
another now dead farmed the Excife ; that the
Money was laid out by Plaintiff on the Behalf
of the Defendant and his Partner, and that Defendant promifed to repay it out of the firft
Profits he received ; and held the Action not
maintained ; the Money being laid out for the
Partners, and the Promife of Payment not abfolute.   2 *Mod.* 279.

Affumpfit in Confideration Plaintiff would forbear his Suit againft *J. S.* for 80 *l.* which *J. S.*
owed him, Defendant promifed to fee him paid ;
and the Evidence was, that *J. S.* owed Plaintiff only 40 *l.*   Held the Plaintiff failed. *Clayton* 111.

Affumpfit, and declared, That *quidam exitus*
in Ejectment of the Demife of the Plaintiff
junctus fuit between the Leffee of the Plaintiff
and *J. S.* Defendant ; the now Defendant, in
Confideration the Plaintiff would not enforce his
Title, but give weak Evidence promifed to
pay the Plaintiff 270 *l.* and avers Performance,
and a fpecial Verdict, that the Agreement was
made as fet out, but that in the Ejectment two
Iffues were joined ; and held a good Verdict for
Plaintiff. *Cro. Eliz.* 337.

The Plaintiff took a Diftrefs for Rent ; the
Defendant promifed, if he would redeliver the
Diftrefs to him, to pay the Sum demanded for
Rent ; and an Action being brought on that
Promife, held that the Plaintiff muft prove the
Rent due. *Clayton* 139. *Gower* v. *Wilkinfon.*

Matters that lie in Account are not to be
given in Evidence on an *Indebitatus-Affumpfit* ;
per *North* Chief Juftice. *Modern Rep.* 270.

Indebt. Affumpf.
Account.

In

Payment.
1 Mod. 210.

In an Action of *Aſſumpſit*, grounded upon a Promiſe in Law, Payment may be given in Evidence, but not where the Action is grounded upon an expreſs Promiſe.

Promiſe.

Upon an *Aſſumpſit*, the Plaintiff declares upon two Conſiderations, and a ſimple Promiſe: If the Jury find but one, or a conditional Promiſe, this doth not maintain the Iſſue for the Plaintiff. *Leon.* 173. *Muſted* and *Hopper's* Caſe.

In *Indebitatus Aſſumpſit*, Infancy may be given in Evidence on *Non Aſſumpſit*.

In *Aſſumpſit* for Money, and likewiſe for Money laid out to the Uſe of the Defendant's Wife *dum ſola*; on *Non Aſſumpſit* pleaded, at the Trial the Defendant offered to give in Evidence the Infancy of the Feme at the Time of the Promiſe, which the Chief Juſtice doubting of, it was referred, by Conſent, to him as a Caſe, who conſulted with the reſt of the Judges; and they all agreed, That upon the General Iſſue, ſuch Evidence hath been of late admitted. *Darby* verſus *Boucher*, *Salkeld* 279.

Parol Promiſe to be performed on a Contingency, is not within the Statute of Frauds, which makes a Promiſe void, that is not to be performed within a Year.

A parol Promiſe was made to pay a Sum of Money upon the Return of ſuch a Ship, which Ship happened not to return within two Years Time after the Promiſe made: It was reſolved by all the Judges, That this was a good Promiſe, and not within that Clauſe of the Statute of Frauds, which ſays, *That no Action ſhall be brought upon an Agreement, that is not to be performed within one Year, unleſs it be in Writing*, for that there was a Poſſibility of the Ship's returning within the Year: And that Clauſe extends only to ſuch Promiſes, where by expreſs Agreement the Thing is not to be performed within a Year. *Anonymus*, *Salkeld* 280.

If

If a Man contracts for Goods, and after carrying them away gives the Seller a Goldſmith's Note for the Money, it does not amount to a Payment; but if it were given at the very Time of the Contract, it would be *prima facie* Evidence, that it was taken in Payment. And if a Man, upon a Contract made before, takes ſuch a Bill, and keeps it till the Party on whom it was drawn becomes Inſolvent, in an Action brought by him againſt the Buyer on that Bill he ſhall be barred; but he ſhall recover the Debt upon the original Contract. *Reports in* Holt's *Time* 298. *Caſes W.* 3. 408.

Upon an *Aſſumpſit*, Covenant under Hand and Seal to pay the Money, is no Evidence, nor is any Specialty or Matter of Record, or any Contract for Rent. *Gilb. Law of Evid.* 182. cites *Cro. Jac.* 506, 598. *Hob.* 284. *Cro. Car.* 343.

In a Declaration on a collateral Promiſe, it is not neceſſary to lay, that it was in Writing, but it is ſufficient within the Statute of Frauds and Perjuries to prove it was in Writing at the Trial. *T. Jones* 158.

In *Aſſumpſit* upon a Note for 10 *l.* 15 *s.* given by the Defendant to the Plaintiff, and *Non Aſſumpſit* pleaded; upon Trial the Plaintiff produced and proved the Note. The Defendant in Diſcharge of himſelf produced the Record of a Foreign Attachment, wherein the ſaid Debt was diſcharged by the City Proceſs, for the Satisfaction of a Debt demanded there of the Plaintiff, and was there condemned: And it was ruled by *Trevor* .C. J. That this was a good Diſcharge, but that if the Plaintiff in this Action could have ſhewed the Original wherein

Record of a foreign Attachment produced to diſcharge the Defendant in Aſſumpſit *upon a Note.*

wherein he declared to be precedent to that
Attachment, ſo that it had appeared, that this
Court was poſſeſſed of an Action for the Demand of this Debt before it was attached, then
ſhould the Plaintiff have recovered his Debt
notwithſtanding ſuch Evidence; but the Declaration in the Record here was betwixt the
Time of the Attachment and of the Condemnation. *Savage's* Caſe, *Salkeld* 291.

Where upon Non *Aſſumpſit* Condemnation in foreign Attachment may be given in Evidence, and where it muſt be plead- ed.
In *Aſſumpſit* Evidence was given, That the
Debt was attached by the Cuſtom of *London*
before the Action brought, and Condemnation
had before the Plea pleaded. And it was
urged, That this ſhould relate to defeat the
Action. But *per Cur.* it was ruled, That if an
Attachment and Condemnation be before the
Writ purchaſed, it may be given in Evidence
on the General Iſſue, becauſe that is an Alteration of the Property before the Action brought;
but if the Attachment only be before the Writ
purchaſed, it ought to be pleaded in Abatement of the Writ; and if the Condemnation
be after the Action commenced, and the Plea
pleaded, then it may be pleaded in Bar, but
ſhall not be given in Evidence on *Non Aſſumpſit*, for that the Property is not altered until
Condemnation, and the Plaintiff had a Verdict.
Brook verſus *Smith*, *Salkeld* 180.

Aſſumpſit on a Bill of Exchange; Defendant
pleads that he was a Gentleman that went
Abroad to travel, and traverſes his being a
Merchant. The Plaintiff demurred; and it
was inſiſted, that it amounted to the General
Iſſue; but held that it was no Rule, that a
Matter, that might be given in Evidence on the
General Iſſue, could not be pleaded ſpecially;
that in Debt for Rent, Entry, and Expulſion may
be

be given in Evidence on *Nil debet*, and ſo on
Nil habuit in Tenementis, but yet are always
allowed to be pleaded ; but the Plea was held
ill in Subſtance, being the Drawing the Bill
made him a Trader. 2 *Vent.* 295. And ſo in
Debt on Bond againſt a Feme Covert, ſhe may
plead Coverture, or give it in Evidence on *Non
eſt factum.* 5 *Mod.* 175.

Winner ſhall not recover on a Bill for Money
won at play againſt an Acceptor ; otherwiſe of
an Indorſee. 1 *Salk.* 344. See 5 *Mod.* 170.
Carth. 356. *Holt* 328. *Caſ. B. R.* 96. *Skin.*
195.

Quarto Jacobi ſecundi, An *Aſſumpſit* was
brought againſt four, who pleaded *Non Aſſump-*
ſer. infra ſex Annos, and the Verdict was, that
one of them did aſſume *infra ſex Annos*, and
the other *Non Aſſumpſer.* And it was held that
no Judgment could be given againſt the Defendant, upon whom the Verdict was found ;
for this is an *Indebitatus Aſſumpſit* for Goods
ſold ; and 'tis an intire Contract, and they muſt
all be found to promiſe, or elſe 'tis againſt the
Plaintiff. 2 *Vent.* 151.

Where the Contract is intire, what Proof is re- quiſite.

Torts are in their Nature ſeveral ; ſo one
Defendant may be found guilty, and the other
not guilty, but 'tis not ſo in Actions grounded
upon Contract. 2 *Vent.* 151.

Torts may be found ſeve- rally.

Caſe on a promiſſory Note againſt the Drawer ; held, that by Stat. 3 *An. c.* 9. the Note
is Evidence of a Conſideration, but not concluſive Evidence, but turns the Proof on the
Defendant, to ſhew that there was no Conſideration given for ſuch a Note ; ſo held by the
Lord Chancellor *King.* *Gilbert's* Reports 154.
M. 8 *G.* 1. *Brown* v. *Marſh.*

· Action against an Indorfor of a Bill of Exchange, Drawer called to prove that he did not draw the Bill ; but held he was not a Witnefs ; but the Party gave him a Releafe, and that was fufficient. *Reports in* Holt's *Time* 297.

Affumpfit against four for Corn fold to them ; the Evidence proved the Sale to be to only two of them. Held that Plaintiff failed as to all. *Clayton* 114.

Of Evidence in Debt.

Non eft factum.   Upon *Non eft factum*, it is no Evidence to fhew that the Bond was made upon an ufurious Contract, or that the Sheriff's Name is miftaken, *&c.* in a Bail-Bond ; or that the Bond is joint or feveral, or delivered at another Place ; or that it is void by Statute, but it muft be pleaded in Abatement.   1 *Inft.* 283. *Hob.* 72.

5 Coke 27.
Roll. Trial,
683. pl. 8.   But to prove that the Seal was broken off, and put on again ; or to prove a Rafure of the Deed, delivered as an Efcrow, *&c.* this is good Evidence, *Lib.* 5. 119. 11. 27. if it were

1 Cro. 120.
Owen 8.   done before the Action brought ; but if the Seal was broke off, *&c.* by Chance, after Iffue joined, the Jury may find it fpecially.

If an Obligation is delivered to the Ufe of another, and he difagrees to it, by this the obligation has no Force, and he can never agree to it afterwards, and therefore this is no Deed, and may be given in Evidence on *non eft factum.* *Gilb. L. of Evid.* 162.

If Witnefs prove Delivery at another Place : *Q.* If that warrants the Iffue. *Ibid.*

Debt on Bond, which was fet forth to be made 15 *November* 25 *Eliz.* and on *Non eft factum,*

factum, the Fact appeared to be, that it was dated 15 *November* 25 *Eliz.* but was delivered 18 *November* 26 *Eliz.* Held the Bond was proved. *Cro. Jac.* 136.

On *Non eſt faƈtum*, the being delivered as an Eſcrow may be given in Evidence, as well as Suſpenſion of Rent, on *Nil debet.* 3 *Keb.* 142.

It was held by *Holt*, C. J. That the Pleading ſpecially a Raſure or Delivery as an Eſcrow, and *ſic non eſt faƈtum*, was impertinent, for thereby the Defendant takes the Proof on himſelf; but on a general *Non eſt faƈtum* the Plaintiff muſt prove whatever is neceſſary to make it a Deed. 6 *Mod.* 218.

In Debt upon an Eſcape, if the Defendant plead *Nul Eſcape*, he cannot give in Evidence no Arreſt. Eſcape.

Debt on a Bond to perform Covenants to deliver Poſſeſſion at the Term's End to the Leſſor or his Aſſigns; Breach was aſſigned in not Delivery to two Purchaſers, Demand being made by both, and Iſſue joined thereon; in Evidence, Demand by one is good. 2 *Cro.* 475.

In Debt upon a Contraƈt, that the Contraƈt was conditional; upon Account, that there was no ſuch Account; *Ne leſſa pas* upon *Nil debet* in Debt for Rent.

In Debt upon the Statute of 21 *H.* 8. of Farms, upon the General Iſſue *Non habuit*, he may give in Evidence the Taking for the Proviſion of his Houſe, according to the Proviſo of that Statute. 27 *H.* 8. 21.

Debt on Bond to perform an Award, *ita quod* the Award be delivered to the Parties; in Evidence Delivery proved to the Wiſe is ſuf-

ficient

ficient for the Jury to prefume the Delivery to the Party himfelf. *Per Hale, Norfolk Summer Affizes,* 1665. *Trice* and *Prat.*

At the fame Affizes, *per Moreton* Juftice, Delivery to the Party's Son is good Evidence. *Violet* and *Cook.*

Debt againft an Heir, *&c. Riens per defcent, &c.* a Feoffment given in Evidence made before the Action, that it was fraudulent may be given in Evidence, though not pleaded. *5 Rep. Co. Gocche's* Cafe, 60 *Hob.* 72. *Vide Fitz.* Tit. *Garranty* 88.

Debt againft Executor, who pleaded *Ne unques, &c.* Plaintiff replied, That he adminiftred as Executor, and gave in Evidence Adminiftration granted to him, by which he adminiftred; good. *Dyer* 305. But a Gift of the Goods the Defendant may give in Evidence.

In Debt againft Executors, and *Plene adminiftravit* pleaded, the Defendant cannot give in Evidence a Bond fatisfied, where the Executor and Teftator were Obligors. *Per Coventry* Lord Keeper, 23 *Jac. Perkins* verfus *Perkins.*

In Debt for Tithes, *Modus* to a Vicar is good againft the Parfon, and fo is a *Modus* to a Parifh Clerk. *Per Moreton* Juftice, *Lent, Cambridge,* 1667. *Barber* verfus *Cofter.*

In Debt againft Executor *de fon tort,* who pleads *Ne unques, &c.* it is fufficient to charge him, by proving he hath adminiftred of never fo little Value. *Clayton* 6.

Debt on Bond againft Executor *de fon tort,* who pleaded Fully adminiftred; the Evidence was, the Inteftate made a Bill of Sale of his Goods to the Defendant; who was bound with him in a Bond as Surety, for his Counterfecurity, but the Goods remained in the Inteftate's ftate's Poffeffion during his Life, for fome few Hours ; ruled a fraudulent Deed by *Barkley* Juftice, at *York.* 11 *Car. Legard* and *Binly, Clayton* 39. *Quære.*

Debt againft Adminiftrator, who pleaded *Plene, &c.* and gave in Evidence Judgments, and good without pleading; *per Henden,* 1638. *York, Clayton* 95. *Quære,* for if Judgments be kept on Foot by Fraud, and given in Evidence, how can a Creditor, who fues for a juft Debt, be prepared to detect this Fraud ? And *Note*; In *Scire facias* againft an Executor on Judgment *per Teftator'*, the Defendant pleaded Fully adminiftred generally, and the Plaintiff demurred fpecially ; and Sir *William Jones* Solicitor General moved to amend the Plea ; and *Hale* Chief Juftice thought he ought to plead fpecially, how fully adminiftred. *Bradford* verfus *Hutchinfon, H.* 25, 26 *Car.* 2. *B. R.*

If the Defen-dant pleads Plene, &c. præter Judgments, &c. The Plaintiff muft prove Affets above the Sum of thofe Judgments. Huntington, by Judge Wyndham, 33 Car. 2.

Debt for Rent on a Leafe; the Evidence to prove the Leafe was, That Plaintiff leafed a Houfe to Defendant at a Rent, but no Time mentioned ; and it was agreed at the fame Time, that the Leffee was not to leave it without Half a Year's Warning. *Per Hale, Norf. Summer Affize,* 1668. It is a Leafe at Will, and the Leaving on Half a Year's Warning, is but a collateral Agreement, and no Part of the Demife.

Debt for Rent.

In Debt for Rent upon a Leafe, and *Nil debet* pleaded, *Ne unques feifie des Terres* is good Evidence; otherwife upon the Plea of *Riens arrere,* or *Levy per Diftrefs.* 2 *Roll. Abr.* 677. *pl.* 21.

Upon

Upon a General Iſſue, you may give Special Matter in Evidence. If you give Colour, you may plead it ſpecially; as in Debt for Rent, you may plead *Nil debet,* and give Releaſe in Evidence; *per Holt* Ch. J. 12 *W.* 3. in Caſe of *Paramour* v. *Johnſon,* cites *Vin. Abr.* Title *Evidence,* 76. *pl.* 72. 12 *Mod.* 412. Ld. *Raym.* 566. S. C. and S. P.

Eviction, Expulſion, and any Suſpenſion of Rent, is good Evidence upon *Nil debet,* for that amounts to diſcharge and falſify in the Caſe of Complaint, for then there was no pernancy of the Profits whereby I could become Debtor to him in Reverſion, and ſo the Act *in Pais* is diſcharged, which goes of neceſſity to the creating of this Debt, though others have held it ought to be pleaded. *Gilb. L. of Evid.* 282.

Debt for Rent.
Dyer 122.

In Debt for Rent upon *Non dimiſit,* that the Leſſor *riens avoit* in the Land at the Time of the Demiſe, may be given in Evidence.

So upon *Nil debet* an Eviction may be given in Evidence. If the Leſſor enter into Part, the whole Rent is ſuſpended; but if a Stranger evict the Leſſee of Part of the Land, the Rent muſt be apportioned.

2 Roll. 641.
pl. 4.

In Eſcape of a Priſoner, and the Iſſue is, If the Gaoler immediately after the Eſcape made freſh Suit; if the Priſoner hath eſcaped a Day and a Night before the Gaoler knew it, and then he makes freſh Suit, it is ſufficient to prove the Effect of the Iſſue, for convenient Purſuit is immediate freſh Suit in Law.

Freſh Suit.
Eſcape.
The Writ, the Warrant, Arreſt and Eſcape are to be proved to an Eſcape.

In Eſcape againſt the Marſhal, the Plaintiff muſt prove the Perſon that eſcaped in actual Cuſtody ſince the *Committitur,* which *Committitur* either in the Marſhal's Book, or on Record,

cord, is not fufficient, without a Proof of being
in actual Cuftody fince. *Keb.* 1 Vol. 375, 775.
See *Keb.* 2 Part 384.   What may be given in
Evidence upon an Information of negligent
Efcape, againft the Marfhal of the King's
Bench, as a Recovery in the Original Action,
and the Plaintiff allowed a Witnefs, becaufe
he neither gains nor lofes.

So upon *Riens per difcent*, by an Heir in *Riens per di-*
Debt upon an Obligation, that the Defendant *fcent.*
aliened the Affets by Fraud and Covin, and fo
void by the Statute of 13 *Eliz.* may be given
in Evidence, becaufe thefe are the General Iffues.   2 *Roll.* 684. *pl.* 4.

In Debt againft the Heir who pleads *Riens* *Riens per di-*
per difcent, Proof that the Father was feifed, *fcent.*
and that the Heir did enter after his Death, is
well enough, for it fhall be prefumed Fee-
fimple till the contrary be fhewn.

In Debt for Tithes, if the Plaintiff declares *Tithes,*
that he is Proprietor of a Farm, it is fufficient, *Crawly verf.*
and may give his Title in Evidence.   *Thorne,*
                                                                        Mich 22
Entry and Sufpenfion may be given in Evi- *Car.* 2.
dence upon *Nil debet* pleaded.   *Mod. Rep.* 35. *Nil debet.*
per Twifden, Brown's Cafe, 1 *Vent.* 258.   *Rent.*

Frefh Suit may be given in Evidence in an *Efcape.*
Action of Debt for an Efcape, on *Nil debet*
pleaded ; *per Hale* and *Wild contra Twifden.*
Hale faid, he always allowed it, and fo faid
Wild Juftice. *Mod. Rep.* 116. *Mofdale*'s Cafe.

Upon a Trial at Bar it was agreed, That in *Efcape.*
Debt upon an Efcape, and *Nil debet* pleaded,
Reprifal upon frefh Suit may be given in
Evidence by the Defendant in Excufe of the
Action.

M 4   Upon

Upon *Non eſt faĉtum*, you may give *Not let-*
tered in Evidence ; for when the Perſon who
delivered the Deed is unlearned, and the Deed
is read and expounded to him in another Senſe
than that which the Deed really contains, then
did not the Party agree to the written Deed,
'tis not the Expreſſion of his Mind, nor to be
accounted his Deed. *Gilb. Law of Evid.* 162.
But it is the beſt Way to plead it, for the
Underſtanding of the Jury. 39 *H.* 6. 9. *Bro.*
Waiver, 2.

Debt on ſingle Bill, on *Non eſt faĉtum* ; one
of the ſubſcribing Witneſſes fully proved the
Executing of it : The Defendant produced a
Witneſs of the ſame Name and Surname as the
other ſubſcribing Witneſs; who ſwore the
Name was like his, but was not his, and that
he never knew either of the Parties, or the o-
ther Witneſs ; neither could the other Witneſs
ſay he was the Man. And *Holt* Ch. J. ordered them to write their Names, and left it
to the Jury, who found for Plaintiff. 6 *Mod.*
167.

Debt on Bond againſt two; on *Non eſt fac-*
tum if it appears to be only the Bond of one,
the Plaintiff fails. 40 *E.* 3. 35. *b.*

If two Men are bound in a Bond jointly,
and one is ſued alone, he may plead this Matter in Abatement ; but cannot plead *Non eſt*
faĉtum; for it is his Deed, though it be not his
ſole Deed. 5 *Co.* 119. 1 *Inſt.* 283. *a.*

In Debt againſt two, if it be proved the
Debt of one, and not of the other, the Iſſue
of *Non eſt faĉtum* is maintained. *Gilb. Law of*
Evid. 162, 163.

Debt

Debt on Bond by *J. S.* againſt *St. John* and *Alice* his Wife, as Heir of her Father ; and on *Non eſt faɛlum* it appeared the Bond was made to *J. S.* and another ; and held that the Plaintiff could not recover ; but the Plaintiff ought to have declared as Survivor of the other. 1 *Leon.* 322. *Sed vide Aleyn* 41. *Houlditch* verſus *Caſe*, the contrary is held, and that it ought to be pleaded in Abatement ; and ſo in *Savile* 92.

One *William Shotbolt* was bound in a Bond to *J. S.* but was named *John* in the Bond ; and the Plaintiff ſued him by the Name of *William Shotbolt*, alias dicɩ' *John Shotbolt* ; and on *Non eſt faɛlum* this Special Matter was found ; held that the Plaintiff failed ; for he ought to have ſued him by the Name of *John*. *Dyer* 279. *b.*

Evidence that the Party was blind, and the Deed miſ-read to him, will juſtify this Iſſue of *Non eſt Faɛlum*.   *Gilb. Law of Evid.* 164.

On *Non eſt faɛlum* a Raſure cannot be given in Evidence, becauſe it was once his Deed, but avoided by a ſubſequent Faɛt. *Mod.* 66.

On *Non eſt faɛlum* it was found, that the Defendant ſealed the Bond and left it on the Table, and the Plaintiff came, and took it up and carried it away ; held this did not amount to a Delivery. *Owen* 95. But if the Defendant had at that Time ſaid, *This will ſerve,* that would amount to a Delivery. 1 *Leon* 140. *Dyer* 192. *b.*

If a Man Seals an Obligation, and commands another to keep it till certain Conditions are performed, and the Bond is delivered to the Obligee before they are performed, this could never be his Bond till thoſe Conditions were performed,

formed, and therefore this Special Matter may be given in Evidence to prove *Non est factum. Gilb. Law of Evid.* 162.

Debt for Rent.

In Debt for Rent upon a Leafe for Years, the Iffue being joined, if the Rent was paid or not, the Defendant gave in Evidence for Part of the Rent, that the Plaintiff was by Covenant to repair the Houfe, and did it not; and thereupon he expended the Rent in repairing the Houfe; and the Queftion was, if this Evidence will maintain the Iffue? *Gaudy* conceived it did, for the Law giveth this Liberty to this Leffee to expend the Rent in Reparations, and recoup the Rent. *V.* 12 *H.* 8. 1. *Fitz.* Tit. *Bar.* 242. 14 *H.* 4. 27. *Fenner :* It is no Evidence, for if the Leffor will not repair it, the Leffee may have his Covenant againft him. *Clench* thought he might well expend the Rent in Repara ions, but he ought to have pleaded it, and cannot give it in Evidence upon the General Iffue; and thereupon they moved the Jury to find the Special Matter. 1 *Cro.* 222.

So that it feemed to the Juftices, That the Defendant had Liberty to expend the Rent in the Reparations (they being to be done at the Plaintiff's Coft) ; but then that he ought to have pleaded this Matter, as it was done in (almoft) the like Cafe, *Fitz.* Tit. *Bar.* 242. Yet why might he not give it in Evidence upon the General Iffue? For if the Law allows this to amount to a Payment of the Rent, then the Defendant owes nothing, which maintains *Nil debet* ; and I think the other Book of 14 *H.* 4. 27. rejects this Sort of Special Plea, upon this Reafon, that the Plea amounted to a General Iffue; but there indeed the Rent

was

was pleaded to be laid out at the Plaintiff's Command, here only by Authority in Law. I fhould be glad if any one would reconcile thofe two Books better.   I know there is another Reafon in the Book (and affigned by *Rolle* in his Abridgment of the Cafe) why the Plea was rejeɛted, *viz.* That the Duty was acknowledged by the Plea, and therefore the Matter of the Plea not good, without fhewing a Deed of it; but I fhould have been better pleafed with him, if he had affigned the other Reafon, *viz.* That it amounted to the General Iffue.   Which made *Cheyne* that he durft not join in Demurrer: For it is not pretended in either Cafe, that the Deed ordered the Rent to be laid out in the Repairs.

And in that Cafe in *F.* where there was no exprefs Order of the Plaintiff; it may be the Judges allowed the fpecial Matter to be pleaded, becaufe the Jury fhould not be intrufted with the Law upon the General Iffue, which may be faid for the fpecial pleading this Matter in our Cafe, although it may amount to the General Iffue.

But as to the Refidue, the Defendant fhewed he paid it to others, by the Plaintiff's Order, which was held clearly good, for what is paid by the Leffor's Appointment, is a Payment to himfelf. *Cro. Eliz.* 223. *Taylor* againft *Beal. Vide Roll.* Tit. *Debt*, 605. 34 *H.* 6. 17. *Bro. Debt*, 27.

Reparations, *Vide* the Cafes of *Recouper, Lib.* 5. 30.

Debt for Rent on a Leafe, the Defendant pleaded Payment; and on Evidence proved Payment to the Sequeftrators of the Common Wealth, the Plaintiff being a Delinquent; and held the Iffue was proved. *Clayton* 129.

In

Debt for Servants Wages.

In Debt for Servant's Wages, *viz.* 20 *s.* or a Robe yearly: The Defendant may plead Payment of the Robe, and shall not be put to the General Issue, where the Payment is of another Thing than Money; but of Money he must plead *Nil debet*, and give the Payment in Evidence. And the Defendant may plead that the Plaintiff departed out of his Service, and shall not be forced to the General Issue. 9 *E.* 4. 36. Though surely that may be given in Evidence upon *Nil debet*, for the Plaintiff must prove he served: So *Indebitatus Assumpsit*, and *non Assumpsit*, upon the Promise in Law, an

Extinguishment.

Extinguishment by taking a Bond (being a Matter of a higher Nature) for the Debt, may be given in Evidence.

And *Note*; If an Infant buy Goods, and afterwards give a Bond, and this Bond be avoided by Infancy, yet it seems the Contract shall not be revived. *Sed dubitatur, Roll.* Tit. *Extinguishment*, 604. For now this Bond which was voidable, is become void, and a void Thing shall not have such Effect: But a Personal Action once suspended is gone for ever; but Acceptance of a Bond shall not extinguish Rent, nor Arrearages of an Account, before an Auditor of Record, because these are of a higher Nature than the Bond, the Rent being real, and the other of Record. But the Bond extinguishes the Contract for the Arrearages upon an *Insimul computasset, &c.*

Acceptance. Rent.

Acceptance of Rent due the last Day, and an Acquittance thereof discharges all the Arrearages due before, *Lib.* 3. 65. Unity of Possession in as high an Estate destroys the Prescription, *&c.*

In

In Debt upon a Bond, conditioned to pay Payment.
20 *s.* at the Houfe of the Defendant the 7th
Day of *May* ; upon a Plea of Payment at the
Time and Place, the Jury found the Payment
before the feventh Day, and prayed the Advice of the Court, if this was a Payment at the
Day. The Court adjudged that the Payment
and Acceptance before the Day, was as well as
if it had been paid at the Day. *Savil's Reports* 1 Cro. 142.
96. *Bond* againft *Richardfon.* And fo fays 1 Anderfon
Coke 1 *Inft.* 212. The Time and Place are but 198.
Circumftances, and if the Obligee or Feoffee Owen 45.
receive the Money at another Place, or before
the Day, it is fufficient ; or a leffer Sum before
the Day. But *Moor* 47. Upon Iffue of Payment at the Day and Place, and Evidence of
Payment a Month before, and Demurrer upon
the Evidence, *Dyer, Brown* and *Welfh* faid
this Evidence doth not maintain the Iffue, becaufe before the Day of Payment there is no
Duty, and the Day and Place are Parcel of the
Iffue, and the Act on one Day is not an Act
done on another Day : As if an Executor pleads
Payment at the Day, it is not good Evidence
to fhew that it was paid before the Day by
the Teftator, for this doth not prove the Iffue,
and yet there was not any Duty remaining at
the Day, and therefore the Pleading ought to
haye been fpecially according to the Truth.
Vide devant ——— And it is not like the Cafe,
where the Circumftances of Time and Place are
only for Neceffity of Trial ; but in Regard that
Payment is the Subftance, why is it not fufficient to prove, as well as to find, the Effect and
Subftance of the Iffue ? And it is not like the
Cafe of collateral Conditions, where the Condition

dition is not to pay Money, but to do some collateral Thing, as to deliver a Horse, a Robe or Ring, &c. or to pay Money to a Stranger; such collateral Conditions are more strictly to be observed. *Vide* 1 *Inst.* 212.

Where pleading Plene administravit admits the Debt. Ruled *per Holt* Ch. J. That in Debt *Plene administravit* admits the Debt; but otherwise in an Action on the Case, or in an *Indebitatus assumpsit*, for there the Plaintiff must prove the Debt; and in Proof of a *Plene administravit*, if the Action be Debt on a Bond, and you offer Payment of the Bond, on *Plene administravit*, Proof must be, it was a Debt by Bond, that it was sealed and delivered: But to Debt on simple Contract, you need only prove Payment, because if no Bond, it is a good Administration in that Action. *Saunderson* versus *Nicholls, Shower* 81.

Where Sealing and Delivery of the Bond paid, must be proved.

It was adjudged *per Holt* Ch. J. That in *Debt* for Rent, upon *Nil debet* pleaded, the Statute of Limitations may be given in Evidence, for the Statute has made it no Debt at the Time of the Plea pleaded, the Words of which are in the present Tense; but in Case on *Non assumpsit*, the Statute of Limitations cannot be given in Evidence, for it speaks of a Time past, and relates to the Time of making the Promise, at *Nisi prius* at *Hertford*, 1690. *Anon'*, 1 *Salk.* 278.

Levy by Distress, & sic non debet, Payment or Release is good Evidence, otherwise of Rasure. In Debt for Rent, if the Defendant plead Levy by Distress, *& sic non debet*, a Release or Payment is good Evidence, for it proves there is no Debt, and that is the Issue; *vide Cro. Eliz.* 140. which agrees: But if the Defendant plead Rasure, and *sic non est factum*, nothing else is Evidence but Rasure. *Per Holt* Ch. J. *Galway* versus *Susach, Salk.* 284.

Per

Per Holt Ch. J. In Debt the Defendant may plead a Releafe, becaufe it admits the Contract, which is a Colour of Action, and yet he might give it in Evidence upon *Nil debet.* So in *Affumpfit,* the Defendant may plead Payment, becaufe it admits the *Affumpfit,* and yet he may give it in Evidence upon *Non Affumpfit. Hatton* verfus *Mors, Salk.* 394.

A Releafe may be pleaded in Debt, or given in Evidence on *Nil debet.*

It was held by *Holt* Ch. J. That if a Bond was of twenty Years ftanding, and no Demand proved, or good Caufe of fo long Forbearance fhewn, he would intend it paid, on *folvit ad diem,* and *a fortiori* in Cafe of a Note. 6 *Mod.* 22.

Debt on a Bond by an Adminiftrator, Defendant pleaded *folvit ad diem,* and infifted on the Bond's being dated 9 *W.* 3. To encounter which, the Plaintiff fhewed an Endorfement, wrote in the Inteftate's own Hand, of the Payment of one Year's Intereft nine Years after the Bond made. *Pratt* Ch. J. refufed this Evidence at *Nifi prius;* and on a Cafe made, the other Judges were of Opinion, it ought to have been allowed as Evidence; but the Chief Juftice continued in his former Opinion. *T.* 10 *Geo.* 1. *Serle* verfus *Barrington, Mod. Cafes in Law and Equity* 278.

Dower.

In Dower, the Iffue was *Ne unques feifie que Dower,* and for the Plaintiff, a Feoffment in Fee was given in Evidence to the Hufband; the Defendant would have given in Evidence, a Seifin in Tail with a Difcontinuance, and then the Feoffment, *&c.* and fo a Remitter, but it ought

ought to be pleaded; *per Cur'. Dyer* 41. Nor an Estate upon Condition.

If an Heir mortgage for Years, and then assign Dower legally, *i. e.* a third Part of the whole, the Assignment shall bind the Mortgagee; *contra*, if the Assignment be illegal, as of one whole Manor, when there were three Manors; that being not as the Law would have done it. And if a Disseisor assign a legal Dower, it is good: But if the Heir mortgage in Fee, and then assign, *&c.* legally, *&c.* that is not good, because the whole Freehold was out of him at the Time of the Assignment. *Per Hugh Wyndham* Just. *Bucks, Lent Assizes* 1668.

Dower. Dower of Rent, *Til. Ne unque seise que Dower la, &c. Horton J. S.* granted the Rent to the Husband, payable at *Michaelmas* next, and the Husband died before the Day, and so he was seized in Law, and demanded Judgment. *Thirning :* You shall say generally, *quod seise que Dower la, &c.* and give our Case in Evidence, *& sic bene,* notwithstanding the Doubt of the *lay Gens,* for they ought to credit the Law, and Evidence is not to be pleaded. 11 *H.* 4. 88.

Ejectment. Title Recovery in Dower ; Defendant offered to prove a Term of Years prior to the Title of Dower, and disallowed.   In Ejectment the Plaintiff made Title by a Recovery in Dower, and produced in Evidence the Record of the Judgment, the *Habere facias seisinam, &c.* The Defendant offered to prove a Term of ninety-nine Years subsisting, and that prior to this Title; but it was disallowed ; for if he had pleaded this in Bar of the Writ of Dower, yet the Plaintiff must have recovered with a *Cesset Executio* ; and the Defendant had a proper Time to have pleaded it then, and has slipped his Opportunity : Also a

3   Chattel

Chattel Intereft was at Common Law bound by a Recovery in a real Action, fo that the Demandant had an immediate Execution, without Regard to the fubfifting Term : And tho' by the Statute *H.* 8. a Termor may falfify, yet it muft be the Termor himfelf, and not another for him. Lady Dowager *Lindfay* verfus *Lord Lindfay, Salk.* 291.

Of Evidence in Ejectment.

If a Leffee affign or make a Leafe to another, the fecond Leffee muft prove the Poffeffion of the firft: *Gilb. Law of Evid.* 230, 231.

The Truftee of a Leafe, Leffor in Ejectment, by his Difclaimer in *Pais* will avoid the Plaintiff's Title. *Ibid.* 231.

The Plaintiff counts of a joint Leafe made by *A.* and *B.* In Evidence it appeared that *A. B.* and *C.* were Joint-tenants, that *C.* leafed to *B.* and that *A.* and *B.* leafed to the Plaintiff; by three Juftices againft two, it is good. 2 *Cro. Jordain's* Cafe, f. 83.

Ne dona pas may be maintained by a Demife; and upon a Feoffment, a Leafe and Releafe; but a Fine and Releafe will not maintain a Demife to Hufband and Wife.

When he that fued an *Elegit* brings an E- *Elegit.* jectment to try the Title, he muft in Evidence fhew the *Elegit* filed.

Count of a joint Leafe made by two; in Evidence it appears they were Tenants in Common; by three Juftices againft one, it is good. 2 *Cro.* 166. *Mantle's* Cafe.

Count of a Leafe by Hufband, Evidence was a Leafe by Hufband and Wife with Letter of Attorney to make Livery, and it is

made

made in Name of both; by three Juſtices a-
gainſt one it is good, for Livery as to the Feme
was void. 2 *Cro. Gardner's* Caſe.

Of a Leaſe made 5 *Maii* 10 *Regis, habendum*
from *Lady-day* laſt paſt, for 21 Years *exlunc
prox' ſequent'.* In Evidence, a Leaſe of 5 *Maii*
10 *Regis, habendum* from *Lady-day* laſt paſt,
for twenty-one Years next following the Date
of the ſaid Indenture, adjudged good, and affirmed in Error. *Hob.* 19.

Ejectment of a Rectory, Evidence of the taking of Tithes only, and not entring into the
Glebe, the Plaintiff was nonſuit. *Latch* 62.
Hems and *Stroud.* 2 *Sid.* 91. *Gilb. Law of Evid.*
225.

In Ejectment, the Leaſe of a Guardian or
Copyholder will maintain a Declaration, tho'
void againſt the Lord and Infant; but a
Leaſe *de Herbage* will not of Meadow. *Hardr.
Rep.* 330.

In Ejectment, a Leaſe to *A.* of Lands in the
Poſſeſſion of three Tenants for Years, was delivered to *J. S.* as an *Eſcrow,* with Letter of
Attorney to enter into all, and then to deliver
the Deed, *&c.* Evidence, that the Attorney
entered upon one Leſſee in the Name of all, and
delivered the Deed, *&c. Per Jones* Juſtice, It
is good enough, for where the Freehold is in
one, his Entry into one Leſſee for Years in
Name of the reſt is good. *Latch* 71. Dame
Argol's Caſe.

In Ejectment the Defendant ſhall not give
in Evidence a former Mortgage or Conveyance
made by himſelf, and therefore in ſuch Caſes
it is left for him that has the former Mortgage
to get himſelf made Defendant before the
Cauſe comes to Trial.

Ejectment,

Ejectment of Tithes; a Leafe for Life of Tithes is good, if there be Church or Church-yard to make Livery in; refolved on Trial at Bar. *Wheeler* verfus *Hancher, Hill.* 14, 15 *Car.* 2. *B. R. Jones Rep.* 321, 322.

Entry and Claim made upon the Land, within five Years after the Death of the Baron of the Countefs of *Peterborough*, to avoid a Fine, fhe being Iffue in Tail, proved by one Wit-nefs, and allowed at a Trial at Bar. *B. R. Mich.* 15 *Car.* 2. *Floyd* and *Pollard*, 1 *Keb.* 620.

Cuftom of Copyholders *in extremis* to furren-der into one Tenant's Hands, in the Prefence of credible Witnefs. A furrender was made accordingly, but pleaded to be done to another Tenant, yet being proved to be done to a Tenant it was holden, by *Wadham Wyndham* Juftice, to be good; and by him, a Glove or a Turf is a Rod to give Seifin by. *May*'s Cafe, *Norf. Summer Affizes* 1663.

A Will under which Title to Land is made, muft be fhewn itfelf, and the Probate is not fufficient. *Contra*, if it were on a Circum-ftance, or as Inducement, or that the Will re-main in Chancery, or other Court, by fpecial Order of fuch Court. *Eden* verfus *Chalkhill, Mich.* 13 *Car.* 2. *B. R. Keb.* 1 Part 117.

Alfo Inrolment of a Deed, which needs no Inrolment, is no Evidence. *Ibid.*

He muft prove Admiffion, Inftitution and Induction, his Reading and Subfcribing the Articles, *&c.* and his Declaration in the Church of his free and full Affent and Con-fent to all thofe Things contained in the Com-mon Prayer; and this ought to be proved done within the Time limited by the Statute, *How a Parfon in Ejectment of a Rectory fhall make out his Title.*

N 2 but

but need not fhew a Right in him that prefent-
ed him. *Poft.* 525.

See *Keb.* 2 Part 484. In Evidence an Inftitution without Prefentation or Copy of it, was
refufed by the Court, albeit a Prefentation may
be made by Parol, but Proof muft be made of
it; if there be Induction upon it, I think it
good Evidence.

The Iffue was Fine uncertain, or certain two
Years Rent and no more, the Evidence was of
Admittances on Surrenders uncertain, but all
under two Years Rent. *Per Williams* Juftice:
You ought to produce Fines on Defcent, and
Fines paid above two Years Rents. 2 *Bulft.* 32.
Allen verfus *Abraham.*

A Leafe was made by Parol, and agreed to
be put in Writing, and Indentures befpoke;
but being held for ten Years, and no Indentures executed, it was ruled for a Leafe Parol.
Per Berkley Juftice, 13 *Car.* 1. *York, Clayton*
53.

By Juftice *Berkley* (1638. *York, Hedges* cont.
Clayton 57.) A Will under Seal, proved, examined by the Original, was allowed good E-
vidence. *Quære*; I think the Practice againft
it.

A Leafe and Releafe were given in Evidence
to intitle the Plaintiff, and they both were named *hæc Indentura*, but were not indented:
Good, *Per Hale* Chief Baron, *Norf. Summer
Affizes* 1668. *Briant* verfus *Trendle.*

After Default (in Ejectment) the Defendant
may confefs Leafe, Entry and Oufter, and may
give Evidence, and have all Advantages (except
Challenges); and if the Plaintiff becomes nonfuit, any one for the Defendant may pray it be
recorded.

Per

Per H. Wyndham Juſtice, *Bucks, Lent.* 68. Dr. *Crawley*'s Caſe. Deprivation in Spiritual Court for Simony, diſables from bringing Ejectment, becauſe he can make no Leaſe ; yet *quære.*

If a Mortgagor continues in Poſſeſſion without Proviſion for that Purpoſe in the Deed, he is Tenant at Will ; and if he levies a Fine, it is no Diſſeiſin by him continued in Poſſeſſion ſtill, becauſe after the Will determined, he is Tenant at Sufferance. *Per Hale* Chief Baron, *Bedford Summer Aſſizes* 1669.

In Ejectment, the Defendant ſhall not give in Evidence a former Mortgage or Contract made by himſelf. *Gilb. Law of Evid.* 231.

Declaration on a Leaſe made 14 *January* 30 *Eliz.* Evidence of a Leaſe ſealed 13 *Jan.* good, for if it was a Leaſe thirteen, it was a Leaſe made fourteen. 4 *Leon.* 14.

If the Declaration in Ejectment be of *Michaelmas* Term, which relates to the firſt Day of the Term, yet it is Matter of Evidence, and examinable what Day the Bill was filed ; and if it was after the Day of the Leaſe, all is well. *Sid.* 432.

Feoffments of forty Years ſtanding, and Poſſeſſion going accordingly, you need not prove Livery, it may be intended *per* Jury. *Roll. Rep.* 132.

If on Not guilty pleaded the Leſſor of the Plaintiff ſhew a Feoffment, the Defendant may give Covin in Evidence. *Gilb. Law of Evid.* 233.

But if the Feoffee by Covin pleads, that he was ſeiſed at the Time of the Judgment by Virtue of a Feoffment, and the Creditor, that

N 3   he

he was not seifed, on this Iffue the Covin may be given in Evidence. *Ibid.* 234.

If the Heir pleads *Riens per Defcent*, and gives a Feoffment in Evidence, the Plaintiff may give Covin in Evidence. *Ibid.* 234, 5.

The common Rock on which fo many have fplit, is laying the Leafe to be *a die datus*, and the Entry the fame Day, which is a Diffeifin, not purged by the Commencement of the Leafe; for where an Intereft paffes, is exclufive, and fo the Entry the fame Day is before the Leafe was to commence, and is a Diffeifin, but in Cafes of Obligation where no Intereft paffes, it is *contra*; *quod nota.* See *Gilb. L. of Evid.* 225.

Ejectione firmæ, and declared of a Leafe by Indenture, bearing Date 6 *December* 19 *Jac. Habendum à die datus Indenturæ præd'.* On Not guilty, the Leafe produced was dated 6 *December* 19 *Jac. habendum à tempore confectionis Indenturæ*; and the Plaintiff was nonfuited, the Leafe proved being different from that he declared on. *Cro. Jac.* 647.

Pafch. 27 Car. 2. in B. R. — *verfus* Cotewell.

In *Ejectione*, upon Not guilty, upon Evidence to the Jury at the Bar, the Cafe was fuch, That *Cotewell* had a Leafe for Years of the Prebend of *Sutton Regis* in the County of *Bucks*, made in the Time of *H.* 8. and being expired, he now claimeth under a Leafe from a nominal Prebendary thereof founded in the Cathedral of *Lincoln*: But the Plaintiff claimed by Letters Patent thereof from King *James*, made the 7th of King *James*, to *Brent* and his Heirs, who granted the fame to the Widow of Sir *W. Rawleigh* and her Heirs, whofe Daughter and Heir Sir *Jervis Elwas* married; and the Poffeffion was according to this Grant: Whereupon

Whereupon the Question was, If they ought to shew how it came to the Crown? *Hale* Chief Justice said, That by the Statute for Confirmation of Patents, *Temp. Jac.* that Prebend did come to the King. And in *Edw.* 1st's Time was a Device, that all that claimed *Terra Regis* should shew how it came to the Crown, which often vanished away. And in the late Times, in a Trial at this Bar, Mr. *Latch* did nonsuit the Plaintiff upon the Claim of Monastery Lands, although he proved the House had it, because he did not make out how it came to the House; but since that Time the Court have intended it well come to the House, the Possession having went accordingly with it: And he said he was of Counsel in a Trial at Bar for an Impropriation, where it was insisted it was presentative until *Edw.* 4th's Time, and could not be appropriated without the King's Licence, *quod Curia concessit,* and he could not produce the Licence, yet because it was enjoyed ever since *Edw.* 4th's Time as appropriate, the Court did intend a Licence, and that the Patent was lost before the Enrolment; and accordingly the Verdict went then.   The Defendant offered to read a Copy of a Lease out of the Leiger-Book of the Dean and Chapter of *Lincoln*; but it was disallowed by the Court; for the Book itself is but a Copy, and a Copy of a Copy is no Evidence. And in this Case the Court did presume the Grant to King *James* to be lost; and thereupon Judgment was for the Plaintiff.

Monastery Lands.

Possession.

Copy of a Leiger Book.

If Copies of Court Rolls be shewn to prove a customary Estate, the Enjoyment of such Estate must be proved. *Gilb. L. of Evid.* 235.

What Poffef-
fion or Entry
will prevent
the ſtatute of
Limitations.

In Ejectment on a Trial at Bar, the Statute of Limitations was inſiſted on, and theſe Points were ruled *per Cur.* 1. That the Poſſeſſion of one Joint-tenant is the Poſſeſſion of the other, ſo far as to prevent the Statute of Limitations. 2. That a Claim or Entry to prevent the Statute of Limitations muſt be upon the Land, unleſs there be ſome ſpecial Reaſon to the contrary. 3. If one makes an Anſwer in Chancery, which is prejudicial to his Eſtate, it may be given in Evidence againſt him, but

Rental of a
Leaſe in a
Releaſe where
it is Evidence.

not againſt his Alienee. 4. That a Recital of a Leaſe in a Deed of Releaſe, is good Evidence of ſuch Leaſe againſt the Releaſor, and thoſe that claim under him ; but againſt others, it is not without proving there was ſuch a Deed, and it was loſt and deſtroyed. 5. If one Joint-Tenant levies a Fine, it ſevers the Jointure, but does not amount to an Ouſter of his Companion. *Ford* verſus *Grey, Salkeld* 285.

In an Ejectment at a Trial at Bar it was held, that the Anſwer of a Guardian of an Infant in *Chancery*, ſhall not be read againſt the Infant ; for 'tis only to bring the Infant into Court, and to make him a Party. 3 *Mod.* 258. *Eggleſtone & al'* v. *Speke.*

In Ejectment, Defendant claimed as a Purchaſer under a Deviſee of a Will, and to prove ſuch Will, produced a Bill in *Chancery*, brought by the Heir at Law (under whom the Leſſor of the Plaintiff claimed) in which the Will was ſet out, and that was confeſſed by the Anſwer ; but held no Evidence though it was proved the Deviſee had enjoyed the Lands accordingly. 2 *Keb.* 35.

A Parſon

A Parſon in Ejectment muſt prove Admiſ-ſion, Inſtitution and Induction, his Subſcribing the Articles, and Declaring a full and free Aſſent and Conſent to the Book of Common Prayer. *Gilb. Law of Evid.* 231. *ſup.* 519.

But after ten or twenty Years Poſſeſſion the Clergy ſhall not be put to the Proof of thoſe Subſcriptions, for the long Poſſeſſion is a Pre-ſumption, unleſs the contrary is proved. *Gilb. L. of Evid.* 232.

But if the Parſon ſhews Admiſſion, Inſtitu-tion and Induction, he need not ſhew any Right in his Patron on the Ejectment. *Ibid.*

Of Evidence in Treſpaſs.

In an Action againſt an Inn-keeper, he may give in Evidence that he told the Plaintiff that his Houſe was full, and that he could not lodge him, and that, notwithſtanding, the Plaintiff, went in and lodged. *Gilb. Law of Evidence,* 259.

Upon Not guilty in Battery, *ſon Aſſault de-* In Battery. *meſne* is no Evidence ; for thereby the Battery is confeſſed. 1 *Inſt.* 283. Neither is Not guilty good Evidence upon *ſon Aſſault demeſne.*

Upon Not guilty in Treſpaſs, Inſufficiency Treſpaſs. of the Plaintiff's Mounds, or to juſtify for a Miſtake of Rent-Charge, Common, Licence, *Son Aſſault* the Day in an *demeſne,* or the like, is no good Evidence. *Ib.* Appeal, is not material upon But to prove a Treſpaſs before or after the Day Evidence. laid in the Declaration, is good to maintain the Action.   1 *Inſt.* 283.

Upon Not guilty in Treſpaſs in the Plain- Warren. tiff's Warren, Evidence that he hath no War-ren is good. 10 *H.* 6. 17. *Kitchin* 119.

In

In Treſpaſs Evidence of Agiſtment of Beaſts taken into the Land of the Defendant, will maintain the Declaration. *Gilb. Law of Evid.* 239.

Treſpaſs.

Upon Not guilty in Treſpaſs, a Leaſe for Years, 12 *H.* 6. 8. or that *locus in quo, &c.* is the Freehold of another, 4 *E.* 3. 45. is good Evidence ; and ſo of a Gift of Goods ; but upon this he cannot juſtify his Entry upon the Place by a Stranger's Licence, or Command, *Br. General Iſſue,* 81. becauſe this is a Juſtification by Way of Excuſe ; neither is a Leaſe at Will good Evidence in this Caſe.

Not guilty in Treſpaſs.

So upon Not guilty in Treſpaſs for Goods, 'tis good Evidence that the Goods were a Stranger's. 9 *H.* 6. 11. But that they were a Stranger's, and that he, as a Servant to the Stranger; or by his Commandment, took them from the Plaintiff, is not good, *Bro. General Iſſue,* 81. becauſe Treſpaſs is confeſſed. But that the Stranger gave them to the Defendant is good. 9 *H.* 6. 11. In *Treſpaſs* the Buttals muſt be proved as they are laid. 2 *Roll.* 677. *pl.* 1, 2.

The Defendant may plead that he came into the Plaintiff's Cloſe to take his own Horſe, but cannot give it in Evidence. *Gilb. L. of Evid.* 253.

A Right to a Way may be pleaded, but not given in Evidence. *Ibid.* 254.

At a Trial at *Hertford Summer Aſſizes* 10 *W.* 3. in Caſe for ſtopping the Plaintiff's Lights, the Defendant pleaded Not guilty ; and gave in Evidence that the Corporation of *Hertford* were Lords of the Soil, where, *&c.* and preſcribed to ſet up Stalls there, being near the Market Place ; and it was admitted by *Holt* Ch. J. to

J. to be given in Evidence upon the General Iffue, becaufe this is to claim Property in the Soil; but where the Defendant, or he under whom he claims, claim only a particular Benefit; as Common or Eafement, as a Way, and not the Property in the Soil; he ought to plead it fpecially, and not give it in Evidence upon the General Iffue, 10 *W. 3. Kent* v. *Wright,* Ld. *Raym.* 732. See *poftea.*

If the Trefpafs were in Truth done the 4th of *May,* and the Plaintiff alledgeth the fame to be done the 5th of *May,* or the 1ft of *May,* when no Trefpafs was done; yet if upon Evidence it falleth out, that the Trefpafs was done before the Action brought, it fufficeth. 1 *Inft.* 283.

Trefpafs another Day.

And fo in Indictments. 3 *Inft.* 230.

If there be two Batteries between Plaintiff and Defendant at divers Times, the Plaintiff is bound to prove the Battery made the fame Day in the Declaration, and fhall not be admitted to give another Day in Evidence, as the Cafe may be: As in Battery the Defendant pleaded *fon Affault demefne*; and the Plaintiff replied *de injuria fua propria abfque tali caufa*; and in Evidence the Defendant maintained, that the Plaintiff beat him the Day mentioned in the Declaration, and in the fame Place; which the Plaintiff perceiving, he gave in Evidence that the Battery was made another Day and Place; to which the Defendant demurred, upon the Difference aforefaid.

If there be two Trefpaffes, and the Defendant pleads a Juftification; if the Plaintiff replies, de injuria fua propria, &c. he cannot give in Evidence a Trefpafs at another Time; but he fhould have replied, that at another Time, to wit,

the fame Day in his Count, the Defendant did the other Trefpafs, &c. to which the Defendant may plead another Juftification, but the Plaintiff cannot then plead a Trefpafs at another Time, but muft conclude, *Sans tiel caufe,* &c. *vide apres.*

2

Brownlow,

Brownlow, 1 Part, 233. 19 *H.* 6. 47. But up-on Not guilty it is otherwise, though there be never so many Batteries between the Parties. *Littleton*, Sect. 485.

In an Action of Assault and Battery, the Defendant pleads *son Assault demesne* ; the Plain-tiff replies *de Injuria sua propria* ; if on this Issue the Defendant can prove any Assault committed by the Plaintiff on him, tho' it be at a different Day from what laid in the Decla-ration, the Verdict ought to be for Defendant, for the Day is not material ; and on such a Justification the Defendant has the Liberty to prove his Plea at any Time ; and the Plaintiff might have made a new Assignment, and then he would have the Election to prove an Assault made on him at any Time ; for peradventure there may have been several Trespasses at se-veral Times, to which the Defendant may have distinct Answers ; and if such Pleading and Evidence were not allowed, the Defendant could not know for which Trespass the Action was brought, nor how to defend himself. 2 *Roll. Abr.* 680. *C. pl.* 3. and 2 *Roll. Abr.* 687. *K. pl.* 3. 1 *Brownl.* 233. and the like held in *Comberb.* 50.

Count of Trespass done in one Acre, Evi-dence of Trespass done but in Half that Acre, good. 2 *Cro. Winkworth*'s Case. *Gilb. Law of Evid.* 236.

The Lady *Hatton* brought Trespass for breaking her Close, and taking away her Horse, &c. against the Defendants ; they plead Not guilty, as to the taking of (Her) Horse ; as to the rest they say, that the Horse of one of the Defendants was in the Close, &c. and they took him out, doing as little Damage as they
could,

could, *quæ eſt eadem, &c.* The Plaintiff replies, *de injuria ſua propria, &c.*

The Evidence was, That the Plaintiff, as Lady of the Manor, took the Horſe as an Eſtray, and it was cryed and marked, *&c.* that the Defendants refuſed to pay for the Meat, and took him away, before the Year and a Day was out.

1. *Per Wadh. Wyndham* Juſtice of Aſſize : A Lord may detain an Eſtray for Meat, yet no Treſpaſs lies if the Owner takes him, but an Action of the Caſe lies for the Meat.

2. If the Action had been brought againſt the Servant only, he muſt juſtify, *&c.* But being brought againſt Maſter and Servant, this joint Juſtification is good.

Cambr. Summer Aſſizes 1667. Lady *Hatton* verſus *Cotes & al'.*

In Treſpaſs, the Evidence for the Defendant was, That the Defendant had a Barn, and purchaſed a Way over the Plaintiff's Land to that Barn ; after the Defendant bought other Lands lying contiguous to that Barn on the one Side, and to a Haven on the other Side, and carried Carriages by that Way to the Barn, and through it over his own new purchaſed Land to the Haven. *Per Hale* Chief Baron, If I purchaſe a general Way to ſuch a Place, I may go from thence on my own Ground whither I pleaſe, though I purchaſe the Ground after the Way purchaſed. *Summer Aſſize Norf.* 1665, *Heynſworth* verſus *Bird.*

Treſpaſs was brought againſt many, by a School-Miſtreſs, for taking away a Child (her Scholar) with a Scarf of the Miſtreſs's. *Per Kelynge* Chief Juſtice : In Treſpaſs for taking (Things) all are Principals that are preſent and

and confenting ; *contr.* in taking (Perfons); and this Action lies not by the Miftrefs for the Child, but for the Scarf only. *Lent Norf. Aff.* 1663. *Mary Cooper's* Cafe.

Trefpafs lies for Leffee in Ejectment on a fictitious Leafe, to recover mean Profits during the Continuance of that Leafe mentioned on Record : And the Recovery fhall maintain it. Otherwife, if brought by the Leffor, for he is no Party to the Action.

But fee *Siderfin* 239. If a Recovery be in Ejectment, and afterwards Trefpafs is brought for the mean Profits before the Leafe, nothing fhall be given in Evidence but the Value of the Profits, and not the Title ; for otherwife Trials would be infinite.

Alfo if it be between the fame Parties, the Record is an Eftoppel ; and fo the Court held it fhould be if it was againft Under-Tenants.

But *Quære*, If the Defendant be one that has a Title, if he cannot give this in Evidence ; for otherwife it would be a great Mifchief.

Trefpafs lies not for pulling down a Pew in a Church, faftned to a Pillar with a Chain. *Contra,* had it been fixed by Nails driven into the Pillar. *Per Glyn* Chief Juftice. *Trevor's* Cafe, *Gilb. L. of Evid.* 238.

Trefpafs *quare fregit liberam Warrenam fuam,* and took his Conies. In Evidence it appeared that the Plaintiff had Liberty of Chafe in the Place ; which, though it includes Warren, yet a general Trefpafs lies not, but an Action of the Cafe. Earl of *Arundel's* Cafe, *Pafch.* 1658. *B. R.*

Per

Per Earl Serjeant, If Beasts be impounded, and the Key lost, the Officer by Replevin may break the Pound, and deliver the Cattle, *per Stat. Marleberge*, 52 *H.* 3. 21.

Tenants in Common must join in Trespass done against them, so Avowry. *Lead* and *Lamstead's* Case, 7 *Car. B. R.* cited by *Finch* in Argument ; or Tenant in Common surviving shall have Trespass.

If one Tenant in Common bring Trespass without the other, the Defendant must plead this in Abatement, and cannot take Advantage of it on the General Issue ; otherwise in Ejectment. *Gilb. L. of Evid.* 237.

But if one brings the Action against the other, he may take Advantage of this on the General Issue. *Ibid.* 238.

In Trespass the Defendant sets forth a conditional Feoffment for Payment of Money at such a Day and Place, and that he paid it accordingly ; Issue joined on the Payment at the Day and Place ; Evidence of Payment before the Day, is not good. *Contra*, had the special Matter been pleaded with Acceptance. *Moor* 47.

In Trespass with *Continuando*, to recover mean Profits, an Entry and Possession of the Land before the Trespass must be proved, and also another Entry after the Trespass. ¹ Leon. 302.

' In Trespass, the Defendant prescribes to dig in the Common for Clay, to repair ancient Houses holden of that Manor, and good. *Berney* versus *Stafford*, *Norfolk Lent Assizes* 1667.

In Trespass they were at Issue on Not Guilty, at the Assizes Defendant left his former Plea, and pleaded an Accord with Satisfaction ;

faction; the Judge would have had it replied to, and tried prefently, but the Council refufed; whereupon the Jury was fworn, and the Plaintiff nonfuited. *Bedford Lent Affizes* 1667. *Green* verfus *Reynolds.* But this was contrary to the Opinion of Sir *Orlando Bridgman* at the fame Affizes, and contrary to 10 *H.* 7. 21. and 1 *Bul.* 92.

Trefpafs lies by Recoverer in an erroneous Judgment in Ejectment for a mean Trefpafs, becaufe the Plaintiff in a Writ of Error recovers all mean Profits, and the Law by Fiction of Relation will not make a Wrong-doer difpunifhable. 13 *Rep. Co.* 22. but *contra,* where Act of Parliament reftores, &c.

Trefpafs for Affault and wounding in *Suff.* Defendant as to *Vi & armis non Cul.* as to the other, Juftification of *molliter manus, &c.* in *Norf.* and feveral Trials, *per Hale* Chief Baron, *Suff. Aff. Summer* 1668. The *Vi & armis* cannot be tried 'till the other be tried. *Contra,* If the firft Iffue of *Non Cul.* was as to the Wounding; and by him Evidence of Livery of Seifin generally, fhall be intended for Life only.

Sen Affault demefne. Defendant proved Plaintiff threatned him, by faying, " Were it not Affize time, he would tell him more of his Mind," which he faid, bending his Fift, and with his Hand on his Sword. *Per Cur.* This is no Affault, as it would be without that Declaration : But it was farther fworn, the Plaintiff with his Elbow punched the Defendant; which, if done in earneft Difcourfe, and not with Intent of Violence, is no Affault, nor then is it a Juftification of Battery after a Retreat. *Keb.* 2 Part 545.

2

The

The Hogs of *B.* were put into the Yard of *A.* and broke into the Land of *C.* and did Trespass: Action lies against *A.* though the Servant of *B.* did look to them and serve them, by which the Owner had the special Possession of them. So if agisted Cattle do trespass, the Agistor shall answer. *Dawtry versus Higgins, Clayton* 33. *per Barkley,* 11 *Car. York.*

A. by Indenture of Uses raised an Estate to *B.* in Fee, who regrants Turbary to *A.* by another Deed, and after *A.* levies a Fine to confirm the Estate and Uses abovesaid declared ; this doth not touch the Turbary. *Per Vernon* 11 *Car. York, Clayton* 42.

Any one employed by an Officer, is an Officer within 7 *Jac.* 5. to plead General Issue, and give the special Matter in Evidence. *Clayton* 54.

Prescription to tether *Equos & Boves* upon such a Balk, *Mares* and *Cows* good Evidence within that Prescription. *Per Berkley, Clayton* 54.

In Trespass Defendant justified, by Reason that he, and all those whose Estate he had in such an House from Time out of Memory had Common for so many Beasts; and Issue being joined on the Prescription, it appeared, that this Common belonged to the House, by Reason of Vicinage ; and held that the Defendant had not proved his Issue ; because that Common, by Reason of Vicinage, does not only begin by the bare Prescription, but there is also with the Prescription this Consideration, that the other Party shall have Common in like Manner in his Land. 13 *H.* 7. 13. *b.*

Trespass *de Clauso fracto.* The Defendant prescribes to have Common, and Issue was joined thereon; the Jury found that the Defendant had Common by Prescription, *prout*, paying for it every Year one Penny to the Plaintiff; held that the Defendant failed in his Prescription; for a Prescription is intire, and Payment of the Penny is Parcel of it. *Croke Eliz.* 546, 563. *Noy* 59.

Trespass for taking away Timber; Defendant pleads a Custom in the Manor, to have the same as Estovers to be burnt *in Terris & Tenementis*; and Issue being taken on the Custom, Defendant only proved the Custom as to the Messuage; and held this did not maintain his Issue. *Godb.* 234. Bishop of *Chichester* versus *Strodwich.*

Per Hale, A Corporation may bargain and sell, though it has been thought an Use upon Use, they being seised to the Use of their House: But I think it rather a Trust than an Use.

If a Justice of Peace send his Warrant to *J. S.* (who is no Officer) to bring one before him, if *J. S.* be no Officer, he is not bound to execute it, yet if he does execute it, it is good, and he may execute it in any Part of the County. And so a Constable of one Town may execute a Warrant in any other Town in the same County, and any such Warrant is as large as the Justice's Commission is. *Per Hale, Norf. Summer Assizes* 1668. *Wrongrie's* Case.

In Trespass against one for gleaning on his Ground; *per Hale, Norf. Summer Assizes* 1668. The Law gives Licence to the Poor to glean, *&c.* by the general Custom of *England,* but

the Licence muſt be pleaded ſpecially, and cannot be given in Evidence on *non Cul. Gilb. L.
of Evid.* 253.

In Treſpaſs *quare Clauſum & Domum fregit
& alia enormia ei intulit* ; after Verdict for
the Plaintiff, and 60 *l.* Damages, 'twas moved for
a new Trial by reaſon of exceſſive Damages;
and upon Affidavit that the Jury intended
great Part of the Damages for the Injury the
Defendant did to the Plaintiff's Daughter,
under Colour of marrying her, *&c.* which
came in under the *& alia enormia*, the Plaintiff had Judgment ; and a Difference was taken, that Damages *ex turpi cauſa* may be given in Evidence under this general Clauſe, *&
alia enormia*, but from nothing elſe. *Siderfin*
225. *Sippora* verſus *Baſſet.*

Joint-tenancy in Treſpaſs cannot be given in
Evidence ; but muſt be pleaded in Abatement.
Jones verſus *Randall, Hill.* 1652. *C. B.*

In Treſpaſs for taking Goods after Judgment 2 Cro. 551.
by Confeſſion, *Non ſum informatus,* or *Nil dicit,*
Property need not be proved to a Writ of Inquiry ; for it would oppoſe the firſt Judgment,
quod querens recuperet, and the Judges might 2 Cro. 220.
have aſſeſſed Damages if they would, *Yelv.* 151.
yet *quære,* if the Defendant may not diſprove
Property in Mitigation of Damages; for the
Jury may find no Damages.

In Treſpaſs *quare clauſum fregit,* with Abut- What ought
tals, all the Abuttals and Deſcriptions muſt be to be proved
proved.   But if the Abuttal be laid North, *&c.* in Evidence.
and it incline North, though not directly, it is Abuttals.
ſufficient, *& ſic de cæteris.*   2 Roll 678.
                                                 pl. 2.
If the Defendant plead *ſon Aſſault demeſne* Son Aſſault
in Battery, and the Plaintiff reply *de injuria* demeſne in
ſua propria abſque tali cauſa, and ſo Iſſue is Battery.

joined; if there was a Battery at another Day than what the Plaintiff and Defendant have affigned, by the Plaintiff, upon the Defendant, the Verdict ought to be for the Defendant; for if the Defendant prove an Affault made upon him by the Plaintiff, this ought to be found for him, although it was at another Day than what he hath alledged, for the Day is not material: For upon fuch fpecial Juftification the Defendant hath Liberty to prove his Plea at any Time, and the Plaintiff might have made a new Affignment at another Time; for peradventure there might be feveral Trefpaffes at feveral Times, to which the Defendant may have feveral Pleas; and therefore if fuch Manner of Pleading fhould not be allowed, and fuch Evidence, the Defendant could not tell how to help himfelf, nor could know for what Trefpafs the Action is brought. *Vide devant hic & apres. Rolle, Trial,* 680. *pl.* 3.

Servant. If my Servant without my Confent put my Cattle in the Land of another, I may plead Not guilty, and give this Matter in Evidence; for by putting the Cattle in, the Servant has gained a Property. *Ibid.* 682. *pl.* 4.

Parcel. In Trefpafs for taking a Stack of Corn, the Evidence may be of Part, and the Verdict as to four Combs or Bufhels, Guilty; and as to the reft, Not guilty. *Ibid.* 684. *pl.* 6.

Mic. 22 Car. 1. For making a Trefpafs *Continuando*, there
Continuando. ought to be a Re-entry of the Plaintiff, and for the not proving thereof, the Plaintiff fhall have Damages only for the firft Entry. *Infra* 547.

Trefpafs. In Trefpafs *quare Claufum fregit,* the Defendant fays, that *locus in quo, &c.* is fix Acres in *D.* which is his Freehold: The Plaintiff replies, that it is his Freehold, and not the Defendant's;

4   fendant's;

fendant's; the Defendant cannot give in Evidence other .six Acres in *D.* which are his Freehold, becaufe the Plea fhall be intended to refer to the fix Acres of the Plaintiff's. *Dyer* 23.

The Defendant cannot give a Licence, or defect of Inclofures, in Evidence. *Gilb. Law of Evid.* 252, 3.

Upon the General Iffue, any Thing may be gi- Regula. *ven in Evidence, which proves the Plaintiff had no Caufe of Action.*

Trefpafs by the Warden of the *Fleet*; upon Trefpafs. Not guilty, you may give in Evidence, that he is not Warden. 4 *E.* 4. 7.

So in Trefpafs of a Houfe, that he had no Houfe there, or the Freehold of another, and not of the Plaintiff, is good Evidence upon Not guilty: But in Trefpafs of Goods, 'tis no good Plea to fay, the Property was in another, although it is in a Replevin; and therefore it feems to be no good Evidence in Trefpafs, becaufe Poffeffion maintains the Action againft all but the Owner; but that the Property was in a Stranger, and he gave them to the Defendant, is good. But in Trover, that they were not the Goods of the Plaintiff, is good Evidence. 5 *H.* 7. 3.

Ceffavit, and **Count** of divers Lands held *Ceffavit.* by intire Service, upon *Non tenuit modo & forma,* held by feveral Services is not good Evidence, for he had no fuch Caufe of Action. 10 *H.* 7. 24.

Upon the General Iffue, for the Defendant by Regula. *Evidence to convey to himfelf the fame Intereft and Title, is good Evidence.*

As

Trefpafs.   As in Trefpafs of Gofhawks, Not guilty, and Evidence, that he had a Leafe of that Wood for Years where they were taken, is good, for it is his Title.

Account.   Account of Receipt by the Hands of *J. S.* the Defendant pleads *Ne unques fon Receiver,* and Evidence that *J. S.* gave this to him, is good. 2 *H.* 4. 13. So in Trefpafs, a Leafe for Years, Tenancy at Sufferance, (but not at Will) that they were a Stranger's Goods, who gave them to the Defendant, is good Evidence upon Not guilty. 22 *Aff.* 73. becaufe by thefe Matters he makes himfelf a Title ; *et fic de cæteris.*

Regula.   *Upon the General Iffue, if by the Evidence the Defendant acknowledge that he did the Wrong, and juftify this, and gives Matter that goes to difcharge him of the Act by Juftification, this Evidence is not good, but he ought to have pleaded it.*

This Rule is demonftrated by thofe Cafes, where, upon Not guilty in Trefpafs, the Defendant would fay the Property was in a Stranger, and that by his Commandment, or as his Servant, he took the Goods. Not guilty, and that he did the Battery *fe defendendo.* Not guilty in Maintenance, and lawful Maintenance. Infufficiency of Mounds. The Freehold of a Stranger, and his Licence. A former Recovery in another Action. So for Common, Rent-fervice, Rent-charge, Licence, *&c.* cannot be given in Evidence upon the General Iffue ; for thefe Matters in Evidence are Juftifications, which go in Difcharge of the Party, not by Title, but by Juftification,

So

So where an Imprisonment or Entry is given by Authority of Law, or by Authority from any Party, as for an Imprisonment by the Statute, against Trespassers in Parks, putting a Man off his Ground, thrusting a Man out of Church that troubles the Congregation in Service, parting an Affray, and keeping the Quarrellers apart, in Defence, of himself or his. Entry in Perambulation. Entry to amend his Gutter leading to his House, as of ancient Time had been used. That it was a common Inn. That he put in his Cattle by the Plaintiff's Agreement. That he entred and took the Emblements after the Death of the Tenant for Life. That the Plaintiff owed him Money, and by his Invitation he went into his House to receive it. That he took the Goods as a Heriot, Waif, Estray, or Wreck. Or the Plaintiff took away the Defendant's Cattle, and he entred into the Close where they were, and took them again. That he took the Cattle Damage-feasant in his Ground, or for an Amercement in a Leet, &c. That the Goods were the Goods of *J. S.* who delivered them to the Plaintiff to keep, and *J. S.* commanded the Defendant to take them; or excuse it, that the Plaintiff delivered them to him. That he took them by a Writ. That as Schoolmaster he gave modeate Correction. *These are Excuses and Justifications without Title, and therefore must be pleaded, and cannot be given in Evidence upon Not guilty.*

So in an Action *de malefactoribus in parcis,* he cannot plead Not guilty, and give a Licence in Evidence. So in an Appeal, if he plead Not guilty, and shews that he was Sheriff, and executed his Office, or that he was Forester,

and

and killed him becaufe he fled, and would not fubmit. *Vide* 12 *H.* 8. *f.* 1. the beft Cafe of this Matter.

Trefpafs *quare Domum & Claufum fregit & bona afportavit.* The Defendant did the Trefpafs by Virtue of a Commiffion of Bankruptcy ; held that the Defendant muft juftify, and cannot plead Not guilty, and give the fpecial Matter in Evidence ; but if the Trefpafs had been only for taking the Goods, he might. *Littleton Rep.* 356.

Trefpafs for entring his Clofe and taking away Corn. Defendant pleads that he was Servant to the Parfon, and that the Corn was Tithes fevered. Plaintiff demurred fpecially, as amounting to the general Iffue ; but the Plea was held good ; for as to the breaking the Clofe, fuch Matter cannot be given in Evidence ; but if the Trefpafs had been only for taking the Corn, it had been only the General Iffue, and the Demurrer had been good. 2 *Keb.* 44.

Trefpafs.

In Trefpafs for Goods taken, the Defendant, upon Not guilty, in Mitigation of Damages, may give in Evidence, That the Plaintiff had is Goods again. 11 *H.* 4. 24. 19 *H.* 6. 34.

Falfe Imprifonment.

Upon Not guilty, the Defendant gave in Evidence, That by the Plaintiff's Agreement he carried him from *D.* to *S.* and held good, becaufe, what is done by the Plaintiff's Agreement, is no Imprifonment. 14 *H.* 6. 2.

In an Action for falfe Imprifonment, the Defendant may give in Evidence, that he took the Plaintiff by Virtue of a Warrant from a Juftice of Peace, by the 7 *J.* 1. *Gilb. Law of Evid.* See *poftea. p.*

See *poftea. p.*

Tenant

Tenant for Life leaseth for Years, who is Emblements.
ousted, and the Tenant for Life is disseised: Knivet s
The Disseisor leaseth for Years, his Lessee sows Case, Lib.
the Land; the Tenant for Life dies; he in Re- 5. 85.
mainder in Fee brings Trespass against the
Defendants claiming the Corn sown by the Lessee
of the Disseisor. Adjudged, That the Defendants
had not the meer Right; but in respect of
their Possession, they should bar the Plaintiff,
who had no Right; and that the meer Right
was in the Lessee of the Tenant for Life, and
that he might bring Trespass against the Lessee
of the Disseisor, and recover all the mean Profits. But as to the Entry into the Land to
take the Emblements, this was good Matter of
Justification; but in regard it was not pleaded,
it could not be given in Evidence upon Not
guilty; and therefore the Plaintiff had Judgment for the Entry, and was barred for the
Residue. *Note,* That the Lessee of Tenant
for Life had Right to the Land, and by Consequence to the Emblements, as Things annexed
to the Land, and the Death of the Tenant for
Life determines his Interest to the Land, but
his Right to the Emblements remains.

Trespass concerning the Rectory of *Norton-* Note Leon.
Pinckney, which belongs to *Oriel College* in *Ox-* 3 Part 210.
ford. The Issue was, if there was a Vicarage admit a Thing
endowed there, or only a stipendiary Curate. *per nient dedire,*
the Jury is
not bound by it; but where upon the pleading a special Matter is confessed, the Jury shall be bound by it.

1. All agreed, That if a Vicarage be erected
and established, if there was no Endowment *de
facto* of the Vicarage, the Vicar could not claim
any Thing.

2. There

Impropria-tion.

2. There was shewed an Impropriation, by the Licence of the Pope, made in the Time of *E.* 2. *Dodderidge* said, That was not good. *Jones è contra.* And it will be perilous to such ancient Impropriations, if now the Consent of the King must be shewed; and at that Time it was held good by the Assent of the Pope without the King. *Dodderidge* denied that the Pope without the King at that Time could make an Impropriation with the Ordinary and Patron. But *Crew* agreed with *Jones.* And in Things of such Antiquity *omnia præsumuntur solempniter esse acta,* and said, that so it was ruled in a Case before: And *Jones* said, it was nothing to the Vicar, for the Vicarage may be endowed without the Consent of the King, and it is not *Mortmain.* *Palmer's Reports* 427. *Erasmus Cope's* Case against *Bedford.*

Trespass; the Defendant pleads, that the Place where was his Freehold; and upon that Issue was joined. The Jury found that the Defendant married a Woman who was seised in Fee of the Place where, and that thereby Baron and Feme in the Right of the Wife were seised. Held by three Judges that Defendant had not proved his Plea. 2 *Anderson* 48.

Hors de son Fee.

Where *hors de son Fee* is pleaded, a Release of the Seigniory is good Evidence. 8 *E.* 2. 262.

Trespass. Freehold.

In Trespass against two for entring into the Plaintiff's Land, if one pleads his Freehold, and the other, that he entred by the Commandment of him that pleads it is his Freehold, here is to be but one Issue joined, *viz.* by him that claims the Interest, for upon that Issue all depends:

depends: If it be found againſt him, his Servant has no Colour.

Defendant may give in Evidence, that the Right of the Freehold was in *A.* and that he entred by his Command. *Gilb. L. of Evid.* 258.

In Aſſault and Battery, if the Plaintiff prove only the Aſſault, he ſhall recover, for an Action of Treſpaſs lies for an Aſſault. Of an Aſſault and Battery, Aſſault and Menace, &c. See *Roll.* Tit. *Treſpaſs,* 545. *F. N. B.* 91. a. &c. [margin: Battery. Aſſault.]

To lay Hands gently upon the Shoulders of a Man, and ſay, that is he againſt whom the Juſtice's Warrant is: Or to ſerve him with a *Subpœna,* proves no Battery.

Theſe Things following are good Juſtifications, but cannot be given in Evidence upon the General Iſſue.

Correction by the Parties, Maſter, or School-miſtreſs; Apprehenſion of a common Cheater at Dice, *Molliter manus impoſuit,* upon one ſetting a Dog upon him. Beating one by the Huſband in Defence of his Wife, by the Maſter in Defence of his Servant; or by the Servant in Defence of his Maſter. Holding a Man that cometh to ſtop the River to his Mill, or to throw down his Booth. Inevitably diſcharging his Muſket in the Plaintiff's Face at a Muſter. Beating one in Defence of his Poſſeſſion of his Goods, Houſe, Lands, Goods diſtrained, &c. by a Foreſter, of one who reſiſted in the Foreſt. That he impriſoned another to prevent Miſchief. As the holding of another with whom he was fighting, (not wrangling with Words) until the Fury be over. [margin: Lunacy will not excuſe in Battery, although it will of Felony. *Note*; a Man may juſtify an Aſſault and Battery, but not wounding or maiming of Life or Member, or Mayhem, in Defence of the Poſſeſſion of his Lands or Goods. 2 Inſt. 316.]

An

Tenant in Common cannot justify to enter into his Companion's Ground to take the Horse they have in Common, altho' he may take him elsewhere.

An erroneous Process to an Officer out of a Court having Jurisdiction, in Aid of the Bailiffs. That the Executor entred the Plaintiff's Ground to take the Testator's Timber there. That he had a Piscary, and put Stakes in the Soil. Taking his Goods stolen, in the Plaintiff's House, upon fresh Pursuit. Entring his Soil to throw down a Nusance. Or to take my Cattle, which the Plaintiff put in his Ground. To throw down the Plaintiff's House on Fire, next mine. Breaking his Windows or House to get out, where he imprisoned me. To take a Handful of Grain out of his Heap, who took one out of mine, and threw it into his. To carry away his Grain or Money which he threw into my Heap. To chase his Cattle with a Dog out of my Ground, Damage-feasant. To throw that into the Plaintiff's Ground which he threw into mine. That my Cattle took a Mouthful, &c. of his Grass passing in the Way I had over his Ground, against my Will. Throwing Goods into the *Thames* out of a Barge, to save the Lives of the Passengers. To fetch out of the Plaintiff's Ground the Trees he granted me. To dig his Ground to mend my Pipe there. That I hunted Cattle out of my Ground with a Dog, which against my Will run into his Ground, I rating and recalling him. A Prescription to cut Grass in the Plaintiff's Ground lying nigh the Church, to estrow the Church, being but an Easement.

Defendant may justify, by reason of a Prescription, but cannot give it in Evidence. *Gilb. Law of Evid.* 257.

Distress

Diſtreſs by a Stranger as Bailiff, and the Aſſent of the Party.   By the Command of the
Chief Juſtice, Order of Chancery, &c.   *Roll.*
Tit. *Treſpaſs*, 559. That the Plaintiff ought to
impale againſt a Foreſt ; and for Default of
Pales, the Beaſts went in, and the Foreſter
fetched them out.

Theſe are Juſtifications and Excuſes that muſt
be pleaded, and cannot be given in Evidence
upon Not guilty, unleſs it be in Mitigation of
Damages.

Treſpaſs lies for Goods ſtolen, although the Treſpaſs.
Thief be convicted of Felony. *Latch* 144.
Markham's Caſe. And ſo I knew my Lord *Hale*
held, although in *Roll.* Tit. *Treſpaſs*, 557, it is
ſaid, if it appears on the Evidence that it was
Felony, Treſpaſs lies not.   Which I think is Felony.
not Law.

A Man who ſows the Lands to Halves with Sows to
the Owner, or three agree to ſow the Land, Halves.
where two of them have no Intereſt, if a
Stranger take the Corn, they cannot join in
Treſpaſs, having no Intereſt but an Agreement ; but the Owner only muſt bring the
Treſpaſs. *Cro.* 3 Part 143. *Goldsb.* 77.

Upon reverſing an Outlawry, the Party is Outlawry
reſtored, and may have Treſpaſs ; but upon reverſed.
Reverſal of a Judgment the Party ſhall only
be reſtored to the Money for which the Sheriff
ſold his Term, upon a *Fieri fac'. Cro.* 3 Part
270.

Upon Not guilty in Treſpaſs *quare Clauſum* Tenancy in
fregit, at the Trial the Defendant ſhall not ſay, Common.
that the Plaintiff is Tenant in Common, he Where Tenants in Com-
mon ſhall join
in an Action, and where not, and what Actions the one ſhall have againſt
the other.   See 1 Inſt. 197, 200, &c.   Godb. 172.

ſhould

should have pleaded this, and hath now loft his Advantage ; and if the Jury find it, their finding is not material. *Cro.* 3 Part 554.

Trefpafs by *Rofs* for breaking his Clofe, and beating his Servants; on Not guilty the Jury found, That Sir *T. Bromley* was feifed in Fee of the Place where, and leafed the fame to the Plaintiff and one *A.* which *A.* affigned his Moiety to *C.* by whofe Command the Defendant entred. Held by the Court, that this Tenancy in Common betwixt the Plaintiff and *A.* under whom the Defendant juftified, might be given in Evidence on this Iffue. 3 *Leon.* 83.

In Trefpafs *quare claufum fregit,* it is a Plea in Abatement to fay, that the Plaintiff is Tenant in Common with another, but cannot be given in Evidence on Not guilty, as it may where one Tenant in Common brings Trefpafs againft the other. 1 *Vent.* 214.

Trefpafs againft *A.* and *B.* for taking Water out of Plaintiff's Well : *A.* pleads in Abatement, that *B.* and the Plaintiff were Tenants in Common of the Well; and Plaintiff replied he was fole feifed. And *Holt* Ch. J. held it was no Plea in Abatement, for a Defendant to fay he was Tenant in Common with the Plaintiff, becaufe he may give it in Evidence on Not guilty ; but that this Defendant, who was a Stranger, might well plead the Tenancy in Common of the Plaintiff and other Defendant. 1 *Salk.* 4. *Farrefl.* 104.

Woods.

A Man fells all his Woods ftanding, growing, *&c.* upon the Premiffes, to hold during the Life of the Vendor, rendring Rent ; the Vendee cuts down all the Trees : If he cuts

Wood

Wood afterwards growing in the same Place, the Vendor may have Trespass. *Leon.* 3 Part 7.

Trespass lies for a Copyholder against the Lord for cutting down Trees, that he the Tenant ought to have for Repairs. *Godbolt* 173. **Copyholder.**

If the Recoveror brings Trespass, though the Judgment be reversed by Writ of Error, he may give this Matter in Evidence, and maintain his Declaration. *Gilb. Law of Evid.* 239.

By Seizure of an Estray, the Lord hath but the Custody and not the Property; and therefore if he works the Horse, Trespass lies. *Yelverton* 96, 97. **Estray.**

Trespass with a *Continuando* cannot be for taking a Horse, nor ten Trees, &c. nor without a Re-entry by the Disseised, unless his Re-entry be taken away by the Act of God, or the estate be determined so as he cannot enter; as if Tenant *pur auter vie* be disseised, and *Cestui que vie* die, for there his Entry is taken away by the Act of God; otherwise if it be taken by his own Act, as if he release to the Disseisor, &c. 19 H. 6. 28. **Continuando. Roll. Trial, 549. & I. 550 sup. 536.**

Upon *Non cul.* no Park by Prescription or Grant is good Evidence. 18 H. 6. 22. **Parco fracto.**

General Trespass for breaking his Park, and taking his Deer, &c. doth not lie at Common Law, but a Writ is given by the Statute *West.* 1. *cap.* 20. So if *A.* have a free Warren in the Soil of *B. A.* shall not have Trespass, but Case, for entring the Warren and stopping the Holes, &c. *Roll. Trial,* 550. L. **Park.** **Warren.**

A Commoner cannot have Trespass for the Grass. After a *Supersedeas* shewed to the Bailiffs, false Imprisonment lies against them, not **Commoner. False Imprisonment.**

against

againft the Sheriff; fo againft the Bailiff of a Franchife, if he takes other Men's Goods in Execution upon the Sheriff's Warrant; not againft the Sheriff, nor againft the Party, unlefs he procure the Plaintiff to take the Wrong. See *ante p.*

Roll. Trial, 552.

Poffeffion.

He that hath the Freehold in Law, unlefs he hath actual Poffeffion, cannot have Trefpafs; therefore the Heir cannot have Trefpafs againft the Abator, nor againft the Tenant at Sufferance before he hath entred, and only from that Time:

Relation.

But an Executor or Adminiftrator fhall, by Relation, have Trefpafs from the Death of the Inteftate, &c. But a Diffeifee after Entry, fhall have an Action for all mean Trefpaffes from the Diffeifin, even againft Strangers, for he is reftored to the Poffeffion *ab initio. Roll. Trial,* 553. *S.* 554. *T.*

Trefpafs.

Trefpafs cannot be maintained againft him who comes by the Goods lawfully, as by the Plaintiff's Delivery, or under that, or by Act in Law, &c. *but Detinue.* But Trefpafs lies againft Tenant at Will, or him that I lend my Goods to, who deftroys them; for thereby the Privity is determined. It lies againft a Miller for taking Toll where none is due; for taking my Servant out of my Service; for refcuing one taken at my Suit out of the Bailiff's Hands, for the Bailiff is my Servant. For beating my Wife or Servant, *per quod,* &c. Not againft him that *J. S.* fells my Horfe to, or has my Goods from the Sheriff, although the Sheriff took them wrongfully. *Roll. Trial,* 555, 556. It lies for hunting a Fox, &c. in my Ground. Againft Churchwardens, who act by the Juftices of the Peace's Warrant, if the Warrant be not good.

For

For digging so near my Ground that it fell into the Defendant's Pit: But not that my House fell into the Pit, for it was my Fault to build so near another Man's Ground: For entring my Ground, to take out his Falcon, which flew thither after Game. For killing my Tumbler in his Warren.

The Defendant may prevail on Not guilty in Trefpafs, by making Title to the Land. *Gilb. Law of Evid.* 242.

Qu. By making Title to the Profits. *Ibid.* 242, 3.

Although I fell the Goods, it lies for a Trefpafs done before. Tender of fufficient Amends before the Action brought, is a good Bar for a *negligent* Trefpafs, not for a *voluntary* one. — Time. — Bar.

If a Man enter into a Place by Authority of Law, and abufe this Authority, he is a Trefpaffer *ab initio*, for his firft Entry fhall be intended for this Purpofe. As if the Leffor enter to view Wafte, and ftay all Night. If the King's Purveyor fells my Goods. If the Searcher abufes my Stuff. If a Man will ftay in a Tavern all Night. If he detains a Diftrefs after Amends tendred before impounding. If a Bailiff refufe Bail, Trefpafs doth not lie againft him *ab initio*, but Cafe; for the Sheriff or Under-Sheriff, not he, ought to take Bail; not againft the Party nor Bailiff, or Perfon in Aid, if the Sheriff doth not return his Writ of *Latitat*, or makes a falfe Return; but it doth againft the Sheriff: So of an Officer of an inferior Court. — *Ab initio.* Roll. Trial, 561. G.

If the Lord work an Eftray, Diftrefs, *&c.* or Executors find a Bond and cancel it, thinking it was difcharged, and it was not; they are

Vol. II.   P   Trefpaffers

Trespassers *ab initio*, although they came lawfully to the Possession at first. *Roll.* Tit. *Trespass*, 563.

Lunatick. The Lunatick (and not the Person to whom he is committed) must bring the Action in his Name for a Trespass done in the Land. *Brownl.* 1 Part 196.

In Trespass on Not guilty the Defendant cannot give Evidence that the Place was a Highway. In Trespass *quare Clausum fregit,* Not guilty was pleaded ; and on Trial the Defendant gave Evidence, that it was in a Highway. *Et per Cur',* It is a special Justification, and ought not to be allowed to be given in Evidence on the General Issue. *Holt said,* in Case for disturbing the Plaintiff of his Common : Upon Not guilty pleaded, he had known the Defendant permitted to give in Evidence, That he had a Right to Common there, but he never thought it right, and had never allowed it. *Watson* versus *Sparks, Salk.* 287. *antea.*

In Trespass for digging a Hole in the Way, whereby his Horse fell in, *&c.* the Plaintiff must prove the Way, and that the Defendant dug the Hole. *Gilb. L. of Evid.* 241.

If a Man be proved dead, when it is declared he assumed, Proof of a Promise at another Day, is good ; but in Trespass, Proof of his Death on the Day discharges the Action. *Gilb. L. of Evid.* 241, 242.

Note; That if upon Evidevce it falls out, the Trespass was done before the Action brought, it suffices. *Gilb. L. of Evid.* 241.

Of

Of Evidence in Affault.

In Trefpafs of Affault, Battery, and Wounding, the Defendant pleaded the Plaintiff began firft, and the Stroke he received, whereby he loft his Eye, was on his own Affault, and in Defence of the Defendant; and on Trial at Bar, now by Evidence it appeared, the Plaintiff threatned the Defendant, and faid, Were it not Affize Time, he would tell him more of his Mind, which was faid, bending his Fift, and with his Hand on his Sword: Yet, *Per Cur.* This is no Affault, as it would be without that Declaration: But it was farther fworn, that the Plaintiff with his Elbow punched the Defendant; which, if done in earneft Difcourfe, and not with Intention of Violence, is no Affault, nor then is it a Juftification of Battery after a Retreat; as *Phineas Andrew*'s Cafe: And the Jury, not believing the Defendant, found for the Plaintiff, and gave 500 *l.* Damages. *Vin. Abr.* Tit. *Evid.* 85. *pl.* 1. cites 2 *Keb.* 545. *pl.* 13. *M.* 21 *Car.* 2. *B. R. Turbervile* verfus *Savage.*

In Action of Battery, which was laid in the Declaration to be 18th Day of *February* 1621. Defendant pleaded *Son Affault demefne, &c.* and Iffue upon that, and the Defendant proved an Affault by the Plaintiff, but at another Day, and ruled that this does not prove this Iffue for the Defendant, becaufe the Juftification fhall refer to the Time laid in the Declaration, if the Defendant do not difference the Times in his Plea; and in fuch Cafe, when the Defendant intends to fhew the Affault was at another Day and Place, he fhall fhew that fuch a

Day

Day before that in the Declaration, as here, 8th *February*, the Plaintiff did affault him, and would have beaten him ; and traverfe the Day in the Declaration. *Vin. Abr.* Tit. *Evid.* 86. *pl.* 2. cites *Clayt.* 110. *pl.* 187. *March* 24 *Car. Turner* Serjeant, Judge of Affize, *Hard-caftle* v. *Lockwood.*

But fee in the Cafe of an Officer who is not tied up to fpecial Pleading; it feems he, upon Not guilty, may vary in his Evidence, to juftify from the Time in the Declaration, &c. *Quod Nota* ; and the Prejudice may come to the Plaintiff's being unprovided perhaps in fuch Cafe to a Reply; whereas when the Matter pleaded is brought to a fpecial Iffue, he knows his Work, &c. 24 *Car.* Hardcaftle ver. *Lock-wood, Clayt.* 110. *Vin. Abr.* 86. *p.* 3.

Concerning Belief.

It is *no Satisfaction for a Witnfes to fay, that he thinks or perfuades himfelf*, and this for two Reafons, by *Coke* ; 1ft, Becaufe the Judge is to give abfolute Sentence, and ought to have more Ground than Thinking. 2dly, That Judges, as Judges, are always to give Judgment *fecundum allegata et probata*, notwithftanding that pri-vate Perfons think otherwife. *Vin. Abr.* Title *Evid.* 86. cites *Dy.* 53. *b. Marg. pl.* 15. *Mich.* 19 *Jac.* in the Star-Chamber. *Adams* verfus *Canon.*

Of

Of Evidence in Trover.

In Trover two Things ought to be proved, Trover. the *Property* and the *Converfion*.

Upon Not guilty in Trover and Converfion, a Demand and Denial of the Goods, is good Evidence of the Converfion (*a*); but when the Goods come to the Defendant by Trover, there muft be an actual Demand and Denial. *Plow.* 14. *lib.* 10. 57. *Cro.* 1 Part, *ult. pub.* 495. *Hob.* 187. *Moor* 460. *Abridg. Roll.* 5. *Gilb. L. of Evid.* 260, 261.

In Trover for Corn to prove a Converfion, it was proved that Plaintiff demanded Satif-faction for the Corn; and held good Evidence, tho' the Corn itfelf was not demanded. *Clayton* 122.

Upon Not guilty in Trover, the Defendant may give in Evidence, That the Goods were pawned to him for 10 *l.* that he diftrained them for Rent or Damage-feafant: That as Sheriff, he levied them upon Execution, or that he took them as Tithes fevered. *Cro.* 1 Part 157. 3 Part 435. *Hob.* 187. A Demand and Denial of the Goods is Evidence of a Converfion.

If Trover be for bare Money, a Requeft and Denial is fo ftrong a Prefumption of Converfion, that nothing can be proved to the contrary; but if it be for Money in a Bag it is not conclufive Evidence. *Gilb. L. of Evid.* 262.

(*a*) If an unjuft taking of Goods be proved, this is good Proof of a Converfion, though there be no Proof of a Demand and Refufal. *Gilb. L. of Evid.* 266.

In Trover, Defendant cannot give a Releafe in Evidence, but he ought to have pleaded it. *E.* 10 *W.* 3. *B. R. Kingfton* v. *Read,* at *Guildhall. Comb.* 473.

In Trover an actual tortious taking of the Goods was proved; and held good Evidence without proving a Demand, for that is an actual Conversion; but *contra* where the Goods are found, there a Demand must be proved. 1 *Sid.* 264. *Brewen* versus *Roe.*

Trover of five Kine; on Not guilty a Special Verdict was found, That *B.* was possessed of these five Kine, and put them to pasture with the Defendant, and agreed to pay one Shilling a Week for each, as long as they continued at Pasture; that afterwards *B.* sold them to the Plaintiff, who demanded them of Defendant, who refused to deliver them, unless Plaintiff would pay for the Pasturage, which came to 10 *l.* and held this Denial a Conversion; for he cannot detain the Cattle against him that brought them, till the 10 *l.* paid, but is drove to his Action against him that put them there; and is not like the Case of an Inn-keeper or Taylor, who may detain till paid. *Cro. Car.* 271.

In Trover it was held, *per Holt,* C. J. at *Nisi prius,* That a Demand and Refusal is an actual Conversion, and not only Evidence of a Conversion; and tho' the Plaintiff on a subsequent Tender refused to take them, yet held, that the Action lay; nay, if on such Tender the Plaintiff had taken the Goods, an Action would have lain on the former Conversion; and his having the Goods again, would only have gone in Mitigation of Damages. 6 *Mod.* 212.

The Citizens of *London* gave in Evidence, on Not guilty in Trover, their Custom to take Toll. *W. Jones* 240.

In

In Trover, on Not guilty the Defendant gave in Evidence, That the Goods were taken and fold by Virtue of a Commiſſion of Sewers; and held it might well be given in Evidence. *Alleyn* 92.

In Trover for an Horſe proved of 15 *l.* Value, the Jury gave but 3 *l.* Damages, upon Miſtake, they thinking that the Plaintiff had his Horſe again.

Per Wadh. Wyndham, If the Jury had not been gone, they ſhould have mended their Verdict; but a new Action of Trover lies for Damages for the Horſe, in which the Jury ſhall prove the 3 *l.* given was only for the Converſion, not the Value of the Horſe; and by him, Trover lies for Goods in the Plaintiff's Poſſeſſion, to recover Damages for the Converſion only. *Tyndal* verſus *Jolliffe, Norf. Lent Aſſizes* 1660.

The Abuſe of an Horſe lent is no Evidence in Trover; but if a Man lends his Horſe to go to *York,* and he goes to *Carliſle,* this Evidence will maintain Trover. *Gilb. L. of Evid.* 265.

In Trover by Adminiſtrator, where the Converſion was in the Time of the Inteſtate, the Plaintiff muſt ſhew the Letters of Adminiſtration; *contr.* where the Converſion was after his Death. *Per Hale, Norf. Summer Aſſizes* 1660.

If an Eſtray be claimed within the Year and the Day, &c. and the Lord refuſes to deliver it; Trover lies, though the Keeping is not paid for, and the Lord ſays, he detains for the ſame; for the Lord cannot detain for the Meat, &c. but muſt bring his Action. *Per Moreton* Juſtice, *Lent Aſſizes Norf.* 1667. *Bond* verſus

Paſton,

Pafton, Quære. Vide Dent. Tit. *Trefpafs; per Wyndham cont.* and I think is Law, *vide Roll.* Tit. *Eftray,* 889.

At the fame Affizes *Daniel* verfus *Berney,* by *Moreton* Juftice, Proclamation may be made of an Eftray by any Perfon, and it is not necef-fary that it fhould be made by the Bell-man or any other Officer. *Vide Co. Entries* 170. *Barber* verfus *Faucet.* In Trover, Iffue was joined on Tender of Amends for Keeping, &c. and Verdict *pro* Plaintiff, and Judgment.

Note; I find Precedents, that in Trover the Matter of an Eftray may be pleaded fpecially, or given in Evidence on Not guilty.

Trover for Goods; the Defendant pleads a Sale in Market Overt; and held ill, becaufe it amounted to the General Iffue. *Cro. Jac.* 165.

Where the Defendant has a *general* Property, he may give it in Evidence on the General Iffue. *Gilb. L. of Evid.* 263.

Trover for Loads of Corn; the Defendant juftifies, and intitles himfelf to them as Tithes fevered; and held ill, becaufe it amounted to the General Iffue, that being fhewn for Caufe of Demurrer. *Cro. Car.* 157.

Trover for an Horfe; Defendant pleads that he was a Common Inn-keeper, that he took the Horfe at Livery, and he died; and held an ill Plea becaufe it amounted to the General Iffue. 1 *Roll. Rep.* 22.

Trover by the Executor of *J. S.* the Defendant pleads that *J. S.* died Inteftate, that Adminiftration was granted to *A.* who fold the Goods to Defendant; and on Demurrer held ill, as amounting to the General Iffue. 1 *Keb.* 318.

In

In Trover for Jewels, it was faid by *Twifden* there is no Plea in Trover but a Releafe, or Not guilty, every fpecial Plea in Juftification being but tantamount. 1 *Keb.* 305.

Oats were taken from the Owner, and carried to a Miller to make into Oat-meal; and before it was done, the Owner prohibits the Miller, &c. and demanded the Oats, who notwithftanding made them into Oat-meal. *Per Berkley,* it is a Converfion in the Miller, 1638. *Clayton* 57. *Holfworth*'s Cafe.

On *Non Cul.* the Defendant gave in Evidence a Seizure of Goods foreign bought and foreign fold. *Per* Cuftom of *Lynn, Norf.* good, *per Hale, Norf. Sum. Affizes* 1668. *Harwich* verfus *Twells.*

In Trover againft Hufband and Wife, the Proving the Goods in the Poffeffion of the Hufband and Wife is fufficient. *Gilb. L. of Evid.* 259, 260.

A Man lends his Horfe to a fpecial Purpofe, the Bailee abufes the Horfe, and over-works him, then the Lender takes the Horfe again. *Per Hugh Wyndham* Juftice, *Lent Aff. Bucks,* Trover lies not. *Conftable*'s Cafe.

Actual prifel eft bone Evidence de prover Converfion fans demand. Sid. 264.

In Trover for Goods, the Proof depended on a *Fieri facias,* and *Venditioni exponas,* which could not be found on Record, and admitted to be proved in Evidence. *Hardres's Rep.* 323, 324.

A Seizure and Condemnation in the Excherquer of forfeited Goods, may be given in Evidence upon Not guilty in Trover, but it muft A Cuftom pleaded in Trover to take Corn to repair a Bridge, and *Cro. Eliz.* 433, and 262. Promife.

Trover.

Record.

Trover.
Trefpafs.
Vide Roll.
1 Part 1, 2.

be

be pleaded in Trefpafs. In Trover of a Horfe, that he is a common Hoftler, and that the Horfe was put to him at Livery and ˙ died, is good upon Not guilty. *Roll.* 1 Part 22.

Per Dodderidge, In Trover and Converfion of Goods, if the Defendant derive a Title from a Stranger, this amounts to the General Iffue; otherwife if from the Plaintiff. *Latch* 186. And Bailment of the Goods to deliver to another, and Delivery accordingly, amounts to the General Iffue, and may be given in Evidence upon it. *Bulft.* 3 Part 209.

Troveragainſt a Carrier.

If a Carrier lofe Goods, a fpecial Action of the Cafe lies againft him, but not Trover, *Roll. Abr.* 6. fo of a common Carrier by Boat. *Noy* 114.

If Goods be delivered by the Owner to *A.* to keep, and he converts them to his own Ufe, this is fufficient Evidence of a Trover. *Gilb. Law of Evid.* 260.

Declaration of a Trover in *Middlefex,* and Proof of one in *Ireland,* good.

Brown verfus *Hedges, Trin.* 7 *A. B. R.* In Trover upon Not guilty pleaded, it appeared in Evidence, that the Defendant was Tenant by the Courtefy of Lands in *Ireland,* and had cut down and fold the Trees off the Eftate, and that the Reverfion belonged to the Plaintiff, and two others in Coparcenary: Upon a Cafe made for the Opinion of the Court, it was refolved, That in local Actions, as in Trefpafs *quare Claufum fregit,* the Plaintiff cannot prove a Trefpafs but where he lays it, nor lay it in any other Place but where it is; but it is otherwife in Actions tranfitory, as Trover; *Ergo* here he may lay the Converfion here, and prove it in *Ireland, vide Stile* 331.

2. One Jointenant or Tenant in Common or

One Jointenant cannot bring Trover againft his Companion, but may againft a Stranger, and it is only pleadable in Abatement.

Parcener

Parcener, cannot bring Trover againſt another; if he does, it is good Evidence upon Not guilty: But if one Joint-tenant brings Trover againſt a Stranger, in that Caſe the Defendant may plead it in Abatement, but cannot take Advantage of it in Evidence. 2 *Lev.* 113. *Cro. Eliz.* 554. *Salk.* 290.

In Trover upon Evidence at a Trial before *Holt* Chief Juſtice, at the Sittings in *Middleſex,* the Caſe was, The Plaintiff proved the Goods to be in his Poſſeſſion, and to be taken away by the Defendant. The Defendant ſhewed that theſe were the Goods of *Jane Blackham* in her Life-time, and that the Defendant had taken out Letters of Adminiſtration to her, and ſo was intitled to the Goods: Upon this the Plaintiff proved, that ſome few Days before her Death ſhe was actually married to him: And in Anſwer to that it was inſiſted, That the Spiritual Court had determined the Right to be in the Defendant; for they could not have granted Adminiſtration to the Defendant, but upon ſuppoſing there was no ſuch Marriage, and that this Sentence being of a Marriage within their Juriſdiction, was concluſive, and could not be gain-ſay'd in Evidence. *Et per Holt* Chief Juſtice, A Matter which has been directly determined, by their Sentence, cannot be gain-ſay'd. Their Sentence is concluſive in ſuch Caſes, and no Evidence ſhall be admitted to prove the contrary, but that is to be intended only in the Point directly tried; otherwiſe it is if a collateral Matter is collected or inferred from their Sentence; as in this Caſe, becauſe the Adminiſtration is granted to the Defendant, therefore they infer that the Plaintiff was not the

Sentence of the Spiritual Court, in a Cauſe within their Juriſdiction, is concluſive Evidence in the Point tried; otherwiſe of a collateral Matter.

the Inteftate's Hufband, as he could not have been taken to be, if the Point there tried had been *married or notmarried*, and their Sentence had been, *Not married*. Salk. 290. *Blackham's* Cafe.

Trover for Million Lottery Tickets; in Evidence it appeared that the Plaintiff gave the Tickets in Queftion to a Goldfmith to receive the Money due on them; and that this Goldfmith had received Tickets of the Defendant, and given a Note to pay him fo many Tickets, and 'that the Plaintiff's Tickets were delivered to the Defendant by the Goldfmith on this Note. Held by *Holt* Ch. J. at *Nifi prius*, that Plaintiff ought to recover, for that the Goldfmith's having Tickets of both Plaintiff and Defendant, and delivering the Plaintiff's to the Defendant was no Change of the Property; for tho' the Goldfmith had Power to receive the Money, he had no Power to change the Tickets. 1 *Salk.* 283. *Ford* verfus *Hopkins*.

If the Nature of the Thing be altered, this is good Evidence of a Converfion, but not of a Writ of *Detinue*. *Gilb. Law of Evid.* 264.

Note; In Trover the Plaintiff muft prove Property, but not in Trefpafs. *Gilb. Law of Evid.* 268.

Of Demurrers upon Evidence.

Middleton againft *Baker, Cro. Eliz.* 42. f. 751. In Ejeΐment, it was held by all the Court upon Evidence to a Jury, that if the Plaintiff give in Evidence any Matter in Writing or Record, or a Sentence in the Spiritual Court, (as it was in this Cafe) and the Defendant offers to demur thereupon, the Plaintiff
tiff

tiff ought to join in the Demurrer, or wave the Evidence, becaufe the Defendant fhall not be compelled to put Matter of Difficulty to *lay Gens*, and becaufe there cannot be any Variance of a Matter in Writing. But if either Party offer to demur upon any Evidence given by Witnefs, the o·her, unlefs he pleafeth, fhall not be compelled to join, becaufe the Credit of the Teftimony is to be examined by a Jury, and the Evidence is incertain, and may be inforced more or lefs; but both Parties may agree to join in Demurrer upon fuch Evidence.   And in the Queen's Cafe, the other Party may not demur upon Evidence fhewn in Writing or Record for the Queen, unlefs the Queen's Council will thereto affent; but the Court in fuch Cafe fhall charge the Jury to find the Matter fpecially, as appears 24 *H.* 8. *Dyer* 53.   But this is by Prerogative. *Vide Lib.* 4. 104. the fame Cafe, and 1 *Inft.* 72. where my Lord *Coke.* fays, If the Plaintiff in Evidence fhew any Matter of Record, or Deeds, or Writings, or any Sentence in the Ecclefiaftical Court, or other Matter of Evidence by Teftimony of Witneffes, or otherwife, whereupon Doubt in Law arifeth, and the Defendant offer to demur in Law thereupon, the Plaintiff cannot refufe to join in Demurrer, no more than in a Demurrer upon a Count, Replication, &c. and fo *è Converfo* may the Plaintiff demur in Law, upon the Evidence of the Defendant, but the King's Council fhall not be inforced to join in Demurrer; but in that Cafe the Court may direct the Jury to find the fpecial Matter.   So that the feveral Sorts of Evidence make no

Joinder in Demurrer.

Difference

Difference as to the joining in Demurrer.   1 Part, *Lecn.* 206.

Darrofe againft *Newbott*, Cro. 4 *Car. f.* 143. In Error of a Judgment in *Bridgwater*, the Error affigned was, for that, in an Action upon the Cafe *fur Affumpfit*, the Parties being at Iffue, a Demurrer was joined upon the Evidence, and thereupon the Jury difcharged, and afterwards Judgment was given for the Plaintiff, and a Writ of Inquiry of Damages awarded, and Damages found, and Judgment thereupon; where the Jurors which came to find the Iffue, although by the Demurrer they were difcharged of the Iffue, yet ought to have affeffed Damages conditionally, if Judgment fhould be given for the Plaintiff. And in Proof thereof, was cited *Newis* and *Scholaftica*'s Cafe, *Plo. Com. f.* 408. and the old Book of Entries, &c.   And it was faid by the Court, if thefe Precedents be good Law, then it may be inquired of by the fame Jury conditionally : But it may be as well inquired of by a Writ of Inquiry of Damages, when the Demurrer is determined, and the moft ufual Courfe is,

Note; He that demurs upon Evidence, admits the Evidence to be true.

when there is a Demurrer upon Evidence, to difcharge the Jury, without more Inquiry. But as my Lord Chief Baron *Montague* held at the Affizes in *Cambridgfhire*, 1612, it may be one Way or other.

In the Affize by *R. Newis* and *Scholaftica* his Wife againft *Lark* and *Hunt*, which was taken by Default ; the Precedent in *Plowd. Com.* as to this Matter runs thus,

‘ Recogn’ Affifæ præd’ exacti venerunt qui
‘ ad veritatem de præmiffis dicend’ electi triati
‘ & jurati

' & jurati fuerunt fuper quo *Willielmus Ben-*
' *lows* Serviens ad legem de confilio prædicto-
' rum *R.* & *Scholaſticæ* in manutentione Affiſæ
' prædict' coram Juſtic' Dom' Reg' de Banc'
' hic in evident' Recogn' Affiſæ præd' dixit
' quod diu ante diem impetrationis Affiſæ præd'
' quidam *H. Clark* fuit feifitus, &c. Et condi-
' dit teſtamentum & ultimam voluntatem fuam
' in fcriptis inter alia unde pars inde in hiis
' Anglicis verbis fequitur videlicet [*Alſo this is*
' *the laſt Will and Teſtament of me the faid*
' Henry Clark, *for and concerning,* &c.] Et
' ulterius idem Serviens ad legem ex parte præd'
' *R.* & *S.* dedit in evident' eifdem Recognit'
' quod, &c. Quorum prætextu idem Servi-
' ens ad legem exigit quod iidem Recogn'
' Affiſæ præd' Affifam præd' de tenementis præ-
' dict' cum pertin' in viſu, &c. pro parte ipſo-
' rum *R.* & *S.* triari & comparere debeant,
' &c. Et veredictum fuum dare debent quod
' præd' *W. Lark* & *J. Hunt* dictos *R.* & *S.* de
' tenementis præd' cum pertin' in viſu, &c.
' diffeiſiverant, &c.

' Et præd' *W. Lark* & *J. H.* in propriis
' perfonis fuis dic' quod evident' & allegation'
' prædict' ex parte præd' *R.* & *S.* fuperius al-
' legat' minus fufficien' in lege exiſtunt ad
' manuten' Affifam præd' ad quos ipfi neceffe
' non habent nec per legem terræ tenentur re-
' fpondere unde pro defectu fufficient' Evident'
' in hac parte pet' Judicium quod Juratores
' præd' de veredicto fuo in præmiffis dicend'
' exonerentur, &c. Et quod præd' *R. N.* &
' *S.* ab Affiſa fua præd' habend' præcludan-
' tur, &c.

' Et

' Et præd' *R.* & *S.* dicunt quod ex quo ipfi
' fufficien' materiam in manutentione Affifæ
' præd' in Evident' recognit' præd' oftend' quam
' quidem materiam præd' *W. Lark* & *J. Hunt*
' non dedicunt nec ad eam aliqualit' refpond'
' petunt Judicium & quod iidem Juraror' inde
' exonerentur, & quod præd' *W.* & *J.* de Af-
' fifa illa convincantur, &c. Super quo dict' eft

' Recogn' præd' quod inquir' quæ dampna
' præd' *R.* & *S.* fuftinuer' tam occafione diffei-
' finæ prædict' quam pro mifis & cuftagiis fuis
' per ipfos circa fectam fuam in hac parte appo-
' fit' fi conting' Judicium pro iifdem *R.* & *S.* io
' placito præd' fuper evidentias prædict' reddi
' Qui quidem recogn' dicunt fupra facram' fuum
' quod fi conting' Judicium in placito præd'
' pro præd' *R.* & *S.* fuper Evidentias prædict'
' reddi, iidem *R.* & *S.* fuftinuer' dampna occa-
' fione diffeifinæ præd' ad 13 *s.* 4 *d.* & pro
' mifis & cuftagiis fuis ad 20 *s.* Et quia Jufti-
' ciarii hic fe advifare volunt de & fup' præ-
' miffis priufquam judicium inde reddant, dies
' datus eft partibus prædict' &c.

Note ; Several Exceptions were taken to the
Manner of giving the Evidence ; Firft, For
that the intire Will was not fhewed, but Part,
and that this being the Foundation of the
Evidence, the whole Will ought to have been
fhewed ; for there might be fome other Matter
of Subftance, as a Condition, Limitation, &c.
in the Parts not fhewed. But all the Juftices
difallowed this Exception, and faid, the Party
in any Title or Bar needs fhew no more than
what makes for him. As in an Act of Parliament, in which are divers Branches, 'tis fufficient to fhew that Branch which ferves one's
Purpofe,

Purpofe, and not like the Cafe of a Fine or Recovery of twenty Acres, where I muft fhew the whole Record, although I am concerned but in one Acre, becaufe the Original is intire, and fo is the Record grounded upon it. See alfo *Fulmerfton* and *Steward*'s Cafe, *Plo. Com.* 102. Another Exception was, That the Fine was not fhewed under the Seal of the Court, or the Great Seal, but one Part indented of the Chirograph was only fhewn, which the Jurors were not bound to believe, becaufe it wanted a Seal. But all the Juftices were againft this, and faid, the Jury might find the Fine of their own Knowledge, without the fhewing of the Parties, or they might find it upon the Credit of any Witnefs that had feen it, and the fhewing the Part indented, is the ufual Evidence of a Fine. (*Note*; A Fine indented, and not exemplified under Seal, *&c.* fhall not be delivered to the Jury. 34 *H.* 6. 25.) And they faid, becaufe it is only the Inducement of the Verity to the Jurors, the Party could not demur upon this; for the Effect of the Matter is, that there is fuch a Fine which is amongft the Records: And this is the Subftance of the Matter, and the Part of the Chirograph is nothing but the Image of the Verity, and therefore there could be no Demurrer upon this.

Another Exception was, That the Recovery was not fhewed under Seal, or at leaft that the Roll of this ought to be alledged certainly; but all the Court (except *Harper*) anfwered, That upon the General Iffue, the Jury might find Things that proved or difproved the Seifin or Diffeifin, be they Matters of Record or otherwife, and the Jury could not give a rightful Verdict, if they could not find them; and whatfoever they may take Conufance of themfelves may be given in Evidence by Words, or Copies, or other Argument of the Truth. 'Tis true,

Style 22.
White and
Pindar's Cafe.
in pleading, a Man cannot make a Title by Record, without fhewing the fame under the Great Seal ; and if a Record be pleaded in Bar, a Day may be given to bring in the Record under the Great Seal ; but fuch Day cannot be given to bring in the Record upon Evidence, but the finding of it by the Jury is fufficient; and they may find it of themfelves, although it be not fhewed them in Evidence. But perhaps they fhall not be bound upon *Pain of Attaint* to find it, if it be not fhewed them under Seal ; but neverthelefs they may find it, and they do well if it be true. And by the fame Reafon that they may find it, they may take Inftruction of it by any Circumftance, which induceth the

Vide Roll.
Tit. Trial,
687.
Truth. (*Note* ; If it be not neceffary to fhew the Record, and the Jury may find it without ; yet 'tis not fit to be permitted to prove it in fuch a Manner, without fhewing the Record, or a true Copy of it.) And the Demurrer upon Evidence goes to the Law upon the Matter, and not to the Verity, which is admitted, and the Effect in Law is denied ; for if the Party will not confefs the Truth of the Matter given in Evidence, then he ought fo to fay, and put it to the Jury to be tried ; and if they find this, where it is falfe, *an Attaint lies* ; but a Demurrer upon Evidence never denies the Truth of the Fact, but confeffes the Fact, and denies the Law to be with the Party which fhews the Fact.

As to a fourth Exception, for Want of alledging and averring, that *H. Clark* had not any other Iffue Male than *John* and *F.* (upon
a Limitation

a Limitation of a Remainder for Want of Iſſue Male of *H. C.* and a Title made to the Plain-tiff's Wife, under that Limitation;) the ſame Judges anſwered, That which the Plaintiff gave in Evidence, is to the Intent to perſwade the Jury that they have a good Title, and what they ſay ſhall be applied as they intended; and as by Preſumption, no Man will ſay any Thing againſt himſelf, ſo it lies on the other Side to ſhew what is againſt him; and although in Pleading, Certainty ought to be ſhewed, (to which the other Party muſt anſwer, and upon which the Court may judge) yet in Evidence, ſo great and exact Certainty is not requiſite; for the Jury may found their Verdict, (if the Matter be ambiguous) upon what is moſt pro-bable, and by the ſame Reaſon that which is moſt probable, is good Evidence, and there-fore it ſhall be intended that *H. C.* had no other Iſſue Male, becauſe the other Party did not ſhew that he had.

The *Precedent* of a Demurrer upon Evi-dence in *Reniger* and *Fogaſſa*'s Caſe, in *Plowd. Com. f.* 1. In an Information upon a Seizure of Wood imported, the Cuſtoms not being paid, nor any Agreement made with the Collector in the Exchequer, where the Iſſue was, whe-ther the Defendant made an Agreement with the Collector of the Subſidies for the Wood, according to the Act, *&c.* or not.

' Ideo fiat inde inquiſ. ac pro eo quod idem
' *A. Fogaſſa* eſt Alien' natus videl' tapud Civi-
' tatem Portus *Portugaliæ* in *Portugalia* ſub
' obedientia præd' *Portugaliæ* Regis petit medi-
' etatem linguæ ſuæ, &c. *A. B. E. M. R. S.*
' &c. qui ad veritatem de præmiſſis dicend'
' electi

' electi triati & jurati dictus *A. F.* in manu-
' tentione exitus præd' superius ad patr' juncti
' & ad proband' exit' ill' pro parte ipsius *A.*
' fore verum produxit præd' *Tho. Wells* Collect'
' Custom' & Subsid' Domini Regis in portu
' villæ *Southampton* ac *J. S.* adtunc & adhuc
' Clericum sive servient' ipsius *Tho. Wells* in
' dicto Offic' Collect' præd' nec non quendam
' *J. D.* Yeoman ad testificand' præmissa in
' placito ipsius *A.* spec' fore vera.   Qui quidem
' *Tho. Wells* examinatus sup' sacram' suum co-
' ram Baronibus hic præstitum in præmissis dicit
' quod, &c. [*Here recite the Evidence.*]

Demurrer.   ' Et præd' Attorn' Dom' Regis pro eodem
' Dom' Rege dic' quod evidentiæ præd' supe-
' rius dat' minus sufficien' in lege exiftunt ad
' manutenend' seu proband' exit' pro parte ip-
' sius *A. F.* superius ad patriam junct' unde ob
' insufficient' earundem evident' ac ex quo per
' evidentias illas non dedicitur forisfactura bo-
' norum præd' in informatione præd' spec' idem
' Attorn' Dom' Regis pro ipso Dom' Rege pe-
' tit Judicium ac quod eadem bona remaneant
' Domino Regi forisfacta juxta formam Statuti
Joinder.   ' præd.   Et præd' *A. F.* dic' quod evidentiæ
' præd' superius ex parte ipsius *A. F.* dat'
' sufficien' in lege exiftunt tam ad manutenend'
' & proband' exit' præd' pro parte dicti *A.*
' *F.* superius ad patriam junct' quam ad exclu-
' dend' Domin' Regem de aliqua forisfactura
' bonor' præd' habend' Ad quas præd' Attorn'
' Domini Regis pro ipso Dom' Rege minus suf-
' ficienter respondit nec aliquod pro ipso Rege
' allegavit unde idem *A.* pet' Judicium ac quod
' præd' bona in dicta informatione spec' ei reli-
                                        ' berentur

'berentur quodque ipſe quoad præmiſſa ab hac
'Curia dimittatur.   Ideo ad Judicium.

Note; In this Caſe, the Agreement according to the Statute, was put in Iſſue generally,
and yet the ſpecial Agreement maintained the
Iſſue.

And whereſoever the Evidence doth not war- Regula.
rant, prove and maintain the very ſame Thing
that is in Iſſue, that Evidence is defective, and
may be demurred upon.

Upon *non eſt factum* to a Bond dated at *Non eſt*
York: It was ſaid in this Caſe, that to prove *factum.*
the Bond made in another Place, doth not
prove the Bond, nor warrant the Iſſue, becauſe
the Delivery is intended to be where the Date
is ; but the Witneſſes cannot prove the contrary, and ſo the Iſſue is not proved.   But
ſurely, if this be found, the Plaintiff ſhall have
Judgment as well as upon a Bond delivered
before the Date.   31 *H.* 6. *Plo.* 7. *Roll. Trial,*
677. *pl.* 24.   But Infancy, or made by *Dures,*
cannot be given in Evidence upon *non eſt factum,*
Lib. 5. *Welpdale*'s Caſe, 119. becauſe thereby
the Bond is not void but only voidable : Otherwiſe of the Bond of a Feme Covert, or Monk,
for there the Bond is void, and ſo *non eſt factum* ;
and ſo of a Bond made to a Feme Covert, and
the Huſband diſagree to it, or by Huſband and
Feme, *non eſt factum* of the Wife.

In an Aſſize, if the Tenant plead *Nul tort,* Releaſe.
nul diſſeiſin, he cannot give in Evidence a Releaſe after the Diſſeiſin ; but a Releaſe before
the Diſſeiſin he may, for then there is no Diſſeiſin upon the Matter.   1 *Inſt.* 283.

Q 3   In

Warranty.

In a Writ of Right, if the Tenant join the Mife upon the meer Right, he cannot give in Evidence a collateral Warranty, for he hath not any Right by it, and therefore it ought to have been pleaded. 1 *Inft.* 283.

Regula.

Regularly, whatfoever is done by Force of a Warrant or Authority, ought to be pleaded.

But *Note* ; In all Cafes where one cannot have Advantage of the fpecial Matter, by Way of Plea, there he may have Advantage of it in Evidence ; as for Example, the Rule of Law is, *That one cannot juftify the Death or Killing of a Man* ; and therefore if one kill another in his own Defence, he cannot plead this fpecially ; but he may give this in Evidence : And fo in Defence of his Houfe againft Thieves and Robbers, &c. 1 *Inft.* 283.

Sewers.

By the Statute 23 *H.* 8. *cap.* 5. any Thing done by the Authority of the Commiffion of Sewers, may be given in Evidence upon the General Iffue. 1 *Inft.* 283.

Regula.

After taking the General Iffue the Defendant cannot give in Evidence any Thing that goes in Difcharge of the Action ; as in Debt upon *Nil debet*, he cannot give in Evidence a Releafe, nor a Grant to cut Trees to repair, upon *Nul waft fait*, nor making of a Ditch to amend the Meadow : But that he only lopped the Trees, he may, if Wafte be affigned *in fuccidendo*

Statute.

Arbores, &c. Neither if a Statute was made, That all Tenants for Life fhould be difpunifh-able of Wafte, could he give in Evidence this Statute. 28 *H.* 8. *Dyer* 28. for the Difcharge ought to be pleaded, becaufe it admits a Caufe of Action without it.

In an Iſſue upon Villenage *regardant* to Villenage. a Manor, a Villein in *groſs* is no Evidence. *Dyer* 48.

In Waſte by the Grantee of a Reverſion, Attornment. by *Montague* and *Fitz.* the Leſſee may plead that he in Reverſion *ne granta pas per le fait,* and give in Evidence, that he never attorned, or he may traverſe the Attornment at his Election. *Dyer* 31.

In Reſcous by the Lord, upon Not guilty, Reſcous. the Defendant ſhall not give in Evidence, That he doth not hold; by *Vavaſour* and *Bryan*; and ſo if he ſaid *Nothing is behind* in Avowry, Avowry. he ſhall not give in Evidence that he doth not hold of him. *T.* 9 *H.* 7. 3.

In Aſſize, Feoffment pleaded, the Plaintiff Feoffment. ſaid he did not *infeoff modo & forma,* upon the Deed and Letter of Attorney to infeoff upon Condition found, if the Attorney made it without Condition, this well proves the Iſſue for the Plaintiff. 13 *E.* 4. 4.

If one plead a Feoffment *jointment* with his Companion, or of a Feme Covert, the other may lay *Ne enfeoffa pas,* and give the Matter in Evidence, and the Court ſhall inſtruct the Jury of the Law. 18 *E.* 4. 29.

Evidence which is contrary to that in Iſſue, or Regula. *which is not agreeable to the Matter in Iſſue, is not good.*

As appears by ſeveral Caſes which you may find in the Chapter of *Evidence.* As upon the Chap. 15. Iſſue, *Nothing paſſes by the Deed,* you cannot give in Evidence, that it is not your Deed, for this is contrary to the Iſſue, and to that which is acknowledged in the Plea by Implication. 5 *H.* 4. *f.* 2.

And

And fo upon Not guilty in Affault and Battery, and Evidence that it was done in his own Defence, is not good.

And fo in Debt upon a Bail Bond, you muft plead, That there is not the Name of the Sheriff in it, *& iffint nient fon fait*, and cannot give in Evicence upon *Non eft factum*, for it is contrariant. 5 *E.* 4. 5.

So upon Iffue of Common appendant, Common *pur Caufe de vicinage* is not agreeable to the Matter in Iffue, and therefore cannot be given in Evidence. 13 *H.* 7. 13.

Roll. Trial, 680. pl. 2. Regula.

Where the Evidence proves the Effect and Subftance of the Iffue, it is good.

As to prove a Grant or Leafe pleaded *fimplement*, a Grant or Leafe upon Condition, and the Condition executed, is good ; for this proves the Effect and Subftance of the Iffue, 14 *H.* 8. 20. So a Promife to the Wife, and the Hufband's Agreement, proves a Promife to the Hufband ; and this you may fee in many Cafes in the Chapter of *Evidence* in *p.* 517.

Other Cafes of Evidence.

Maintenance. Juftifiable Maintenance cannot be given in Evidence upon the General Iffue, but muft be pleaded. The Mafter may juftify for his Servant. Any Man for his Kindred, *&c.* or to give Money to the Poor, *&c.* But that he was of his Council may be given in Evidence upon the General Iffue ; for to give Council, is not Maintenance. 22 *H.* 6. 35. 28 *H.* 8. 6.

A Witnefs may prove the Contents of a Deed or Will. Vaughan's Rep. 77.

In an Iffue upon a Prefcription traverfed, the Plaintiff gave in Evidence a Deed, bearing Date after the Time of Limitation, *fcil.* after the Time of *R.* 1. And the Defendant would have Demurred in Law upon it, and well he might ; *per Cur.* Whereupon the Plaintiff would

4

would not give this in Evidence, but gave other Evidence. 34 *H.* 6. 37. See Chapter *Evidence*, where a Grant fhall be taken as a Confirmation of a Prefcription. *Prefcription.*

Note; The Opinion 12 *H.* 4. 21. That a Deed made before the Time of Memory, may be given in Evidence, although it cannot be pleaded. *Ancient Deeds.*

Vide Repl. in *Fitz.* 34. *Repl.* of a Sow and Pigs; the Defendant juftified for the Sow; and to the Pigs pleaded, he did not take them; the Jury found that the Sow was with Pig when fhe was taken, and after caft her Pigs in the Cuftody of the Defendant; and the Plaintiff recovered Damages: For fays *Bro. Abridg.* Tit. *General Iffue,* 88. This is a fpecial Taking in Law. *Sow pigged, being taken in Diftrefs.*

It fufficeth to prove the Subftance, without any precife Regard to the Circumftance. As if an Indictment be, That with a Dagger the Offender gave another a mortal Wound, *&c.* And in Evidence it is proved to be done with a Sword, Rapier, Club, Bill, or any other W , the Offender upon this Evidence ought to be found guilty; for the mortal Wound is the Subftance, and the Manner of the Weapon is but the Circumftance; yet fome Weapon ought to be mentioned in the Indictment. And fo if *A. B.* and *C.* be indicted for killing *J. S.* and that *A.* ftruck, and the other were Abettors; to prove that *B* ftruck, is fufficient, *&c. Regula. Subftance. Circumftance. Indictment.*

Manflaughter upon an Indictment muft be found, if proved, becaufe the Killing is Subftance, upon which Judgment fhall be given.

Indictments for Murder of Minifters of Juftice in Execution of their Office, may be general, *viz.* That the Prifoners *felonice, voluntarie*

luntarie & ex malitia sua præcogitata, &c. percuſſerunt, &c. without alledging the ſpecial Matter, which may be given in Evidence, for the Law implies malice prepenſed. So if a Thief in robbing kills a Man that reſiſts him, or a Man is killed without any Provocation, or without Malice prepenſed that can be actually proved, the Law adjudges this Murder, and implies the Malice; and in theſe Caſes, the Offenders may be indicted generally, That they killed of Malice prepenſe; for the Malice implied by Law, given in Evidence, is ſufficient to maintain the general Indictment. *Lib.* 9. 67. *Mackalley*'s Caſe.

So if an Indictment as Acceſſary to two, to prove Acceſſary to one, is ſufficient. *Lib.* 9. 119.

In *Cromwel*'s Caſe, *Lib.* 4. 12. Although it was objected, That in an Action of Slander, if the Defendant will juſtify, he muſt juſtify the ſame Words, and in the ſame Senſe, as is laid in the *Nar*', or elſe he muſt plead Not guilty, and give the ſpecial Matter, that is the Variance, in Evidence. Yet the Court held, That the Defendant ſhould not be put to the General Iſſue, but might juſtify, although he varied from the Plaintiff in the Senſe and Quality of the Words; and might ſet forth the coherent Words. As for calling the Plaintiff Murderer, the Defendant may ſhew that they were ſpeaking of Hares, and the Words were ſpoken in Reference to killing of Hares.

Copyhold. In *Pilkington*'s Caſe, *Style* 450. Upon the Iſſue, if the Lord of the Manor granted the Lands *per Copiam rotulorum Curiæ manerii præa' ſecundum conſuetudinem manerii præd'*;

præd; to prove that there were cuftomary Lands in the Manor, and that the Lord of late granted the Land, &c. *per copiam Rotulor. Curiæ*, where it was never granted by Copy before, is no good Evidence to find the Cuftom, or that the Lands, &c. were grantable or demifeable by Cuftom. *Leon.* 55. *Kemp* and *Carter*'s Cafe.

Rolle faid, if Copies of Court-Roll be fhewed to prove a Cuftomary Eftate, the Enjoyment of fuch Eftates muft alfo be proved, otherwife the Proof is not good.

Forger of a Deed, in which is contained a Demife of the Scite of the Manor of *R.* and *terras dominicales*, &c. A Deed of the Scite and all the Demefnes of the faid Manor, *exceptis duabus claufuris*, &c. is good Evidence; for it is not neceffary to conftrue *terras dominicales*, &c. *omnes terras dominicales*, &c. for Lands not excepted are *terræ dominicales*; and fo the Court is fatisfied by that Evidence. 1 *Leon* 139. *Atkins* and *Hale*'s Cafe.

Forger. *Totum & pars.*

In a Replevin, the Taking was fuppofed in *R.* The Defendant faid, That the Place where is forty Acres, Parcel of the Manor of *R.* which is his Freehold, and avowed for Damage-feafant; the Plaintiff faid, That the Place where is Parcel of the Manor of *R.* in *R.* and conveyed Title to himfelf in that; *Abfque hoc*, that the Manor of *R. unde*, was the Freehold of the Defendant. It was the Opinion of the Juftices, that the Plaintiff is eftopped to give Evidence that the Defendant had not any Manor of *R.* for the Words *abfque hoc* and *unde* imply he had fuch a Manor, but he ought to have taken it by Proteftation, that the Defendant had no fuch Manor of *R.* in *R. abfque hoc*, that the forty Acres were the Freehold of the Defendant. *Dyer* 183.

No Evidence to be given againft what is admitted upon the Record.

Where

Eftoppel.

Where a Man is eftopped in Pleading, to fpeak againſt his own Deed, yet he ſhall not in Evidence; as in *Ifeham*'s Cafe againſt *Morris, Cro. 4 Car.* 109. Upon Evidence at Bar, it was held by all the Juſtices of the Common Pleas, That where one makes a Leafe for Years of Land by Indenture, and hath nothing in the Land, and afterwards purchafeth the Land and aliens it; although it be a good Leafe for Years by Eftoppel againſt him and his Alienee, by way of Pleading, and ſhall bind them, yet it ſhall not bind the Jury, but they may find the Truth; and if they find the Truth, the Court ſhall adjudge it to be a void Leafe. *Vide tamen Rawlin*'s Cafe *Lib.* 4. 53. *Sutton* and *Dicken*'s Cafe, *Leon.* 1 Part, f. 206. 1 *Inſt.* 47. 227. *Edwards* againſt *Omellballum, March* 64. *James* and *Landon*'s Cafe, *Cro.* 27 *Eliz.* f. 36. *Leon.* 3 Part 210. *Bulſt.* 2 Part 41.

Demurrer.

Note; That if a Demurrer be made upon the Evidence, the Evidence ought to be entred *verbatim, Keilway* 77. where in Account againſt one generally as Bailiff, the Evidence that charged him fpecially by Reafon of his Tenure to collect, &c. was upon Demurrer held not good.

Surplufage.

Matter of Surplufage ſhewed in Evidence ſhall not hurt. *Keilway* 166.

Will.

Iſſue was upon a Devife to *A. Harding* and her Heirs, *modo & forma*, and the Will given in Evidence was, *A. H. ſhall have all my Inheritance if the Law will allow it*; and held fufficient to maintain the Iſſue. *Hob.* 2. So upon *Ne unques receiver per Mains J. S.* a Delivery from *J. D.* by the Appointment of

Account.

J. S. to the Plaintiff's Ufe, is good Evidence. *Hob.* 36.

Iſſue

Issue whether *A.* was taken by a *Capias ad* Arrest.
sat. at the Suit of *B.* and Evidence of a Taking
at the Suit of *C.* and then a Delivery of a *Capias ad sat.* at the Suit of *B.* to the Sheriff, is
good. *Hob.* 55.   But a Taking upon a *Capias
utlagat.* or *Capias pro fine*, with a prayer of the
Plaintiff, that he remain for his Satisfaction, is
not. *Ibid.*

In a *Confimili casu*, where the Demandant *Confimili casu.*
counts of an Alienation in Fee, yet the Defen- Substance.
dant shall make his Traverse to the Alienation
modo & forma; and then the Demandant shall
maintain the Issue by an Alienation in Fee, or
in Tail, or for Life, for they are all alike material. *Hob.* 105.

In an Assize, the Defendant pleaded the Warranty.
Deed of the Brother of the Plaintiff with
Warranty; a Deed of the Father with War-
ranty, will not maintain the Defendant's Issue.
Hob. 55.

In an Action on the Case, for digging a Demurrer
Hole in the Highway, into which his Gelding upon Evi-
fell, *&c.* upon Not guilty, this Evidence dence.
given, that the Plaintiff's Servant was driving
the Plaintiff's Gelding in the Way, and that
by Reason of the Hole he fell, *&c.*   Upon
which it was demurred, because it was not
proved that there was such a Highway, or
who digged the Hole. *Rolle* Chief Justice,
That Evidence is no more than a special *Action sur*
Verdict, and it ought to find the Way and *Case.*
the Hole digged, and all the Matter con-
ducing to the Issue, and therefore it is not
good as it is, and a *Venire de novo* was a-
warded. *Style* 335.

In

In Trover and Converfion, there was a Demurrer joined upon the Evidence, and thereupon the Court directed the Jury to find Damages for the Plaintiff, if upon the Argument
of the Demurrer, the Law fhould be adjudged
for him; and then the Parties defired the Jury
might be difcharged, and referred the Matter
to the Judges, to determine the Law upon
the Evidence.   In this Cafe *Rolle* Juftice took

this Difference: If a Record be pleaded, it
muft be *fub pede figilli*, or elfe the Judges cannot judge of it; but it may be given in Evidence, and the Jury may find it, though it be
not *fub pede figilli*. And the Court advifed
the Parties, for their own Expedition, to let a
Venire facias de novo be iffued out, and to wave
the demurrer upon the Evidence, becaufe it
was not good, nor could not bring the Matter in Queftion before them, that they might
determine it; for one Party fays there is a
Writ, and the other faith there is not a
Writ, which is bare Matter of Fact for the
Jury to determine, and not for the Court; and
the Demurrer ought to have been, whether the
Writ be good or bad, and fhould have admitted that there was a Writ *tiel quel*; and
then had the whole Matter come legally before
the Court, to wit, Whether the Evidence given
to the Jury be fufficient for them to find a
Verdict for the Plaintiff, upon the Iffue joined, or not? for the Matter of Fact ought to
be agreed in a Demurrer to an Evidence, otherwife the Court cannot proceed upon the De-

murrer. And he faid, if a Deed be pleaded,
the Party muft fhew it in Court; but in Evidence, it is not abfolutely neceffary to fhew it,
if it can otherwife be proved to the Jury,

and

and so it is of a Record; and concluded, that Record. the Demurrer was not good, and that there ought to be a *Venire facias de novo* to try the Matter again. *Bacon* Justice said, there ought not to be a *Venire facias de novo*, but that Judgment ought to be given against one Party, to wit, the Defendant, for ill joining in the Demurrer, to the Intent the Party that is not in Fault may be dismissed; and the Parties here have waved the *Trial per Pais*, by joining in the Demurrer. But *Rolle* answered, That no Judgment at all could be given, for both Parties be in Fault, one by tendring the Demurrer, and the other by joining in it; and the Defendant might have chosen whether he would have joined or not; but might have prayed the Judgment of the Court, whether he ought to join? The Court advised to search Precedents for a *Venire facias de novo* after Demurrer upon an Evidence; and if there be any, they hold that the same Jury ought to come again, and not another. *Rolle* said, If a special Verdict be found insufficient, a new *Venire facias* ought to issue; and he saw no Difference between that and this Case. *Wright* and *Pindar*'s Case, *Style* 22 and 34.

Where the Issue is not perfect, no Evidence Imperfect can be applied, neither can the Justices of *Nisi* Issue. *prius* proceed to the Trial of such an Issue. As whether the Money be paid after the Date of the Obligation, and the Date was left out and did not appear in the Record. *Brown* 2, 47.

Note; If there be a Demurrer, yet there Pleas puis dar- may be a Plea *puis darrein Continuance*; and rein Continu- if the Plaintiff take Issue, or demur to this ance. Plea, yet the Court must also consider of the

firſt

firſt Demurrer; for if upon that ſtanding confeſſed by the Demurrer, the Plaintiff could not
have his Action, the Court cannot give Judgment for him, howſoever the latter Iſſue or
Demurrer paſs. But otherwiſe if the firſt had
been an Iſſue; for then nothing were confeſſed
to his Prejudice, and then that had been utterly relinquiſhed by a ſecond Iſſue, or Demurrer.
Hob. 18. with a *Quære, &c.* When this Plea
is pleaded, (the Juſtices of *Niſi prius* cannot proceed to take the Inqueſt, neither can the Plaintiff reply there, but in Bank. *Bulſtr.* 92, 93.

Of Averments.

Averment.

And in regard what may be averred, may be
proved and given in Evidence, it will not be
impertinent to draw a ſhort Scheme of Averments.

**Averment
had upon or
againſt a
Deed.**

To alter, qualify, or abridge the Operation
of it, if there be any apt Words in the Deed,
whereupon to ground it. As a Grant to *A.*
the Son of *B.* and he hath two Sons of that
Name, of the Manor of *S.* and he hath two
Manors of that Name, which Son or Manor
was intended may be averred. And ſo may

Conſideration.

a Conſideration of a Deed that is beſides,
but not that is againſt the expreſs Conſideration of the Deed; nor can any Thing againſt
the Words of the Deed either inlarge or re-
ſtrain it.

Uſes.

Nor can a Uſe againſt or beſides the expreſs
Uſes in the Deed; but where no Uſe is expreſſed, or incertainly expreſſed, it may; and
alſo to reconcile a Fine, and the Indentures to
lead the Uſes of the Fine. *Lib.* 2. 75.

But

But when a Deed is utterly incertain, no A-verment ſhall help it. As a Grant to one of the Sons of *J. S.* to two *& Hæredibus, &c.*

An Eſtate to a Woman for her Life may be averred to be made for her Jointure, *Dyer* 146. Upon or a-*lib.* 4. 4.   And that the Thing granted to me gainſt a Re-by a new Name, is all one Thing with that cord. which hath another, or an old Name. *Dyer* 37. 44.

A thing that is againſt or beſides a Record, or any Thing that is within it, ſhall not be averred; therefore the Date of a Recogni-zance expreſſed to be taken at *Dale* cannot be averred to be taken at *Sale.*   But ſuch an Averment as may ſtand with the Record may be admitted.   As that the Fine was before the Inrollment (being both in one Term,) the A Fine taken Uſes of a Fine or Common Recovery may be by *R. M.* Eſq; averred ; or what, or who was meant, where and returned there are two of a Name, *&c.   Lib.* 8. 155. *litem* upon The Heir in Tail cannot aver againſt a Fine the *Ded. p.* levied by his Anceſtors, That *partes finis nihil* the Record *habuerunt, Lib.* 3. 84, 85.   *Leon.* 75, 76, *&c.* not to be a-But when Tenant in Tail accepts of a Fine, verred againſt and grants and renders the Land by the ſame Yelv. 33. Fine, which is executory; there, if no Ex- Cro. 2 Part ecution be ſued in the Life of Tenant in Tail, 11. his Iſſue may aver Continuance of Poſſeſſion, *&c.* in his Father ; for this ſtands with the Fine, and the Acceptance of the Fine alters not the Eſtate.

If a Man and his Wife ſell her Land for Money, and after levy a Fine to the Vendee and his Heirs, it may be averred it was for Money, and ſo carry the Uſe to the Vendee, without any Declaration of Uſe, which other-wiſe would reſult to the Woman and her Heirs :

And fo other Ufes may be proved, than what are in an Indenture of Ufes fubfequent to the Conveyance, &c. *Lib.* 9. 8. 5. 26.

Tenant in Tail with Remainder in Tail to *A.* Reverfion in Fee to himfelf, bargains and fells Land, &c. and levies a Fine to him with Proclamation, with general Warranty. The Conufee infeoffs *A.*

Refolved, The Bargainee had an Eftate determinable upon the Death of the Tenant in Tail, (and alfo the Reverfion in Fee, which the Bargainor had) and his Wife fhall be endowed; but this determines upon the Death of the Tenant in Tail.

Refolved, the Fine doth not difcontinue the Remainder, for this doth not pafs any Eftate, but this Eftate of the Bargainee is durable, &c. fo that it fhall not determine until the Tenant in Tail die without Iffue; and the Conclufion may be confeffed and avoided.

Refolved, That Warranty doth not bar the Remainder; for this was annexed to the Fee determinable, &c. and to the Reverfion in Fee, and doth not extend to the Remainder, for the Conufee cannot inlarge, &c. It is a Maxim, that a Warranty bars no Freehold, which is *in effe,* Poffeffion or Remainder, &c. and not difplaced before, or that the Time of the Warranty, although it be devefted before the Defcent.

Refolved, a Warranty cannot inlarge the Eftate.

Refolved, The Feoffment of the Conufee was not a Difcontinuance of the Remainder, becaufe he was not Tenant in Tail; fo of the Grantee of *totum ftatum fuum,* &c.

Refolved,

Refolved, A collateral Warranty may be given in Evidence, and found by the Jury.

The Chief Juftice held, That by the Feoffment of the Conufee, the Remainder was not difplaced, nor put to a Right, for his Fee-fimple and his Fee determinate pafs ; and the Feoffment, which in itfelf is not tortious, cannot be tortious to another. Otherwife it is when Tenant for Life, or Remainder in Tail, &c. makes a Feoffment, for the Feoffment itfelf is tortious.

Note ; There are fome Titles to which a Warranty doth not extend ; as in the Cafe of an Exchange, Condition upon a Mortmain, Confent to a Ravifher, &c. for in thefe Cafes no Action lies, in which Voucher or Rebutter may be ; neither fhall a Defcent take away Entry in thefe Cafes, and cannot be difplaced out of their original Effence. Collateral Warranty fhall bar Dower, and yet an Action is given for this. But a Fine, &c. and five Years bar thefe Titles and Dower alfo, if an Action be not brought in Time. *Seymour*'s Cafe, *Lib.* 10. 96.

Buckler and *Harvey*'s Cafe, *Lib.* 2. 55.

Tenant for Life leafes for four Years, and afterwards grants the Lands to *C.* from *Midfummer* next for Life ; after the Feaft the Leffee for Years attorns, then the Grantee enters and leafes at Will ; to which Tenant at Will the Tenant for Life levies a Fine *come ceo, &c.* Remainder in Fee enters.

Refolved, the Grant was void, for an Eftate of Freehold cannot commence *in futuro,* and the Grant being void at the Commencement, the Attornment afterwards cannot make it pafs ; and that the Grantee was a Diffeifor. But if

R 2   the

the Grant had been good at the Commencement, and was only to have its Perfection by a subsequent Act, as by Livery upon a Charter of Feoffment, &c. and the Grantee enter before the Perfection, he is not a Disseisor, but a Tenant at Will.

Resolved also, If the Fine had been levied to the Disseisor himself *come ceo,* &c. he which had the Right of Remainder, may enter for the Forfeiture ; for it was agreed that the Right of a particular Estate may be forfeited, and Entry given to him who had but a Right. As if Lessee for Years be ousted, or Tenant for Life disseised, and the Lessee for Years brings an Assize, or the Lessee for Life a Writ of Right, &c. it is a Forfeiture.

Resolved also, That the Fine being levied to the Tenant at Will, it is a Forfeiture, and he which had Right of Remainder may enter, and the Tenants for Life and at Will also shall be estopped to say, *quod partes finis nihil hab.* &c. and of such Estoppels which are by Matter of Record, and trench to the Disherison of them in Reversion, &c. they shall take Advantage although they are Strangers to the Record, for they are Privies in Estate.

Resolved also, if the Disseisee levy a Fine to an Estranger, the Disseisor shall retain for ever ; for the Disseisee against his own Fine cannot claim the Land, and the Conusee cannot enter, for the Right of the Conusor cannot be transferred to him ; but by the Fine the Right is extinct, whereof the Disseisor shall have Advantage. But in *Croke,* 1 Part 482. 13 *Car.* it was moved, If the Disseisee, not knowing of the Disseisin, levied a Fine to a Stranger, whether that should bar his Right,

and

and move to the Benefit of the Diffeifor, according to *Buckler's* Cafe; and faid, if admitted, it would be of very mifchievous Confequence; and by two Judges held, That it fhould not enure to the Benefit of the Diffeifor, but to the Ufe of the Conufor himfelf; for otherwife a Diffeifin being fecret may be the Caufe of Difherifon of any one who intends to levy a Fine for his own Benefit, for Affurance of his Lands upon his Wife and Children, or otherwife 1 *Inft.* 277.

Not againft fuch Certificates as are a defini- Againft a Certificate. tive Trial of the Thing certified, as the Bifhop's Certificate of Excommunication, Baftardy, lawful Marriage, &c. So Certificates of the Marfhal of the Hoft, which is a Trial; but againft Certificates only of Information it may be: As againft Certificates upon Commiffion out of any Court, or of the Commiffioners that affirm a Man a Bankrupt, which are not triable in a Courfe of Law, but Informations. *Lib.* 7. 14. *Lib.* 8. 121.

So of a Return, if it is a definitive Trial Upon a Return. of the Thing returned, no Averment lieth againft it. As the Return of a Sheriff upon fome Writs, as a Writ of Partition, *Elegit*, and of *Hab. Corp.* from a Mayor, &c. But if the Return is not definitive, as upon a Refcous, &c. an Averment doth lie; and upon this you may go to Trial: So if there be a Return to endanger a Man's Life, or his Inheritance, an Averment may be had againft it. *Dyer* 348. 117. So it lieth againft the Returns of Bailiffs of Franchifes, fo that the Lords be not prejudiced in their Franchifes thereby. *Goldsb.* 129, 139. *pl.* 23.

In Action for a falfe Return, an Averment doth lie againft the Sheriff's Return, *Winch* 100. and fo it doth in any other Action, than in that the Return was made.

Upon or againft a Will or Adminiftration, it lieth altho' they be under Seal of Court.

Any Averment may be upon a Will, or any Part of it that may help to expound it; and of fuch a Thing that may ftand with the Will, and may be collected out of the Words. As which Son he meant, &c. *Lib.* 8. 31, 41. But no Averment againft or befides that which is expreffed in the Will, or which cannot be gathered to be the Mind from the Words, nor of any Thing that doth not cohere with the Will; efpecially if it be about Lands, as in the Lord *Cheyney's* Cafe, *Lib.* 5. 68. A Devife to *A.* and the Heirs of his Body, the Remainder to *B.* and the Heirs male of his Body, on Condition, *that he or they, or any of them, fhall not alien, &c.* no Averment fhall be taken to prove by Witneffes or other Evidence, that the Devifor intended to include *A.* within this Condition, by the Words *he or they*; for the Conftruction of Wills ought to be collected out of the Words of the Will in Writing, and not by any Averment or Proof out of it.

Againft Court Rolls, or upon them.

It lies againft the Rolls or Records of County-Courts, Hundred-Courts, Courts-Baron. As that there is no fuch Record, or it is not as it is certified. 34 *H.* 6. 42. 9 *E.* 4. 4.

Againft common Prefumption or Reafon.

No Averment or Proof is to be admitted againft common Prefumption, as that there was more Rent behind, when the Acquittance of the laft Rent was made. 1 *Inft.* 373. Nor againft common Reafon, as that Common is appendant to a Meadow, or to a Meffuage. *Plow.* 170. *Lib.* 4. 37.

If

If the Matter contained in an Award, and Upon an A-
the Matter in the Submiffion do not agree, it ward.
will hardly be fupplied by an Averment. *Dyer*
242. 52.

If the Defeafance of a Recognizance be Date.
dated before the Recognizance, it may be
averred to be delivered at or before the Time
of the Recognizance entred into. *Perkin*'s
Cafe, 147.

Things apparent, or neceffarily intendable by
Law, need not be averred : *Manfefta non proba-*
tione indigent : Quod conflat clare, non debet ve-
rificari. Lib. 11. 25. *Plo.* 8.

Chief Juftice *Anderfon* held, *Godbolt* 131. Devife.
That if one devife Lands to the Heirs of *J. S.*
and the Clerk writes it to *J. S.* and his Heirs,
that the fame may be holpen by Averment,
becaufe the Intent of the Devifor is written,
and more; and it fhall be naught for that
which was againft his Will, and good for the
Refidue. But if a Devife be to *J. S.* and his
Heirs, and it is written but to the Heirs of
J. S. there an Averment fhall not make it
good to *J. S.* becaufe it is not in Writing,
which the Law requires; and fo an Averment
to take away any Surplufage is good, but not
to increafe that which is defective in the Will
of the Teftator. But with Submiffion, if the
Law fhould admit of fuch Averments, it would
be as mifchievous one Way as the other, and
no Man could know by the Words of the
Will, what Conftruction to make, nor what
Advice to give; but this fhall be controuled by
collateral Averments out of the Will, and in-
ftead of proving the Teftator's Will, it would
be the deftroying of it.

Partition.

If the Partition be by Writ, although it be unequal, yet it ſhall not be avoided by Averment, but ſhall bind the Feme Coverts. And ſuch Averment againſt the Return of the Sheriff ſhall not be good. 1 *Inſt.* 171.

Conſideration.

A valuable Conſideration in a Bargain and Sale not expreſſed, may be averred. 2 *Inſt.* 672.

A Conſideration which conſiſts with the Deed, and not repugnant, may be averred; as in a Bargain and Sale, if a particular Conſideration be expreſſed, and the general Clauſe of *other good Cauſes and Conſiderations*, or without that general Clauſe, yet other Conſiderations may be ſhewed: So if the particular Conſideration be Love and Affection, yet Payment of Money may be ſhewed: ſo a precedent Intent of Uſes, and to levy a Fine, may be ſhewed to guide the Uſe of the Fine. *Roll.* Tit. *Uſes*, 790.

Uſes.

As if I covenant by Deed to purchaſe Land, and then to levy a Fine, or make a Feoffment thereof to the Uſe of another, and afterwards purchaſe and levy a Fine, or make a Feoffment, this Uſe ſhall riſe; for the Deed is an Evidence of the precedent Intent, and the Uſes of a Fine or Feoffment may be directed by the precedent Intent, and yet ſuch Intent is countermandable. But a Covenant to purchaſe and ſtand ſeiſed of Lands to Uſes, ſhall not raiſe the Uſe after the Purchaſe, becauſe the Uſe is to riſe by the Deed, and at the Time when the Deed was made, there was no Eſtate in the Land. *Ibid.*

So if one Joint-tenant covenant to ſtand ſeiſed of his Companion's Part, if he ſurvive, yet no Uſe ſhall riſe if he did ſurvive, becauſe

at

at the Time of the Covenant, he could not grant nor charge the Land. *Ibid.*

'Tis true that a Fine *sur Grant & Render*, *Fine sur Grant* unless it be in special Cases, cannot be averred *& Render.* by Parol to be to any other Use or Intent than what is expressed in the Fine, Feoffment, or other Conveyance: But there is a Diversity betwixt a Use and Consideration; for when a Fine, Feoffment, or other Conveyance, import an express Consideration, a Man may aver by Word another Consideration, which may stand with the Consideration expressed; but the Parties cannot by Parol aver any other Use than is contained in the same Conveyance. Also no Averment shall be against the Consideration expressed; but yet in some Cases a Fine *sur Grant & Render* may be ruled and directed in Part by Averment *per parol:* And this is when the original Bargain and Contract betwixt the Parties is by Indenture or other Deed; as where it is agreed by Indenture, that a Fine shall be levied of certain Lands, by the Name of a certain Number of Acres, to divers Persons, and that they shall grant and render the Land again in Fee-simple, which shall be to certain Uses, the Fine is levied of the Land; but there is some Variance betwixt the Number of Acres comprized in the Fine; or the Fine is levied to one of the Parties only, who grants and renders the Land, so that there is a Variance betwixt the Covenant and the Fine, either in the Number, Time, or Person, *&c.* yet this Fine shall be averred to be to the Uses in the Indentures. For the Intent of the Parties, and the Substance and Effect of their original Bargain and Agreement, is chiefly to be regarded in all Con-

4   veyances;

veyances; and therefore the Law allows an Averment by Parol, to reconcile the Fine and Indentures, although this Sort of Fine imports a Confideration in itfelf, and regularly by a naked Averment by Parol cannot be averred to be to any other Ufe or Intent, than is comprized in the Fine itfelf; but by Deed it may be. *Lib.* 2. 77.

And although the Fine be of fo high a Nature, that it will not permit naked Averments againft the Purport and Conufance of the Fine; yet when the Law requires one of Neceffity, and for Conformity, to join with another in a Fine, the Law permits to fhew the Verity of the Matter, to avoid Prejudice and Confufion. As where Baron and Feme an Infant levy a Fine, which is reverfed for the Nonage of the Wife, the Baron and Feme fhall have Reftitution prefently, and the Conufee fhall not detain this during the Coverture; for all the Eftate paffes from the Feme, and the Baron joins for Neceffity and Conformity; and therefore the Law permits that the Verity of this fhall be fhewed, and that the whole Eftate fhall be reftored to the Wife, during the Life of the Hufband. *Worfely* and his Wife againft *Charnock*, 30 & 31 *Eliz. Lib.* 2. 77.

What may be averred *contra & præter* Records, Fines, Recoveries, Deeds, Wills, &c. is very requifite for a good Practifer to be ready in, and therefore I have here given this Tafte, referring him to the Books at large, where he may fee what Averments he in Remainder, the Heir in Tail, the Wife, her Heirs, Eftrangers, Privies, Parties, &c. may have to Fines, Recoveries, &c. *Lib.* 1. 76.

Lib.

Lib. 2. 77. *Lib.* 4. 71. *Lib.* 9. 140, 141. *Lib.*
2. 55. *Lib.* 2. 88. *Lib.* 10. 50, 96. *Lib.* 3.
51, 88. *Lib.* 4. 74, *&c.*

   The Knowledge of Evidence is fo benefi- *Note*; The
cial and neceffary for all Practifers in the Law, Chapter of
that none can know too much, be too well Verdicts gives
verfed, or too often converfant in it. There- to know what
fore to compleat this Treatife, efpecially in Evidence is
this Particular, I have drained the Law Books good, and
of all, or the moft principal Cafes relating to what not.
it ; and have added fome Obfervations very fit
for the Unlearned to know ; and I hope not
fit for the Learned to reject.

C H A P,

CHAP. XVI.

Brief Observations relating to Trials in Capital Cases.

Accessary.

1. IF the Principal be acquitted, or convict only of Manslaughter, or' *se Defendendo*, or before Attainder hath his Clergy or Pardon, or die, the Accessary shall not be arraigned. So if the Principal stand mute. *Hale P. C.* 221.

2. If the Principal appears not, the Accessary shall not be tried, unless he will. *Ibid.* 222.

3. Where a new Felony is made by Statute, it seems that there is no Accessary, unless specially enacted. *Ibid.* 223. *Quære*, for *Co. 3 Inst.* 72. is otherwise.

4. A Man being acquitted as Principal, cannot be arraigned as Accessary ; but if acquitted as Accessary, he may be arraigned as Principal. *Ibid.* 224.

5. Where there are two Principals and one Accessary, if one of the Principals be found Not guilty, the Accessary is discharged. *Co. 2 Inst.* 183.

Accessary to be tried when the Principal is pardoned or admitted to his Clergy.

By 1 *Annæ, cap.* 9. it was enacted, That if the Principal be convict of Felony, stand mute, or challenge peremptorily above twenty Jurors, the Accessary may be proceeded against as if such Principal Felon had been attainted, notwithstanding such principal Felon be admitted
ted

ted to his Clergy, pardoned or otherwife delivered before Attainder.

Such Acceffary being convicted, or if he ftands mute, or challenge as aforefaid, fhall fuffer as if the Principal had been attainted. *And fuffer as if the Principal was attainted.*

By 5 *Annæ, cap.* 31. it is enacted, That if any Perfon fhall receive or buy knowingly any ftolen Goods, or knowingly harbour or conceal Felons, he fhall be taken as Acceffary to the Felonies, and being convicted fhall fuffer Death as a Felon. *Receivers of Felons or ftolen Goods deemed Acceffaries.*

If the principal Felon cannot be taken, fo as to be convicted, yet the Perfon buying ftolen Goods, or receiving a Felon knowingly, may be profecuted for a Mifdemeanor, to be punifhed by Fine or Imprifonment, or other corporal Punifhment, as the Court fhall think fit; which fhall exempt the Offenders from being punifhed as Acceffary, if the Principal be after convict. *Such Acceffaries may be profecuted before the Principal is taken.*

Vide *Attainder* 3. *Bar* 1.

Accufation.

1. By the Statute 37 *E.* 3. *c.* 18. Promoters of Suggeftions to the King were to incur the Pain which the Accufed fhould fuffer, in cafe the Suggeftion hold not; but that Claufe was repealed by 41 *E.* 3. *c.* 9. and the Penalty changed into Fine and Imprifonment, and Damages to the Party grieved.

Action.

1. Action lies after Trial and Acquittal (of Felony) for unjuft and malicious Profecution. 400 *l.* Damages were recovered in the Com-

mon

mon Pleas after Trial in the King's Bench.
The Caſe of the five *Frenchmen*. *Vide* Lord
Hollis's Narrative, p. 42.

Appeal.

1. An Appeal for the Death of her Huſ--
band is proſecuted in the Office of civil Pleas-
in the King's Bench, and not in the Crown--
Office; and the Woman may proſecute by
Attorney, made by Warrant under Hand and
Seal, acknowledged by the Party in Court,
or proved by Witneſſes. 2 *Jones* 210. *Warren*
and *Verdon.*

2. Principal or Acceſſary in Murder being
acquitted within a Year and a Day after the
Fact, the Juſtices ſhall not let them go at
large, but either remand them to Priſon, or
bail them till the Year and Day be up, in which
Time the Wife or next Heir of the Party ſlain
(whether the Offender be attaint or acquitted)
may proſecute their Appeal, in Caſe the Benefit of Clergy hath not been allowed. The
Appellant muſt commence the Appeal in proper Perſon, but may after appoint an Attorney to proſecute it (ſave only in ſuch Caſes
where Battle lieth). *Stat.* 3 *H.* 7. *c.* 1. *ſect.* 15.
& *infra.*

3. No Man ſhall be taken or impriſoned
upon the Appeal of a Woman for the Death
of any other than her Huſband. *Mag. Chart.*
c. 34.
Vide *Particeps Criminis* 1.

Arraignment.

Arraignment.

1. A Prifoner at the Time of his Arraignment ought not to be in Irons. *Hale P.C.* 212. *Quære.*

2. After an Attainder of Felony, the Prifoner may be arraigned of Treafon. *Ibid.* 231.

3. When the Defendant hath pleaded to the Indictment, *Not guilty*, the Clerk on Behalf of the King, or his Attorney General, by Way of Replication, fays *Culprit, i. e. Culprift*, which is an Averment of his Guilt; and a taking of Iffue thereupon, as much as *paratus eft verificare quod Culpabilis eft*; the like as in Civil Actions, *& hoc paratus eft verificare, prift* in *French* fignifying the fame with *paratus* in *Latin*; then the Prifoner being demanded how he will be tried, anfwers, *By God and thē Country*, which is the fame with a Rejoinder and joining Iffue in a Civil Action, concluding *& de hoc ponit fe fuper Patriam.* So that upon all Arraignments, there is a Formality of Pleading obferved, in Effect the fame as in Civil Actions.

Vide *Trial* 6.

Arreft of Judgment.

1. Four Days are regularly given to move in Arreft of Judgment; but the Court may enlarge the Time if they pleafe, and accordingly eight Days were given to *Oates.* *Oates*'s 2d *Trial* 56, 57.

2. Of old Time the Party convicted had at leaft thirty Days, to fhew fome Matter to arreft Judgment, which now (fays Sir *Ed. Coke*)

is

is gone *in diffuetudinem*; and great Expedition is now made in Pleas of the Crown concerning the Life of Man. *Sed de morte hominis nulla eft cunctatio longa. Co. Lit. f.* 134. *b.*

Attainder.

1. Attainder may be falfified by the Party, by Writ of Error; or by others, as a Purchafor in fome Cafes, if he purchafed before the Attainder, and after the Time of the Felony fuppofed. *Vide Hale P. C.* 270.

2. If the Attainder was by fuch as had no good Commiffion, the Party himfelf may falfify. *Id. ibid.*

3. Principal is attaint, and then the Accef-fary; Principal reverfes his Attainder, the At-tainder of the Acceffary is *ipfo facto* avoided. *Id. Ibid.*

4. Attaint of Treafon, and then the Trea-fon is pardoned by Act of Parliament, the Party or Heir fhall falfify. *Ibid.* 271.

Bail.

1. BY the Statute of 31 *Car.* 2. *cap.* 2. a Writ of *Habeas Corpus* may be granted in Vacation Time by the Lord Chancellor, or any Judge or Baron of the Coif, returnable *im-mediate*, who are impowered to bail the Pri-foner (if bailable) to appear at the King's Bench the next Term or Affizes, *&c. Sect.* 3. The Prifoner who wilfully neglects two Terms, fhall not have the Benefit of a *Habeas Corpus* in the Vacation Time, *Sect.* 4. Perfons com-mitted for Felony or Treafon, if not (upon
their

their Petition in open Court, the firſt Week
of the Term, or firſt Day of Seſſions, &c.) indicted the next Term or Seſſions, &c. ſhall be
bailed, unleſs it appear by Oath, That the
Witneſſes for the King cannot be produced ſo
ſoon; and if not indicted the ſecond Term or
Seſſions, &c. he ſhall be totally diſcharged,
Sect. 7. If the Lord Chancellor, or any of the
Judges aforeſaid, ſhall in the Vacation Time,
upon View of the Copy of the Commitment,
or Oath made that ſuch Copy was denied,
deny a Writ of *Habeas Corpus*; he ſhall forfeit
to the Priſoner or Party grieved 500 *l. Sect.* 10.
Sheriff or Officer neglecting or refuſing to
obey the Writ, or to deliver a true Copy of
the Commitment within ſix Hours after Demand, ſhall forfeit to the Priſoner, for the
firſt Offence 100 *l.* for the ſecond Offence
200 *l.* and loſe his Office, *Sect.* 5. (unleſs the
Commitment be for Felony or Treaſon plain-
ly and ſpecially expreſſed in the Warrant of
Commitment).

2. Perſons taken for the Death of a Man,
or by Command of the King or his Juſtices,
Perſons outlawed, abjured, Provers and ſuch
as are taken in the Manner, Priſon-breakers,
Thieves openly defamed and known, Appel-
lees by Provers, (during the Life of ſuch Provers) Houſe-burners, Counterfeiters of the
King's Seal or Coin, excommunicated Perſons, and Traitors, are not repleviable (or
bailable) by common Writ, or without Writ.
Weſm. 1. (3 E. 1.) *c.* 15. *Vide Hale P. C.* 98.
& *infra.*

3. Perſons guilty of Larceny by Inqueſts taken before Sheriffs or Bailiffs, or of Petty Larceny, not before detected, or acceſſary unto

VOL. II.   S   any

any Felony, or only guilty of fome Trefpafs, for which he ought not to lofe Life or Member, are bailable by good Sureties. *Stat. ubi fup'.* To bail thofe who are not bailable, and refufe to bail thofe who are, is punifhable by Fine and imprifonment. *Stat. ubi fupra. Hale P. C.* 97.

4. Yet the Court of King's Bench has bailed one indicted for Murder at the Quarter-Seffions in *Suffex*, the Indictment being removed by *Certiorari* into that Court, after he had been arraigned, and pleaded Not guilty. The Bail were four fufficient Perfons, *Corpus pro Corpore. Farrington's* Cafe, *Mich.* '34 *Car.* 2. 2 *Jones* 222.

5. Juftices of Peace cannot bail but where they have Cognizance of the Caufe, and therefore if a Man be taken upon a Procefs of Rebellion out of Chancery, they cannot bail. *Id.* 105.

6. By the Statutes of 3 *H.* 7. *c.* 2. and 1 & 2 *Ph.* & *M. c.* 13. two Juftices of Peace are impowered to bail in Cafe of Felony. *Hale P. C.* 105.

7. A Bail for a Prifoner cannot be a Witnefs for him, unlefs the King's Counfel confent. *Hambden's Trial* 32.

8. By *Stat.* 1 *W.* & *M. Seff.* 2. *c.* 2. it is declared and enacted, *(inter alia) That exceffive Bail ought not to be required, nor exceffive Fines impofed, nor cruel and unjuft Punifhments inflicted, and that all Grants and Promifes of Fines and Forfeitures of particular Perfons before Conviction are illegal and void.*

Vide *Appeal* 2.

3

Bar.

Bar.

1. Where a Man is convict upon an Indictment of Manflaughter, and hath had his Clergy, this is a Bar to an Appeal after brought, though it be of Murder, for the Fact is the fame. *Hale P. C.* 247.

Baron. Peer.

1. A Baron of the Realm being a Witnefs, fits covered after his Evidence is over.   So alfo where he hath been a Party in Treafon, if he hath his Pardon. *Hamb. Trial* 17.

2. Evidence againft the Honour of a Peer of the Realm who gives Evidence for the King, thereby to render him incredible, as to make him an Atheift, &c. not admitted. *Hamb. Trial* 37, 38.

Vide *Trial* 16.   *Clergy* 4.

Challenge.

1. PRifoner may challenge peremptorily in Capital Cafes, where his Life is concerned, but not in leffer Offences.   *Reading's Trial* 8.

2. Allowed for a good Caufe of Challenge to one of the Petty Jury, if he hath been of the Grand Jury that found the Bill. *Oates's 1ft Trial* 1.

3. In Treafon the Prifoner accufed may challenge thirty-five ; and therefore there is a Return generally of fixty or eighty, and when he has challenged as many as he pleafes, the

twelve

twelve Men that ftand next are to be of the
Jury.   Lord *Ruffel's Trial* 31.

4. Peremptory Challenge is not allowable,
but where the Life of Man comes in Queftion.
At Common Law he might have challenged
peremptorily thirty-five, that is under three full
Juries; if he challenged above, he fhould be
hanged: But by the *Stat.* 22 *H.* 8. *c.* 4. made
perpetual by 32 *H.* 8. *c.* 3. it is reduced to
twenty; and if he challenge above twenty, he
fhall not be therefore hanged, but his Challenge
fhall be over-ruled, and put upon his Trial:
Yet *quære Hale P. C.* 259. But in Cafe of
Treafon or Petty Treafon, the Challenge of
thirty-five is reftored by *Stat.* 1 *&* 2 *Ph. & M.*
10. *Hale P. C.*

Vide *Mute* 1.

Clergy.

1. Where Clergy is allowable, it is to be
allowed as well where the Party is convict by
Confeffion, as by Verdict, and where he ftands
mute. *Hale P. C.* 231.

2. One admitted to his Clergy fhall, notwithftanding his Purgation, anfwer for other
Offences formerly committed, *Stat.* 8 *Eliz. c.* 4.
Before, (by Reafon of the *Stat.* 25 *E.* 3. 5.
which fays, a Clerk fhall be arraigned of all
his Offences at once) *Auterfoits convict* and
Clergy had been a Bar to an Arraignment of
any other Felony, though not within Clergy.
Hale P. C. 249.

This poffibly may be the Occafion of that
Error, which the leffer Criminals at the *Old
Baily* fo often ufe, when they plead Guilty to
this and all other Felonies within the Benefit
of

of Clergy ; though they are as often told they can plead only to what they are indicted.

3. None shall have the Benefit of Clergy twice, unless he be really in Orders. *Stat.* 4 *H.* 7. *c.* 13. *Hale P. C.* 239.

4. Ecclesiastical Persons being convict of Manslaughter, and having their Clergy, shall not be burnt in the Hand, *propter ordines*, *Hob.* 288, 294. Neither shall a Baron of this Realm, in the like Case, be burnt in the Hand, *propter bonorem. Stat.* 1 *Ed.* 6. *c.* 12. *sect.* 14.

5. The King may pardon Burning in the Hand after Conviction, and that as well in an Appeal as upon an Indictment : And the Burning being pardoned, he shall be delivered out of Prison of Consequence. *Co. Rep. l. 5. f.* 50. *Biggin's* Case.

6. A Man discharged of Burning in the Hand shall be immediately discharged of his Imprisonment. *Co. ubi sup'.* Yet the Justices, if they see Cause, may detain the Party in Prison for some Time, not exceeding a Year. *Stat.* 18 *Eliz. c.* 7. *sect.* 2, 3.

7. By the 3 & 4 *W.* & *M.* 9. it was enacted, That if a Woman should be convicted of any Offence, for which a Man might have the Benefit of his Clergy ; upon her Prayer to have the Benefit of this Statute, Judgment of Death shall not be given against her, but she shall suffer the same Punishment a Man should suffer in the like Case. *Women to have the Benefit of Clergy.*

8. By the same Statute, Clergy was taken away from such as should break any Dwelling-house, Shop or Warehouse thereunto belong-ing *Persons break-ing Houses, Shops, &c. and stealing the Value of 5 s. excluded Clergy.*

S 3

ing, or therewith uſed in the Day-time; and feloniouſly take away Money or Goods to the Value of five Shillings, though no Perſon were therein.

Perſons ſtealing the Value of 5 s. out of any Shop, Warehouſe, &c. though not broke open, are excluded Clergy.

9. By 10 & 11 *W.* 3. *cap.* 23. it was enacted, That all Perſons who by Night or Day after the 20th Day of *May* 1699, ſhould in any Shop, Warehouſe, Coach-houſe or Stable, privately and feloniouſly ſteal any Goods, &c. to the Value of five Shillings, though ſuch Shop, &c. were not broken open, and whether the Owner or any other Perſon were or were not in ſuch Shop, &c. And whoever ſhall aſſiſt in the committing ſuch Offence, being thereof convicted, ſhall loſe the Benefit of Clergy.

Reading taken away.

10. By 5 *Annæ*, *cap.* 6. If any Perſon ſhall be convict of ſuch Felony, for which he ought to have the Benefit of Clergy, and ſhall pray the Benefit of this Act; he ſhall not be required to read, but ſhall be puniſhed as a Clerk convict.

Perſons ſtealing the Value of 40 s. out of a Dwelling-houſe excluded Clergy.

11. By 12 *Annæ*, *cap.* 7. Perſons ſtealing Money or Goods to the Value of 40 s. out of any Dwelling-houſe or Out-houſe thereto belonging, though ſuch Houſe or Out-houſe are not broke open, they and their Accomplices are excluded the Benefit of the Act which comes in the Room of Clergy: Provided it do

Not to extend to Apprentices under fifteen.

not extend to Apprentices under fifteen Years of Age, who rob their Maſters. Perſons getting into a Houſe by Day or Night, with an

Breaking out of a Houſe, excluded Clergy.

Intent to commit Felony, who in the Night-time ſhall break the ſaid Houſe to get out, ſhall be deemed guilty of Burglary, and excluded the Benefit of Clergy. *Ibid.*

Commitment.

1. People apprehended upon Suspicion of Robbery, and had before a Justice, ought not to be committed without Oath. Lord *Hollis's Narr'* of the Trial of five *French Gentlemen*, 4. 31.

2. Subjects of this Realm committed for any Crime, shall not be removed into Custody of any other Officer, unless by *Habeas Corpus*, or some other legal Writ in due Course of Law, or in Case of Fire, Infection, or other necessity. *Stat.* 31 *Car.* 2. *c.* 2. *sect.* 9.

3. No Person, who shall be delivered or set at large upon any *Habeas Corpus*, shall be again re-committed for the same Offence, by any Person or Persons whatsoever, other than by the legal Order or Process of such Court wherein he shall be bound by Recognizance to appear, or other Court having Jurisdiction of the Cause. *Stat.* 31 *Car.* 2. *c.* 2. *sect.* 6.

4. No Subject inhabiting in this Realm, shall be sent Prisoner into *Scotland*, *Ireland*, *Jersey*, or any Foreign Parts, except Persons contracting to be transported, or Felons praying Transportation. 31 *Car.* 2. *c.* 2. *sect.* 12, 13, 14.

Confess.   V. *Overt-Act* 5.

1. Parties have sometimes confessed themselves Guilty, falsly. The Case of *Harrison* of *Campden* in *Gloucestershire*, who appeared alive many Years after three had been hanged for his Murder, one of which confessed. Also the Truth of Witches confession against

S 4   themselves

themselves hath been often doubted; it seems therefore that there ought to be good Circumstances concurring.

Copy.

1. Copy of Indictment, or Council, in Cases of Treason, not grantable by Law. *Sidn. Trial* 7. And this, notwithstanding 46 *E.* 3. which (as Mr. *Sidney* alledged) provides that *tout gents* shall have a Copy of every Record. *Ibid.* 9, 10.

2. But now by the *Stat.* 7 *W.* 3. *c.* 3. Every Person accused or indicted for High Treason, whereby any Corruption of Blood may be made, or for Misprision of such Treason, shall have a Copy of the whole Indictment (but not the Names of the Witnesses) five Days at least before the Trial; his Attorney or Agent requiring the same, and paying Fees for Writing, not exceeding 5 *s.*

3. Also by the said Statute, such Person shall have a Copy of the Jurors who are to try him, at least two Days before the Trial.

4. Before the said Statute, the Prisoner might not have a Copy of the Indictment, but was sometimes indulged a Copy of the Panel, though it was not his Right. Lord *Ruffel's Trial* 29, 30.

Council.

1. In collateral Matters, any one may be of Council with the Prisoner, without Affignment. 2 *Jones Rep.* 180. *O Carny's* Cafe.

2. Prisoner

2. Prifoner hath not Council in Treafon, becaufe the Proof muft be plain. *Colm. Trial* 17. *Co.* 3 *Inft.* 137.

3. In thofe Cafes where a Man can have no Council, (as Treafon, *&c.*) the Court is of Council for him; but where he may have Council the Judges are not of Council for the Prifoner. *Oates's* 1ft *Trial* 66.

4. Council in Treafon not grantable, except in fome fpecial Point of Law; there Council may be granted. *Sidn. Trial* 7. *Co.* 3 *Inft.* 137.

5. But now by the Statute of 7 *W.* 3. *c.* 3. If any Perfon indicted for High Treafon, whereby any Corruption of Blood may be made, or Mifprifion of fuch Treafon, fhall defire Council, the Court before whom he fhall be tried, fhall affign him fuch Council as he defires, not exceeding two, who fhall have free Accefs to him at feafonable Hours.

6. A Prifoner indicted, and demanding Council, and having it, if he refufes to plead as his Council advifes, Judgment fhall go againft him as his Crime requires. 3 *Cro.* 175. *Jeffe's* Cafe.

7. What the Prifoner may alledge to obtain Council as to Matter of Law, fee *Co.* 3 *Inft.* 137. *viz.* Such Matters as may make the Proceedings erroneous, and of fuch it is lawful for any Man then prefent in Court, to inform the Court. *Co.* 3 *Inft.* 29 *&* 137.

County.

1. In Trials of Treafon, it is not material that the Fact be proved to be done in the particular Parifh laid in the Indictment; it is
sufficient

fufficient if proved to be done in the County, in any other Parifh. *Charnock's Trial* 71 & *alibi.*

Vide *Place* 1. *Trial* 11, 12.

Defence.

1. BY *Wi. Williams,* in all Cafes where a Perfon fwears directly againft a Defendant, the Defendant, or his Council, (in Cafe the Caufe admits of Council) muft endeavour to fhew from Circumftances arifing out of the Fact, and farther Circumftances attending the Fact, and by probable Arguments, and reafonable Inductions out of the Evidence, that the Defendant is Not guilty: This where direct Evidence of his Innocence cannot be had. *Hambden's Trial* 19.

Demurrer.   Vide Plea.

Depofitions.

1. In Trial for Murder, Depofitions taken before the Coroner may be read for Evidence, if the Party be either Dead or beyond the Seas. *Secus,* Depofitions taken before a Juftice of Peace, 2 *Jones Rep.* 43. yet *Hale P. C.* 263. fays, Depofitions before a Juftice may be read; but in Prudence the Juftice or his Clerk ought to be fworn to the Truth of the Examinations.

Evidence.

Evidence in Criminal Matters.

1. IF a Man be indicted upon the Stat. of Stabbing, 1 *Jac.* 1. *c.* 8. and the Evidence is, that the dead Person struck first, whereby he is out of the Statute ; yet this will maintain a general Indictment for Manslaughter ; for this is an Indictment at Common Law as well as by the Statute; and though the Prisoner proves himself out of the Statute, yet he is not out of the Charge in the Indictment. *Gilb. Law of Evid.* 272.

2. A Witness may make use of Notes to refresh his Memory, but his Testimony must not be meerly to read them. *Coleman's Trial* 48.

3. A Man may give Evidence though he be sworn of the Jury. *Reading's Trial* 11.

4. Printed Trials not allowed to be cited for Evidence. 5 *Jes. Trial* 45. *Langhorn's Trial* 17, 50.

5. Hearsay, or a Report of what another Man said, is no Evidence against the Prisoner. *Lang. Trial* 22.   Lord *Russel's Trial* 48. See *postea.*

6. If a Woman were indicted for killing her Bastard, formerly the Evidence ought to have been, that she actually killed it ; but now by the 21 *Jac.* 1. *c.* 21. the very endeavouring to conceal the Death is Evidence of Murder, unless she contradict it by another Proof, and prove at least by one Witness that the Child was Still-born. *Gilb. Law of Evid.* 271, 272.

7. An Approver (who is one that confessing himself guilty of a Felony accuses another of the same Crime) hath a Penny a Day ; by

North

North Chief Juſtice, to ſhew that *Oates* and *Bedlows*'s Maintenance from the King was no Objeƈtion againſt their Evidence. *Lang. Trial* 27.

8. A Copy of a Record in the Lords Houſe would not be admitted to be given in Evidence at *Langhorn's Trial*, (*p.* 44.) nor was he allowed to prove by Witneſſes what *Oates* had affirmed in Relation to him at another Trial. *Lang. Trial* 45, 49.

9. The Journal of the Houſe of Commons, no Evidence; becauſe they have no Power to give an Oath, but the Proceedings of the Houſe of Peers are Evidence, becauſe that is a Court of Record. By *Jeffreys* Ch. Juſtice, *Oates's* 1ſt *Trial* 55. An Order of Court-Baron no Evidence, otherwiſe of the Judgment of a Court-Leet. *Id. ibid.*

10. If a Witneſs be ſworn to a particular Thing, and ſpeak to another Matter which he was not ſworn to give an Account of, this can never be Evidence; by *Jeffreys* Chief Juſtice. *Oates's* 1ſt *Trial* 65.

11. Hearſay is admitted for Evidence where it is to eſtabliſh another Witneſs's Teſtimony; as where a ſecond ſwears that he heard the firſt Witneſs declare the ſame Thing formerly. *Oates's* 1ſt *Trial* 70.

12. Where two Faƈts are alledged of the ſame Man, and it be queſtioned whether it be the ſame Man, it is ſufficient that it is ſo reported; and this is good Evidence, unleſs ſome one elſe of the ſame Name be produced. *Oates's* 2d *Trial* 15.

13. Indiƈtment that *A.* gave the mortal Blow, and that *B.* and *C.* and *D.* were preſent and abetting, the Evidence that *B.* gave the

2   mortal

mortal Blow, and that *C.* and *D.* were prefent abetting, maintains the Indictment. *Gilb. L. of Evid.* 271.

But if two are indicted as Principals, and the Evidence proves one Acceffary, he muft be difcharged. *Gilb. L. of Evid.* 271.

14. By *Jeffreys* Chief Juſtice. Though in Strictnefs we do not chufe to admit of what others have fworn at another Trial, unlefs the Party be dead that fwore it, yet the Prifoner is fometimes indulged fo far as to be admitted to prove it. *Oates's 2d Trial* 40.

15. If a Man be indicted of Poifoning, Evidence of Stabbing does not maintain the Indictment. *Gilb. Law of Evid.* 270.

16. On an Indictment of Murder, *Self-defence* fhould be given in Evidence, and not pleaded, becaufe nothing can juftify a private Man's Killing another. *Gilb. Law of Evid.* 270.

17. If the Indictment be of Felony at one Day, and the Evidence of Felony at another, yet the Jury may find generally againſt the Prifoner; but if they give a general Verdict, the Prifoner may falfify. *Gilb. Law of Evid.* 268.

If the Indictment lay the Evidence at one Place, and the Evidence of the Fact done at another, in the fame County, this will maintain the Indictment. *Ibid.* 269.

18. Evidence may be given in Treafon, to fhew the Temper of the Prifoner's Spirit, and how his Inclination hath been all along, tho' that be not the Thing for which he is directly called in Queftion. *Roufe, Tri.* 69, 70.

19. Hearfay from others is not to be applied immediately to the Prifoner; however, thofe Matters that are remote at firſt, may

serve

ferve to prove there was a general Confpiracy to deftroy the King and Government; and fo was the conftant Rule and Method about the Popifh Plot, firft to produce Evidence of the Plot in general. By Ch. Juftice. *Sidn. Tri.* 56.

20. No Witnefs admitted to prove what another had formerly faid in Evidence, tho' that Party be now difabled to come into Court himfelf. *Hamb. Trial* 31.

21. The Opinion of a Third Party againft the King's Witnefs, on Behalf of the Prifoner at the Bar, not admitted as Evidence. As to prove that the Lord *E.* had no good Opinion of the Lord *H.* who gave Evidence againft Mr. *H.* makes nothing for Mr. *H. Hamb. Trial* 36.

22. It is not regular to produce any Evidence without firft opening it. *Rockwood's Trial* 63.

23. By the late Act for regulating Trials in Cafes of Treafon, 7 *W.* 3. *c.* 3. no Evidence is to be admitted of any Overt Act, that is not exprefsly laid in the Indictment; but it does not exclude Evidence in order to prove an Overt Act laid, though fuch Evidence be not laid. *Rock. Trial* 74.

24. Indictment for Murder *ex Malitiâ*, and the Evidence is for Killing without Provocation or an Offence, or that the Party was committing an unlawful Act; this is proof of Murder, for in this Cafe the Law implies the Circumftance of Malice. *Gilb. Law of Evid.* 273.

25. Indictment for Murder; if it be proved the Words arofe on a Provocation, the Jury may

may find him guilty of Manflaughter. *Gilb. Law of Evid.* 272.

Vide *Baron* 2. *Depofitions* 1. *Examination* 3. *Trials* 3, 5.

Examination.

1. Perfons accufed of Manflaughter or Felony, who for want of Bail are to be fent to Prifon, muft be examined before the Juftice before he commits them, and the Accufers bound over to appear and give Evidence againft them at the next Gaol-Delivery, whofe Examination muft be taken and committed to Writing within two Days at the fartheft, and certified by the faid Juftice, with the Bonds or Recognizances of the Accufers at the faid next Gaol-Delivery. *Stat.* 2 & 3 *P. & M. c.* 10.

2. Examination before a Juftice muft be only fubfcribed to by the Offender, and not upon his Oath; but Examination of others muft be upon Oath. *Hale P. C.* 262.

3. Thefe Examinations, if the Party be dead or abfent, may be given in Evidence; but not Examinations relating to a forcible Marriage; in a Trial upon the *Stat.* 3 *H.* 7. *c.* 2. *Hale P. C.* 263.

4. Prudence requires that the Juftice or his Clerk be fworn to the Truth of the Examinations. *Vide ibid.*

Exception.

Exception.

1. No Exception to Witneffes in Treafon, becaufe they have been concerned by their own fhewing in the fame Crime; for they are the moft proper Perfons to be Evidence, none being able to detect fuch Councils but them. Lord *Ruffel's Trial* 61.

Vide infra *Quafhing* 1. *Indictment.* 3.

Execution.

1. Executions muft be purfuant to the Judgment, and cannot be altered by the King, as in Felony from Hanging to Beheading. *Hale P. C.* 268, 272. But the King may pardon Part of the Execution, as in Treafon he may pardon all but Beheading. *Hale P.C.* 272. Yet there have been fome inftances of beheading after Judgment in Felony; as of *Edward* Duke of *Somerfet* in the Reign of *E.* 6. and *Mervin* Lord *Audley* in the Reign of *Ch.* 1. fo of fome Women who have been beheaded, though the Judgment is not fo, neither in Felony nor Treafon. *Vide Co.* 3 *Inft.* 211.

2. If the Sheriff or other Officer, where he ought to hang the Party attainted, according to his Judgment, or Charge, will burn or behead him, or *è converfo*; the Law in this Cafe implieth Malice. *Co.* 3 *Inft.* 52.

3. If a Lieutenant or other, in Time of Peace, hang or otherwife execute any Man, by Colour of Martial Law, this is Murder. *Id. Ibid.*

Feme

Feme Covert.

1. THE Wife (nor the Wife's Examination) is not to be produced or ufed, neither for or againſt her Huſband. *Hale's P. C.* 263. *Co Lit. fo.* 6. *b.* Nor the Huſband againſt his Wife, except in Treaſon. *Raym. Rep. p.* 1. *Mary Grig's* Caſe.
Fines. V. *Bail* 9.

Habeas Corpus. V. *Bail*·1.

Hearſay.

See *Evidence* 4, 9, 13, 14, 15.

1. THE two Witneſſes required in Treaſon, muſt not give Evidence only by *Hearſay.* *Hale P. C.* 262.

Homicide.

1. The Preſence, and abetting at Homicide done by another, makes a Man guilty in that Caſe, as well as in the Caſe of Murder. 2 *Jones Rep.* 55.

Impriſonment.

1. BY *Stat. M. Cb.* 29. No Freeman ſhall be taken, impriſoned, diſſeiſed of his Freehold, or Liberties or free Cuſtoms, outlawed, or exiled, nor otherwiſe deſtroyed, unleſs by

legal Judgment of his Peers, or by the Law of the Land. And by the *Stat.* 25 *E.* 3. *c.* 4. none fhall be taken, unlefs it be by Indictment or Prefentment of lawful People of the Neighbourhood in due Manner, or by Procefs made by Writ original at the Common Law.

2. No Serjeant at the Mace, Bailiff, or other Officer whatfoever, fhall convey or carry any Perfon in his or their Cuftody by Writ, Procefs or other Warrant whatfoever, to any Tavern, Ale-houfe, or other Victualling or Drinking-houfe without the voluntary Confent of the, Party. *Stat.* 22, 23 *Car.* 2. *c.* 2. *fect.* 9.

3. If the Keeper or Under-keeper of a Prifon, by too great *Durefs* of Imprifonment and by Pain, make a Prifoner that he hath in Ward to become an Appellor (or Approver) againft his Will, and thereof be attainted, he fhall have Judgment of Life and Member. *Stat.* 14 *E.* 3. *c.* 10. Every Imprifonment is taken and deemed in Law *Duritia, Durefs*; a little Addition to it by the Gaoler is *too great Durefs* in this Cafe. *Co.* 3 *Inft.* 91.

4. If a Gaoler keep the Prifoner more ftrictly than he ought of Right, whereof he dieth, this is Felony in the Gaoler by the Common Law; and this is the Caufe that if a Prifoner die in Prifon, the Coroner ought to fit upon him. *Id. ibid.*

5. In all Offences fineable, the Imprifonment is o:ly to be until the Fine is paid; if the Fine be tendred, there is to be no Imprifonment at all. 1 *Vent.* 116.

Vide *Commitment* 4.

Indictment.

1. The Word *Proditorie* is neceſſary in all In-dictments of Treaſon, *Reding's Trial* 8.   In all Indictments of Death, the Word *Percuſſit* is neceſſary, except in Caſe of Poiſoning.   *Co. Rep. lib. 5. fo.* 122.   So in Rape, *Rapuit* ; in Larceny, *Felonice, Hale P. C.* 207. In Murder, *Murdravit*; for theſe are *Vocabula artis. Co.* 5 *Rep.* 121. *b.*

2. An Indictment is no more than an Ac-cuſation, and in the Nature of the King's Count, and may be true or falſe.   *Co.* 9 *Rep. f.* 118. *a.*

3. *By the* Stat. 7 W. 3. c. 3. *No Indictment in Caſes of Treaſon and Miſpriſion of Treaſon, or any Proceſs or Return thereupon, ſhall be quaſhed on the Motion of the Priſoner, for miſ-writing, falſe or improper Latin, unleſs Excep-tion for the ſame be made by the Priſoner or his Council, before Evidence given in Court* ; *yet any Judgment given upon ſuch Indictment may be reverſed upon a Writ of Error.* The Court underſtood this to be before Plea pleaded, or at leaſt before the Jury ſworn. *Rookw. Tri. p.* 20. *uſq*; 36. But the Advan-tage of the Priſoner's Council ſlipping that Time was waived, and the Council admitted to except as to miſ-writing, miſpelling, falſe and improper *Latin*, before the Evidence opened ; but they did not, for their Exceptions were ſaid to be ſubſtantial, which might be moved in Arreſt of Judgment after Verdict, *ub. ſup'*.

Vide *Place, County.*

Infant.

Infant.

1. Examination of an Infant of thirteen, nay of nine Years of Age, allowed in fome Cafes. *Hale P. C.* 263.

2. Infant within Age of Difcretion kills a Man, no Felony; as if he be nine or ten Years old: But if by Circumftances it appears he could diftinguifh between Good and Evil, it is Felony; as if he Hide the Dead body, make Excufe, *&c.* but in fuch Cafes, Execution in Prudence is refpited, to obtain a Pardon. *Hale P. C.* 43, 44.

Interruption.

1. The Prifoner and his Council have been heard in the midft of fumming up the Evidence by the Court, to rectify a Miftake. *Rookwood's Trial* 71.

2. No Obfervations ought to be made upon the Prifoner's Evidence, till he hath concluded to give all his Evidence, admitted for good Practice in Lord *Mohun's Trial* 33, 36.
Vide *Trial* 8.

Jury.

1. In Capital Cafes a fpecial Jury fhall not be ftricken by the Clerk of the Crown in the King's Bench, as is ufual by the Secondary in Civil Caufes on Trials at Bar: Thus it was ruled in the feveral Cafes of *Fitz-Harris, O Carny* and *Farrington*. 2 *Jones Rep.* 222.

2. There

2. There is no Panel made in *London* of Freeholders, there being few Freeholders there capable of being impanelled, becaufe the Eftates of the City belong much to the Nobility and Gentry, who live abroad, and to Corporations; therefore in the City of *London* the Challenge of Freeholders is excepted.   Lord *Ruffel's Trial* 31.   And the *Stat.* 2 *H.* 5. *c.* 3. extends not to this Cafe; and fo ruled in the Lord *Ruffel's* Cafe at the *Old Baily*; and it was there faid, That at the Common Law Trials for Treafons might be without Freeholders of the Jury; and for Treafon, Trials fhall be according to Common Law; by *Stat.* 1 *&* 2 *P. & M. c.* 10. Lord *Ruffel's Trial* 36.   But now by the *Stat.* 1 *W. & M. Seff.* 2. *c.* 2. it is declared and enacted, (*inter alia*) *That Jurors ought to be duly impanelled and returned, and Jurors which pafs upon Men in Trials for High Treafon ought to be Freeholders.*

3. No *Medietas Linguæ* is allowed in Treafon, nor in any Appeal of one Alien againft another; nor fhall a *Scot* be accounted an Alien to have a *Medietas Linguæ,* nor *Egyptians. Medietas Linguæ* muft be prayed by the Prifoner, and the Jurors need not to be of the fame Nation, but any Aliens. *Hale P. C.* 260, 261. *Vide Dyer* 144, 145.

Vide *Challenge* 2, 3.

Means.

1. IF the Indictment be of poifoning with one Poifon, and it is proved with another; or killing with a Dagger, and it is proved with a Staff, yet it maintains the Indictment; for

it agrees in Subftance and Kind, though not in the Means. But if the Indictment and Evidence differ *in fpecie Mortis,* as Indictment of Poifoning, Evidence of Stabbing, this maintains it not. *Hale P. C.* 265.

Medietas Linguæ. Vid. *Jury* 3.

1. By the *Stat.* 28 *E.* 3 *c.* 13. *fect.* 2. all Enquefts made among Aliens and Denizens, be they Merchants or other, although the King be Party, fhall be one Half Denizens, and the other Half Aliens, if there be fo many in the Town; if not, fo many as are; and thefe Aliens are not required to have 40 *s.* Freehold *per Annum.* 9 *H.* 6. *c.* 29. *n.* 13.

Mute.

1. To challenge above thirty-five, is the fame as to ftand Mute, and he fhall have *Pain fort & dure.* But in an Appeal, ftanding Mute, Judgment is to be hanged; fo for Felony within the Verge; and in Treafon it is a Conviction. *Hale P. C.* 226. *Co.* 2 *Inft.* 178. This forfeits no Land, nor works any Corruption of Blood. *Co Lit. fo.* 391.

Noli profequi. Vide *Trial* 14.

Non Compos.

1. IF a Man that is *Non Compos* kills another, this is no Felony; fo of a Lunatick during his Lunacy. But he that incites a Madman

to

to kill another, is a principal Murderer. A Man that is drunk killeth another, this is Felony. *Hale P. C.* 43.

Oath.

1. EVidence for the King always upon Oath, not fo for the Prifoner till the Statute of Q. *Ann.* But in fome Cafes heretofore by the Statute, Evidence is to be upon Oath for the Prifoner; as 31 *Eliz. c.* 4. *fect.* 2. & 4 *Jac.* 1. *c.* 1. *fect.* 27.   *Hale P. C.* 264.

2. Witneffes in Capital Cafes againft the King for the Prifoner, cannot be fworn, but the Jury is to take heed of what they fay, and to be governed by it according to the Credibility of the Perfon and of the Matter. Lord Chief Juftice in the 5 *Jef. Trial* 45. *Co.* 3 *Inft.* 79. fays, there is not fo much as *Scintilla juris* againft it, and that Evidence againft the Prifoner fhould be fo plain, that nothing could be anfwered againft it; and therefore no Evidence to be fworn againft the King. 5 *Jef. Tri. ibid.*   But this was before the Stat. of Q. *Ann.*

3. Now, by the Statute of 7 *W.* 3. *c.* 3. It is provided and enacted, that Perfons accufed, or tried for High Treafon, whereby any Corruption of Blood may be made, or Mifprifion of fuch Treafon, fhall be admitted to make any Proof by lawful Witnefs or Witneffes who fhall then be *upon Oath*.

4. To take a Man's Life away by a falfe Oath, is Murder; by *Scroggs* Chief Juftice. *Coleman's Trial* 17.

Vide *Commitment* 1.   *Examination* 2.

T 4	*Overt-*

Overt-Act.

1. Compassing the King's Death is Treason by the Words of the Statute 25 *E.* 3. And meeting in Council to raise a Rebellion, is an Evidence of Compassing, and an *Overt-Act* declaring the same. Lord *Ruffel's* *Trial* 51, 57.

2. If a Man should be indicted only for High Treason in levying War; here a contriving to levy War is not a sufficient Evidence, without an actual War levied; but if he be indicted for compassing and imagining the Death of the King, there the contriving such a War is an *Overt-Act* of the compassing and Imagining. *Sidn. Trial* 56.

3. Though some Judges have been of Opinion that Words of themselves are not an *Overt-Act*, yet no Sage of the Law ever questioned, but that a Letter was an *Overt-Act* sufficient to prove a Man guilty of High Treason, for *Scribere eſt agere.* Sidn. Trial 56.

4. Loose Words spoken without Relation to any Act or Design are not Treason; but Arguments and Words of Persuasion to engage in a treasonable Design and Resolution, and directing and proposing the best Way for effecting it, are *Overt-Acts* of High Treason; so consulting together for such a Purpose is an *Overt-Act* of High Treason: For it is the Imagination, the Compassing and Designing the Death of the King, that is the Treason; but there is no Way of Discovery of those Imaginations in order to punish a Traitor, but by some external Act. Chief Justice in *Charnock's Trial* 65. And that which is a sufficient Ma-
nifeſtation

nifeftation of fuch a Defign is an *Overt-Act.*
Id. ibid.

5. By the late *Stat.* 7 *W.* 3. *c.* 3. no Perfon
fhall be indicted, tried or attainted of High
Treafon, whereby Corruption of Blood may
be made, or Mifprifion of fuch Treafon, but
by the Oaths and Teftimony of two lawful
Witneffes, either both to the fame *Overt-Act,*
or one to one, and the other to another *Overt-*
Act of the fame Treafon ; unlefs the Party willingly in open Court confefs, ftand mute, or
peremptorily challenge above thirty-five.

Outlawry.   Vide *Witnefs.*

Panel.

1. BY the *Stat.* 7 *W.* 3. *c.* 3. the Prifoner for
High Treafon, or Mifprifion, *fhall have*
a Copy of the Panel of the Jurors, who are to
try him, duly returned by the Sheriff, and deli-
vered to him two Days before the Trial. This
fhall be underftood two Days before the Trial,
after the Panel is made, and not after it is returned into the Court ; for then the Trial is to
commence. *Rookwood's Trial* 13.

Pardon.

1. A Pardon is good and fufficient after Indictment, though it doth not recite the fame, if
it hath other Words tantamount, fuch as *five*
fuit Indictatus five non. 2 *Jones Rep.* 56.
vide 1 *Vent.* 207.

2. A Par-

2. A Pardon takes away as well all Calumny as Liableneſs to Puniſhment, and ſets an Offender right againſt all Objection. *Reading's Trial* 53. It takes away not only *Pœnam* but *Reatum* alſo. *Hob. Rep.* 81.

3. A Pardon of a Felony (though after burning in the Hand) reſtores a Man to be a Witneſs; but in caſe he had been convicted of Perjury, and afterwards pardoned, that would not enable him to be a Witneſs 1 *Vent.* 349.

4. Charter of Pardon, no Bar of Appeal, *Hale P. C.* 251. yet the King may pardon burning in the Hand upon an Appeal. *Id.* 252.

5. He that hath a Pardon, muſt ſue forth a Writ of Allowance, ſpecifying that he hath found Surety for his good Behaviour; which he is obliged to do by the Statute of 10 *E.* 3. *c.* 3. and if he afterwards breaks the Peace, the Pardon ſhall be void by the Statute, and he hanged for the firſt Offence, unleſs the Pardon be with a *Non obſtante* to the Statute. *Hale P. C.* 252.

6. Pardon after Attainder does not make a Felon capable of being a Juryman, nor a Witneſs; *ſecus*, if burnt in the Hand. 2 *Brownlow* 47. 2 *Bulſt.* 154. *Brown* and *Craſhaw's* Caſe urged in *Rookwood's Trial, p.* 41. But overruled, *p.* 42, 43. yet allowed by the Chief Juſtice, that this may be objected againſt his Credit; but this is not to be urged againſt his being a Witneſs. *Ibid.* 44.

Vide *Clergy* 5. *Particeps Criminis* 1, 3.

Particeps Criminis.

1. *Langborn* urged at his Trial, That if an Approver (*i. e.* one who confeffes Felony committed by himfelf, and appeals or accufes others to be guilty of the fame) be pardoned, the Appellee ought to be difcharged; and for the fame Reafon, if thofe who have been *Participes Criminis* have got their Pardons, they ought not to be accounted fubftantial Witneffes againft a Prifoner at the Bar. But this was over-ruled. *Langborn's Trial* 27.

2. No Exception to a Witnefs in Treafon, becaufe they have been concerned, by their own fhewing in the fame Crime; for they are the moft proper Perfons to be Evidence, none being able to deteft fuch Councils but them. Lord *Ruffel's Trial* 61.

3. *Particeps Criminis*, whether pardoned or not, admitted as a Witnefs for the King, in High Treafon, *Sidney's Trial* 13, 30. So alfo upon a Penal Statute, 2 *Jones Rep.* 155. the King and *Benifon*.

Vide *Witnefs* 5, 9.

Peer.   Vide *Baron.*

Place.

1. If the Indiftment lay the Felony at one Place, the Evidence proving the Faft at another Place in the fame County, maintains the Indiftment. *Hale P. C.* 264.

2. Regularly he that pleads any fpecial Matter in Cafes capital, and confeffeth not the Felony, if the Plea be found againft him, the Felony

lony notwithftanding fhall be inquired of, and therefore he fhall plead over to the Felony. *Hale P. C.* 254. *Secus,* where the Prifoner demurs to the Indictment; for that amounts to a Confeffion of the Fact.   *Co.* 2 *Inft.* 178. *Hale P. C.* 243.

See *Clergy* 2.

Proof.

1. To prove a Hand-Writing by Similitude, and by thofe who have known the Hand, though the Party was not feen to write it, was allowed fufficient Proof of a treafonable Writing, in *Sidney's* Cafe; for this is faid to be as much Proof as the Thing is capable of, efpecially where the Writing was found in his Poffeffion. *Sidn. Trial* 51.   Yet *Sidney* faid, it had been declared in the Lady *Car's* Cafe, to be no lawful Evidence in Criminal Cafes.   *Sidney's Trial* 32.

Quafhing.

1. INdictment of Manflaughter not to be quafhed upon Motion, 1 *Vent.* 110. Nor Indictments of Perjury, Nufance, or the like, but the Party muft plead. *Id.* 370.

See *Indictment* 3.

Time.

1. IF the Indictment be of Felony, *&c.* at one Day, though the Evidence be of another Day, the Jury may find generally against the Prisoner, and leave the Person concerned in Point of Time to falsify; or the Jury may find the true Day upon their Verdict. *Hale P. C.* 264.

Vide *Trial* 9.

Treason.

1. All Persons indicted and tried for High Treason, must either be convicted of that Crime or acquitted; they cannot be found guilty of Misprision of Treason. *Wakeman's Trial* 83.

2. In Case of Treason, two Witnesses are required by the Statute of 1 *E.* 6. *c.* 12. except Treason for counterfeiting Coin. *Hale P. C.* 262.

3. The Statute of 7 *W.* 3. *c.* 3. intitled, *An Act for regulating of Trials in Cases of Treason and Misprision of Treason*, hath enacted several Matters in relation to such Trials; for which, see *Council* 4. *Evidence* 16. *Indictment* 3. *Copy* 2. *Oath* 4. *Overt-Act* 5. *Panel* 1. *Witness* 20. By the said Statute there is a Limitation of Time for finding the Indictment, *viz.* within three Years after the Crime committed, or three Years after the 25th of *March* 1696, for Treasons committed before that Time: Excepted out of this Limitation, Persons designing or attempting any Assassination on the Body of the King by Poison

or

or otherwife. This Act not to extend to any Impeachment or other Proceedings in Parliament, nor to Treafons for counterfeiting the King's Coin or Seals.

Trial.

1. To defire a Trial by *Ordeal* (there being no fuch Trial now ufed) was faid to be an artificial Varnifh to take with the Auditory. 5 *Jef. Trial* 68.

2. By *Scrogs* Chief Juftice, the Jury muft not take Notice of any Thing that was done at a former Trial, unlefs it be fpoken of now. 5 *Jef. Trial* 69. And a Prifoner muft not call any Witneffes to prove what was faid then, but to difprove what is faid now. *Ibid.* 70.

3. Regularly the Prifoner fhould not afk Queftions, but the Court, and the Prifoner propofe the Queftion to the Court. *Langhorn's Trial* 14.

4. The fame Matter may be examined and tried over again, by another Jury in another County, though tried the Day before. *Lang. Trial* 15.

5. Incoherent Evidence hath been fome Times taken favourably, and feeming Contradictions reconciled. *Wakeman's Trial* 15.

6. A Prifoner may be arraigned and tried at the fame Time in Capital Crimes. *Lord Ruffel's Trial* 59.

7. The King's Council are to have the laft Word. *Oates's 1ft Trial* 52.

8. By *North* Chief Juftice, the Prifoner muft have Liberty to afk Queftions while the Evidence is giving, becaufe there are fome Queftions that elfe may be forgotten, and the Opportunity

portunity will be loft ; but when he hath afked thofe Queftions, he is to make his own Obfervations upon them in private to himfelf, and afterwards it will be Time for him to argue upon it, when the King's Council have done their Evidence. Before, it will do him little Service, and cannot be permitted. *Wakeman's Trial* 19. Vide fupra *Interruption* 2.

9. A Criminal can demand no Time to prepare for Trial, for thofe who will commit Crimes, muft be ready to anfwer for them, and dcfend themfelves. *Roufe's Trial* 63.

10. Upon good Caufe fhewn, a Verdict for the King in an Information for Perjury has been fet afide, and a new Trial awarded. 2 *Jones Rep.* 163. *The King* and *Smith*.

11. A Perfon examined before the King's Council, or three of them, upon any Treafon, Mifprifion of Treafon, or Murder, and confefling the fame, or vehemently fufpected by the faid Council, the King may direct his Commiffion of *Oyer* and *Terminer* for trying the fame, into fuch County or Place as he pleafeth ; and here no Challenge for the County or Hundred fhall be allowed. *Stat.* 33 *H.* 8. *c.* 23. *fect.* 1.

12. Where any Perfon is felonioufly ftricken or poifoned in one County, and dieth of the fame in another County, an Indictment or Appeal may be brought in the County where the Party dies. *Stat* 2, 3 *E.* 6. *c.* 24. *fect.* 2, 3.

13. Juftices of Peace, and *Oyer* and *Terminer*, cannot make their *Venire facias* to try an Iffue returnable the fame Seffions; but Juftices of Gaol-Delivery may, for their Panel is returned by the Sheriff without any Precept. *Hale P. C.* 256.

14. At-

14. Attorney General may enter a *Noli pro-sequi*, and stop Proceedings upon an Information, at the Trial after the Jury are sworn. 1 *Vent.* 33.

15. Prisoners for Treason were indicted, arraigned, and in their Trial, and then the Jury were discharged of them, because but one Witness against them ; and the same Persons were afterwards tried again for the same Fact, and condemned. *Ireland's Trial* 55. This was because they had not been before in Jeopardy of their Lives, (as the Court said) because the Charge of the Jury is not full, 'till the Court give them their Charge at last after the Evidence; and the Jury are sworn to try such Prisoners *as they shall have in Charge.* 5 *Jef. Trial* 5. By *North* Chief Justice. *Bedlow* being sworn to say *the Truth, the whole Truth, and nothing but the Truth, in Relation to* Whitebread, *&c. at* Ireland's *Trial, said afterwards, that he did not then say all, nor half that he could have then said.* 5 Jef. Trial 32. *He also said in Court, I cannot prove it without bringing some Witnesses that I have behind a Curtain, and I will not discover them until another Trial (then intended). They shall not know who they are.* 5 Jef. Trial 34. *This though it will not take away his Evidence, yet it goes to the lessening the Credit of it* ; *by* North *Chief Justice,* 5 Jef. Trial 76. *It was urged by* Whitebread, *that* Bedlow *being sworn to say the Truth, and the* whole Truth ; *if he did not say the whole Truth, he is perjured* ; *if he did, he can say nothing against me now.* 5 Jef. Trial 76. But it seems a Man shall not appear perjured by a Logical Argument or Dilemma, so as to take off his Evidence, without producing a Record of his Conviction

Vide infra Witness 12.

3

viction of Perjury. Yet this Cafe of *White-bread*, and the Jury's being difcharged of him, being cited many Years after, was faid to be a fingular Precedent, and the Authority hardly allowed. *Rookwood's Trial* 24.

16. By the Statute of 7 *W.* 3. *c.* 3. All Peers who have Right to fit in Parliament, fhall be fummoned upon Trials of any Peer or Peerefs for Treafon, at leaft twenty Days before fuch Trial.

Verdict.

1. THE Verdict in Cafes Capital muft be given openly in Court, and no privy Verdict. *Hale P. C.* 267.

Witnefs.   Vide *Evidence.*

1. TWO Witneffes to the fame Fact, tho' at feveral Times, fufficient. *Ireland's Trial* 55.

2. If a Witnefs denies what he formerly dif-covered upon Oath, he is not allowed to be perjured, fo long as that Denial is not upon Oath. *Green's Trial* 23.

3. In Cafes not Capital, a Witnefs for the Pri-foner fhall be fworn. *Reading's Trial* 43. But in Capital Cafes, before the Stat. 2 *Ann.* a Witnefs again ftthe King for the Prifoner could be fworn; but the Jury is to take Heed of what they fay, and to be governed by it according to the Cre-dibility of the Perfon. 5 *Jef. Trial* 45.

Vol. II.   U   4. *Roman*

4. *Roman Catholicks* lawful Witnesses, unless such Objection can be produced to invalidate their Evidence, as would have the same Force against Protestants. *5 Jef. Trial* 46, 64, 70. *Oates's* 2d *Trial* 51, 52. It was objected against Mr *Langhorn's* Witnesses, that they were Papists, and spake in a general Cause : To which he replied, That if they were not to be believed because Papists and Friends, then the other, on the contrary, are not to be believed, because they are Enemies. *Langh. Trial* 58. *Oates* cited *Bulstrode's Rep.* 2 Part 155. as my Lord *Coke's* Practice, that a Popish Recusant is not to be admitted a Witness between Party and Party. Over-ruled, as against Law. *Oates's* 1st *Trial* 73.

5. If a Man stand charged with the same Crime with the Prisoner, though he be not convicted, his Evidence on Behalf of the Prisoner is of little Weight. *5 Jef. Trial* 73. *Vide infra* 9.

Vide antea Evidence by Witnesses. 6. A Man that hath stood in the Pillory, is counted an infamous Person, and cannot be taken for a Witness, by *North* Chief Justice. *Langhorn's Trial* 28.

7. One Attaint of Conspiracy, Forgery, or Perjury, or duly set in the Pillory, not allowed to be a Witness. *Hale P. C.* 263. One convict of Perjury can never be a Witness, tho' he hath a Pardon. *Sid.* 52. A Party outlawed (*of Felony*) is no *legalis Testis. Trin.* 32 *Car.* 2. *B. R.* in *Cellier's* Case, *Sid. vid. Co. Lit. f* 6. *b.*

8. One convict of Perjury, *Præmunire*, Forgery, *Stigmaticus*, Pillorized, or other infamous Person ; an Infidel, *Non compos*, or a Party interested, and regularly all such as lose their

liberam

liberam Legem, are not fufficient Witneffes. *Co Lit. f. 6. b.*

9. In an Information in the Crown Office for a Riot, two of the Defendants (no Witneffes appearing againft them) were allowed and fworn as Witneffes in Behalf of the other Defendant. *Sid.* 237. *The King* and *Bedder.*

10. A Man retained of Council for the Prifoner, or his Attorney or Solicitor, may not be examined againft him, for he is obliged to keep his Secrets. 1 *Vent.* 197. *Cuts* and *Pickering.*

11. It is a Maxim in Law, That Witneffes cannot teftify in the Negative, but in the Affirmative only. *Co.* 2 *Inft.* 662.

12. A Matter may be fworn falfe, and yet the Witnefs is not guilty of Perjury 'till he be indicted, and another Jury pafs upon him; for it is one Thing to be forfworn and perjured, and another Thing to be proved fo; and he is not proved to be fo, but by a Record for that Purpofe: By *Scrogs* C. J. 5 *Jef. Trial* 70.

13. Lord Chief Juftice *Jeffreys* would not admit a Witnefs to fwear, that he was forfworn at a former Trial: For he that has once forfworn himfelf ought not to be a Witnefs after that in any Cafe whatfoever. *Oates's* 1ft Trial 68.

14. A Man is not compellable to be a Witnefs, unlefs he be *fubpœna'd* (and tendered Charges, *Vide Stat.* 5 *Eliz. c.* 9. *fect* 12.) but if a Man will come without a *Subpœna*, and give Evidence in a Caufe, this is no Objection to his Teftimony. *Oates's* 1f. *Trial* 14.

U 2   15. It

15. It is very unjuſtifiable, and indeed a very horrid Thing, and ſeverely to be puniſhed, for Witneſſes that come on Behalf of the Priſoner, to be hindred of free Ingreſs and Regreſs, or moleſted or abuſed. By *North* Ch. J. and *Atkins* Juſtice, *Langhorn's Trial* 45.

16. *Langhorn* deſired that he might examine ſome of his Witneſſes, after the King's Council had done, but he was told he might then ſay what he would for his Defence, but not examine any new Witneſs. *Langhorn's Trial* 47.

17. Witneſſes may be examined to give an Account of the general Tenour of the Converſation of a Witneſs againſt a Priſoner, but not of particular Crimes. *Rookwood's Trial* 64, 65.

18. Two Witneſſes, one to one particular Fact of Treaſon, and one to another, have been held ſufficient in Law, for they are both *Overt-Acts* of the Treaſon. Sir *Henry Vane's* Caſe, and *Gaven's* Caſe, 5 *Jeſ. Trial* 87, 88. So if the *Overt-Acts* were in two ſeveral Counties, *College's Trial* 12. The two Witneſſes, that the Statute (5, 6 *E*. 6. *c*. 10. *ſect*. 8.) requires in Treaſon, are not to the ſame individual Act, but to the ſame Treaſon ; for if there be ſeveral Acts declaring the ſame Treaſon, and one Witneſs to each Act, it is ſufficient. *Sidney's Trial* 47, 56. Lord *Ruſſel's Trial* 50, 59. And this was the Lord *Stafford's* Caſe.

19. If in Caſe of Treaſon there be but one Witneſs to prove a direct Treaſon, and another Witneſs to a Circumſtance that contributes to that Treaſon, that will make two Witneſſes. Reſolved by all the Judges of *England*, *Sid. Trial* 59.

20. Now

20. Now, by the Stat. 7 *W.* 3. *c.* 3. Witneffes for the Prifoner fhall be upon Oath, in Cafes of Treafon whereby Corruption of Blood may be made, or of Mifprifion of fuch Treafon ; and no Perfon fhall be attainted in fuch Cafes, but by the Oaths and Teftimony of two lawful Witneffes, either both to the fame *Overt-Act*, or one to one, and the other to another *Overt-Act* of the fame Treafon, unlefs the Party willingly confefs in open Court, ftand mute, or challenge above thirty-five peremptorily, or be attainted by Outlawry ; yet if the Party outlawed comes in, and is tried, he fhall have the Benefit of this Law ; and where two or more diftinct Treafons of divers Kinds fhall be alledged in one Bill of Indictment, one Witnefs to one, and another Witnefs to another Treafon fhall not be deemed two Witneffes within the Meaning of this Act ; and the Prifoners fhall have like Procefs to compel their Witneffes to appear for them, as is ufually granted for Witneffes againft them.

Words.

Vide *Overt-Act* 4.

Writing.

Vide *Proof* 1.   *Overt-Act* 3.

F I N I S.

N. B. The READER is defired to take Notice, That *Pages* 373 to 378 are twice Numbered in the preceding Pages; but if the Matter in the INDEX be not found in the one, it will be found in the other.

THE

TABLE.

A.

Amendment,

The TABLE.

Arrefting

The TABLE.

Assumpsit.

Assumpsit.

Averment.

Award.

If

The TABLE.

The TABLE.

In

The TABLE.

Copy.

A Copy

The TABLE.

D.

When

E.

Court

The TABLE.

Evidence by Witneſſes, Chap. 15. p. 372.

The TABLE.

In

Witnefs

Bills

The T A B L E.

The TABLE.

Payment

The TABLE.

The TABLE.

In

The TABLE.

An

The TABLE.

F.

G.

H.

The TABLE.

Inquefts.

Jury. See *Tales.*

The

The TABLE.

Where

The TABLE.

Y 3 Tranfitory

The TABLE.

Y 4

The TABLE.

One

Jurors, Punishments they are liable to.

K.

Knights.

Anciently

No

O.

Pardon.

P.

Pardon.

WHETHER one attainted of Felony and pardoned, may be of a Jury *Page* 386

Whether one convicted of Felony and pardoned, may be a Witnefs 391, *&c.*

A Felon pardoned may be a Witnefs, but one that has been convicted of Perjury never can 377, 391, 397, 630

Where one fues out his Pardon, what is necef-fary to be done 622

Parifhioner 394, 400

Parol-Promife 498

See Evidence.

Particeps Criminis 298, 623

Partition 588

Partners 501

Peers.

Who fhall be tried as Peers 12

How Peerage fhall be tried 16

A Peer cannot be challenged in a Trial by Peers 176

A Peer exempted from ferviug on Juries 179

A Peer produced as a Witnefs muft be fworn 372

May be covered after his Evidence is over 599

No Evidence to be admitted againft the Honour of a Peer who is a Witnefs for the King *Ibid.*

Perjury.

The T A B L E.

Q.

R.

SEALS

S.

The TABLE.

T.

Tales.

Challenge

Treason.

Trials.

Trials

The TABLE.

U.

Of

The TABLE.

Wager

W.

Wager of Law.

WHERE a Trial may be by Wager of
Law, and the Manner of it *Page* 21
In Wager of Law none can be challenged for
Favour or Insufficiency   192
Warranty   582
Waste   358

Way.

If one purchase a Way to a Barn, and after purchase other Lands beyond, he may
use that Way to the new purchased Lands
                                       529
Wills   17, 519
       See Evidence.
Witness. *See* Evidence.
Writs and Record after a Verdict *lost*, and how
supplied   79

F I N I S.

LAW-BOOKS just published,

By T. WALLER, Fleet-ftreet.

PRACTICE of the King's Bench, Common Pleas, Chancery, and Ecclefiaftical Courts, in 6 Vols. or each feparate.

A General Abridgment of Cafes in Equity, 2d Vol. argued and adjudged in the High Court of Chancery, &c. with a large Collection of Cafes never before publifhed; which brings the Work down to the prefent Time. By a Gentleman of the Middle-Temple.

Where may be had alfo the 1ft Vol. of the above Work, either feparate or together.

Cafes in Equity during the Time of the late Lord Chancellor Talbot. 2d Edit.

Lilly's Modern Entries and Select Pleadings in the Courts of King's Bench, Common Pleas, and Exchequer; alfo a Collection of Writs in moft Cafes now in Practice.

Sir Thomas Raymond's Reports in the Courts of King's Bench, Common Pleas, and Exchequer.

Barnardifton's Reports in Chancery.

Rules, Orders and Notices in the Court of King's Bench and Common Pleas; alfo Reports and Cafes of Practice in the Common Pleas, 2 Vols.

Treatife of Equity.

Baron and Feme.

The

The prefent Practice of Fines and Recoveries, wi h the Theory belonging to each.

Law of Commons and Commoners.

Bohun's Law of Tithes.

Hawkins's Abridgment of Coke upon Lit-leton.

New Returna Brevium: Collected from the many printed Law-Books extant, concerning the Return of Writs in the Courts of Chancery, Exchequer, King's Bench, &c.

Gilbert's (L. C. B.) Law of Devifes, Revocations and laft Wills. To which are added Choice Precedents of Wills.

———— Law of Ejectments.

———— Ufes and Trufts.

———— Hiftorical View of the Exchequer.

———— Tenures.

———— Reports in Equity and Exehequer.

Baco 's New Abridgment of the Law, 4 Vols.

Wa ton's Complete Incumbent: Or, The Clergyman's Law.

Levinz's Reports.

A few remaining Copies of Hale's Pleas of the Crown, 2 Vols.

———— Hiftory of the Law.

Vernon's Reports in Chancery from the 33d of King Charles II. to the 5th of King Geo. I. 2 Vols.

Cu nberbach's Reports in the King's Bench.

Saunders's Reports in the King's Bench, 2 Vols.

Hobarts Reports.

Sir Thomas Jones's Reports.

Cafes in Chancery, 3d Edit.

Tenants

Tenants Law: or, the Laws concerning Land-lords, Tenants and Farmers, viz. 1. Of the several Kinds of Tenants and Tenures. 2. Of Leases, Covenants, Surrenders, and Assignments, &c. 3. Of Rent: Acceptance and extinguishment thereof. 4. Of Crops growing, and Trees blown down, &c. who are entitled to them. 5. Of Distresses, Replevins, and Rescous. 6. Of Waste; what is so, and what not. 7. Of Common for Cattle. 8. Of Frauds in buying and selling Lands or Goods. 9. Of Trespasses and Nusances. 10. Modern Observations relating to Covenants on Leases. 11. Of the late Act to prevent Fires; and Rules to be observed in erecting of new Buildings in and about London. Useful for all Landlords Tenants, Farmers, Stewards, Agents, Solicitors and others, concerned in the buying, selling, or letting Estates. The Fifteenth Edition, with all the Modern Cases: In which are added all such Acts of Parliament and Resolutions, as relate to these Subjects, down to the present Year; and likewise plain Directions for distraining for Rent.